Gender and the Political

Gender and the Political

Deconstructing the Female Terrorist

Amanda Third

To my Spectrum Sister & all
round Wonder Woman, Kati'mon
May you be inspired by &
recognise yourself in the
women you find between
these pages.
Love you to bits.
Amanda (A3)
xox

GENDER AND THE POLITICAL
Copyright © Amanda Third, 2014.

Softcover reprint of the hardcover 1st edition 2014 978-1-137-40275-2

First published in 2014 by PALGRAVE MACMILLAN® in the United States—a division of St. Martin's Press LLC, 175 Fifth Avenue, New York, NY 10010.

Where this book is distributed in the UK, Europe and the rest of the world, this is by Palgrave Macmillan, a division of Macmillan Publishers Limited, registered in England, company number 785998, of Houndmills, Basingstoke, Hampshire RG21 6XS.

Palgrave Macmillan is the global academic imprint of the above companies and has companies and representatives throughout the world.

Palgrave® and Macmillan® are registered trademarks in the United States, the United Kingdom, Europe and other countries.

ISBN 978-1-349-48680-9   ISBN 978-1-137-40276-9 (eBook)
DOI 10.1057/9781137402769

Library of Congress Cataloging-in-Publication Data

Third, Amanda, 1972–
  Gender and the political:deconstructing the female terrorist/Amanda Third.
    pages   cm.
  Includes bibliographical references and index.

  1. Women terrorists. 2. Terrorism. 3. Feminism. I. Title.
  HV6431.T56687 2014
  363.325082—dc23   2014015561

A catalogue record of the book is available from the British Library.

Design by SPi Global.

First edition: October 2014

10 9 8 7 6 5 4 3 2 1

For Dimitris Vardoulakis

Contents

Acknowledgments

In a project that has spanned more than a decade, there have been countless shows of support for which I am enormously grateful. My sincere thanks go:

To Jon Stratton and Ron Blaber, who helped me to conceive this project and supported the journey that unfolded.

To colleagues who have facilitated the publication and presentation of this work: Stathis Gourgouris, Neni Panourgia, Jeremy Varon, Peg Birmingham, Rosie Cox, Nickianne Moody, Shelley Godsland, Diane Negra, Carole Ferrier, Susanna Scarparo, Katrina Schlunke, Elizabeth Presa, Jill Carrick, Paul Magee, Cesare Casarino, Amy Kaminsky, and Karen Dubinsky.

To friends and colleagues who have provided valuable feedback on the work as it progressed: Joke Hermes, Jane Stadler, Kelli Fuery, Anne McGuire, Barbara Caine, Maryanne Dever, Margaret Henderson, Alison Bartlett, Ina Kerner, Natalya Lusty, Tania Lewis, Ned Rossiter, Angi Buettner, Michael Goddard, Zenon Banachowski, Nina Philadelphoff-Puren, Sharon Pickering, Janemaree Maher, Jo Lindsay, Rebecca do Rozario, Ann-Louise Shapiro, Helena Grehan, Richard Johnson, and Rocky Jones.

To senior colleagues who have helped me secure the forms of institutional support necessary to complete this book: Ien Ang, Peter Hutchings, Greg Noble, Gar Jones, Andrew Cheetham, Bev Thiele, Gail Phillips, Geoff Craig, Stephi Hemelryk-Donald, and Chris Smyth.

To family, friends and colleagues who provided love, injections of humor, and timely reality checks: Bob Third, Jo Third, Cameron Third, Sally Pinder, Katie Third, Bas de Jong, William Stibbs, Ethel Third, Shirley Lewis, Maggie Third, Jane Lewis, Janita Radford, Judi Stanley, Lamonta McLarty, Jo (VSF) Lamb, Amanda Cinanni, Lyn Dale, Kate Fitch, Saba and Sam el Ghul-Bebawi, Nerillee Miller, Tania Lewis, Karen Cunningham, Giancarlo Mona, Johan Lidberg, Jon Watts, Mark Gibson, Andrea Witcomb, Jane Armstrong, Manu Madan, Scott and Mihali Gotsis, Julie Marriott, Pam Williams, Jo Gray, and Marian Quigley.

To Urszula Dawkins, who edited this manuscript as if it were her own, artfully balancing kindness, respect, patience, and humor throughout. And to Harriette Richards, Vanessa Mendes Moreira de Sa, Bettina Rösler, Kristen Phillips, and Kathryn Locke, for their outstanding research assistance.

To Brigitte Shull and Ryan Jenkins at Palgrave for their professionalism and support of this project during the publication process.

And lastly to Dimitris Vardoulakis, whose unfaltering support has enabled me to complete this book, and whose love and generosity of spirit makes every day singular; and to little Lukás, who has taught me how to love and be loved in unprecedented ways. Thank you.

Introduction

Experience has shown that woman as terrorist must be dealt with after the fashion of the Gorgon if those responding would survive.

—H. H. A. Cooper[1]

Terrorism is a highly gendered phenomenon, producing the figure of the female terrorist that circulates within contemporary Western culture as an object of fascination and heightened concern. This book analyses how the discourses about terrorism and those of femininity are overlaid.[2]

In 1979, H. H. A. Cooper admonished that the female terrorist should be "dealt with after the fashion of the Gorgon,"[3] signaling two things simultaneously. First, the female terrorist constitutes a significatory threat. Medusa represents the decisive rupture of signification; whoever sighted Medusa, the ancient Greek Gorgon, was instantly turned to stone. The Gorgon is unimaginable; she can never be comprehended. Second, the only response to this inscrutability is in the manner of Perseus, namely by the slaying of Medusa: the significatory threat must be eliminated. Contrary to Cooper's suggestion that we annihilate her, the present study seeks to scrutinize and interpret the figure of the female terrorist and to revitalize understandings of her importance in the construction of both femininity and the idea of terrorism.

Why this vehement, almost hysterical, rejection of the female terrorist? I argue that the female terrorist represents a particularly acute, if not monstrous, threat to social order because she registers as *hyperterrorist* (and therefore not properly feminine) and simultaneously *hyperfeminine* (and therefore not properly terrorist but nonetheless highly dangerous).

Constructed in always extreme but fundamentally ambivalent ways, the female terrorist presents in the popular imagination as liminal and therefore "ambiguous." She at once disrupts idealized notions of Western femininity and represents the ever-present potential of women to subvert the categories that subtend gendered order in Western (post)modernity. Despite attempts in popular culture to "fix" the meanings of the figure of the violent woman, she remains elusive, always threatening to exceed the limits of the categories that are called upon to make sense of her. She is not only a figure that marks the limits of the discourse of femininity, enabling this discourse to be called into being, but also the site upon which this discourse dissembles. This makes her a slippery, highly unstable, and, consequently, politically potent figure. She manifests as a malevolent threat to (gendered) cultural order with the capacity to generate an excess of affect, problematizing the boundaries of legitimate femininity as they are prescribed by Western culture. As a consequence, the female terrorist is the ideal figure through which to interrogate the gendering of the political.

My argument has a historical specificity. The representation of politically active women in the United States during the 1960s and 1970s is intricately linked with the genesis of contemporary terrorism studies discourses. In the Western world, the female terrorist first became a preoccupation for governments, law enforcement agencies, and popular culture more generally during this period. At this time, in response to the "new" threat of both "international terrorism" and "terrorism at home," a new discourse on terrorism emerged in Western cultures. Simultaneously, women gained prominence in the so-called terrorist activities of a range of underground organizations operating in the West, such as the Weathermen and the Symbionese Liberation Army (SLA) in the United States, the *Brigate Rosse* (Red Brigades) in Italy, and the *Rote Armee Fraktion* (Red Army Faction, also known as the Baader-Meinhof gang) in West Germany. At this historical moment, the institutions of Western culture began their project of delineating the specific threat of female terrorism, and the female terrorist became the subject of various forms of dominant cultural knowledge production, from counterterrorism, law enforcement, and psychology to the news media, pulp fiction, and film.

In the past two decades, there has been a resurgence in the visibility of, and interest in, women involved in terrorism in the late 1960s and early 1970s in the United States. In 1996, the film *I Shot Andy Warhol*, which traces the events leading to Valerie Solanas' near-fatal shooting of pop art icon Andy Warhol, was released.[4] In June 1999, after 23 years on the run, Kathleen Soliah, a former member of the SLA, which had kidnapped and "converted" Patricia Hearst in 1974, was captured in America's Midwest, where she was living a peaceful life as the mother of three teenage daughters. Amid the furor of the Bush Administration's war on terror in early 2003, in what might be construed as a gesture of punishing "their own" as harshly as "the Other," a US court sentenced Soliah to 20 years in prison.[5] By contrast, on the eve of surrendering the US presidency to George Bush Junior in January 2001, President Bill Clinton granted Patricia Hearst a formal pardon. Hearst served

23 months of a seven-year jail sentence for her infamous involvement in a 1974 SLA bank robbery before her sentence was commuted by President Jimmy Carter in 1979. In 2003, two independently produced documentaries dealing with the terrorism that grew out of the social protest movement in the United States in the late 1960s and the early 1970s—*Guerrilla* and *The Weather Underground*—were featured in film festivals around the globe.[6]

But these recent representations of the female terrorist fall short of taming the Gorgon. In their discussion of cultural memory production in relation to the *Rote Armee Fraktion* in West Germany, Gerrit-Jan Berendse and Ingo Cornils argue that, produced primarily by the younger generation, the swell of 1990s artistic and popular cultural texts addressing *der Deutscher Herbst* (the German Autumn) of 1977 evidenced "a tendency in the culture industry to fuel and then satisfy the demand for sublimated violence in a decade that can be classified as relatively uneventful in terms of politically motivated violence."[7] The same might be said of the new wave of text production pertaining to post–Summer of Love terrorism in the United States. In this reading, the recent disinterment of the 1960s and 1970s US female terrorist as the subject of a range of popular memory texts unfolds according to a cultural trajectory that predates events such as September 11, 2001. Her rehabilitation thus appears to occur at the expense of any explicit link to the construction of the idea of the terrorist today. But this is the equivalent of obscuring Medusa's inscrutable face with a mask. The discourses that shaped the construction of the female terrorist in the 1960s and 1970s—indeed, that called her into being—continue to constitute terrorism as a gendered phenomenon today.

In the aporia induced by 9/11, the cultural memory processes pertaining to 1960s and 1970s terrorism throughout the Western world—processes which began in the mid-1990s and have continued into the present day—gained new interpretive significance. As Berendse and Cornils argue, "the wave of memory texts in the maiden years of the new millennium, concerning 1970s terrorism . . . was forcefully confronted with the 9/11 paradigm shift and its aftermath."[8] Drawn into dialogue with the sudden and "incomprehensible" absence of the Twin Towers on the skyline of downtown Manhattan, cultural memory texts began to resonate in a new register, constituting an important component of the fabric of meaning that sought to subordinate the "radically unfamiliar" to a regime of knowing.[9]

Indeed, one of the striking aspects of institutional responses to the destruction of the Twin Towers was the alacrity with which Western culture turned to (frequently conservative) commentators with counterterrorism credentials established at the height of "international" and "home-grown" terrorism in the 1970s to explain and formulate responses to al Qaeda's strikes "against Western democracy." The "experts" of terrorism studies, a discipline overwhelmingly aligned with state objectives that emerged in the early 1970s, populated the landscape of mainstream media commentary in the immediate aftermath of 9/11 and became an important touchstone in the subsequent development of government responses to terrorism. In the intervening years, in the burgeoning publishing subindustry on terrorism that has emerged, many of these protagonists have (re)published commentaries which, although they, to varying extents, address the new conditions shaping terrorism/counterterrorism, rehearse traditional 1970s perspectives on the phenomenon of political violence. Thus, post-9/11, the discursive machine driving the Western allies' mainstream symbolic war on terrorism has been reliant on the weight of historical wisdom.[10] It is thus the historical roots of mainstream discourse on terrorism that this book addresses.

Feminist analyses have traditionally contended that the extreme responses elicited by the female terrorist can be attributed to her disruption of the idealized form of femininity (passivity, nurturance, pacifism, and so on) traded in Western culture. While this idea has had considerable traction, it relies upon a disavowal of the ways in which, within the spaces of everyday culture in Western (post)modernity, reified femininity is shadowed by a set of equally entrenched ideas about women's inherent corruptibility and deception. Is the female terrorist simply non-feminine? How might the female terrorist, in disrupting idealized femininity, also confirm a Western historical preoccupation with femininity as subversive?

I argue that the female terrorist represents one manifestation of the Western cultural anxiety that femininity (as excess) inevitably slides into criminality. She both *marks the limits of legitimate femininity*—circulating as a site of containment and control of the meanings of femininity—*and operates to disrupt those limits*. She enables the system of gender representation underpinning Western modernity to constitute itself as relatively coherent and stable, and is simultaneously a site of that system's instability. For this reason, the female terrorist generates an excess of fear within the popular imagination, and is thereby radically othered. This reading of the female terrorist provides the backdrop against which I situate my analysis of the specificities of US female terrorism in the late 1960s and early 1970s.

If the female terrorist is the shadowy figure of excess or deviance that, albeit tenuously, demarcates legitimate femininity from its Other, so, too, does she mark the limits of *feminist* agency. Within dominant discourse in the United States in the late 1960s and early 1970s, a female terrorist was always already presumed to be a feminist. The female terrorist became a preoccupation within both official and popular culture at the precise moment when second-wave feminism began to present as a formidable (and increasingly publicized) force for social change. In this context, "feminism" and "terrorism" began to present in the US popular imagination as twin practices. Indeed, given the high ratio of women to men engaging in the terrorism of the period, the word "terrorism"—and specifically that of left-wing, "white," middle-class, urban terrorist groups—came to signify as *feminist terrorism*.

In 1992, Gilda Zwerman suggested that "critical scholars have paid little attention to the . . . relationship between the image of the 'female terrorist,' as constructed in counterinsurgency literature, and the growing backlash to American feminism."[11] More than two decades on, this connection remains largely unexplored. What are the implications of this discursive intertwining of feminism with terrorism across the representational field that calls her into being? How does gender operate as a mechanism of political affect, both historically and into the present? How does the crosswiring of feminism with terrorism within the popular imaginary illustrate the tenuousness of the distinction between legitimate and illegitimate forms of political resistance, particularly in times of perceived (inter)national crisis? And, how does it illuminate the limits of our conceptualizations of the political?

* * *

The first two chapters of *Gender and the Political* explicate the conceptualization of terrorism that underpins my argument and analyze the generic representation of the female terrorist.

First, I demonstrate that the origins of "dominant discourse" on terrorism in the United States, or "the terrorism industry,"[12] can be traced to the late 1960s and early 1970s, when the institutions of government and law enforcement organized themselves to combat what was perceived as a "new" problem plaguing Western nations. Although the idea of terrorism is constitutive of modernity, understandings of terrorism underwent a significant transformation at that time due to the emergence of "urban terrorism"—left-wing terrorism carried out by US citizens on US soil—from the social protest movements of the 1960s and 1970s. In this context, terrorism signified as a practice of left-wing political violence besieging Western democratic nations. This conceptualization of terrorism has been consolidated by the "discipline" of terrorism studies, and in turn shapes the popular imagination of terrorism in the United States.

Second, to account for the affect generated by the female terrorist, it is necessary to understand terrorism as a communication practice. This enables the theorizing of the affect terrorism generates in terms of its disruption and destabilization of the cultural narratives that traditionally legitimize social organization in the West.

In Chapter Two, I also track the rise of the female terrorist threat specific to the late 1960s and early 1970s in the United States by analyzing the era's counterterrorist formulations of the female terrorist. In these texts, the female terrorist presents as a particularly nefarious figure of excess that both challenges and confirms dominant cultural understandings of femininity. Thus, the construction of the female terrorist rehearses the limits of both femininity and feminist agency.

Chapter Three addresses the discursive crosswiring of feminism with terrorism, showing how the threat of feminism in the late 1960s and early 1970s is mapped onto the female terrorist. In this sense, the female terrorist constitutes a site upon which dominant culture enacts a struggle for the discursive containment and control of the feminist threat to (patriarchal) order. The threat of female/feminist terrorism to which the counterinsurgency literature and, by extension popular culture, responds is in fact the specific threat of *radical feminism*. Historically, radical feminists often spoke in terms of rage and retribution, and practiced a style of politics that frequently mobilized around a notion of spectacle. As such, radical feminist activism succeeded in gaining mainstream media coverage and, as it gained momentum, began to present in the popular imagination as a violent and dire threat to the structure of gender relations underpinning social organization in the United States—a threat that resonated closely with the contemporary practice of terrorism. Consequently, radical feminism and terrorism in this era were regarded as fundamentally *similar in form*.

Chapters Four to Seven interrogate the discursive terrain across which radical feminism could be crosswired with feminism. From the late 1960s to the mid-1970s the United States experienced the most intense campaign of terrorism carried out on its territory. The historical coincidence of radical feminism and terrorism thus provides the fertile ground upon which the figure of the female terrorist is constructed. I thus analyze the stories of two women whose participation in political violence bookends the rise and fall of radical feminism—namely, Valerie Solanas and Patricia Campbell Hearst (between 1968 and the mid-1970s).

Chapter Four analyzes how terrorism resonates as an acute threat to order in modernity. Terrorism's discursive power derives from its disruption of the linear and routine time of the everyday, which is central to modernity's constitution as a project of order.[13] Further, terrorism forces upon its audiences a fundamentally unsettling experience of time—that of apocalyptic time. Representing the annihilation of linear and routine time that characterizes order in modernity, terrorism invokes the apocalyptic implosion of modernity itself. Through an analysis of some of the key foundational texts of political theory, I show that the organization of everyday life in modernity is in fact based on the democratization and circulation of terror. Thus, when terrorism attacks on the temporal plane, it simultaneously politicizes the terror at the heart of modernity and signals modernity's *dénouement*.

Chapter Five analyzes radical feminist activist practice to demonstrate that, throughout the era in question, radical feminism deployed a range of tactics that paralleled those of the "revolutionary terrorism" of the era. Whereas other forms of feminism have sought to find a place for women within historical time, radical feminism, like terrorism, refuses the linear and routine temporality of modernity. I analyze radical feminist writings through the lens of modern discourses of apocalypse and utopia, focusing in particular on Valerie Solanas' *SCUM Manifesto*, which argues that the solution to the age-old problem of women's subordination lies in the annihilation of men—what I term "sexocide." I suggest that Solanas' manifesto can be read as a feminist critique of the state that advocates an apocalyptic methodology for forcing the door of utopia. Thus, it epitomizes how the radical feminist posture explicitly articulates a nexus between feminism and terrorism. Seeking to contain the threat she posed, dominant culture responded by constructing Solanas as mad.

Chapter Six further elaborates why radical feminism was perceived as particularly terroristic; positioned, as it was, within dominant discourse as an excessively angry and vengeful movement for gender-based retribution. The source of this rage lay in the racial politics that framed both the New Left and radical feminism. I argue that radical feminism took shape via the abjection of whiteness, which operates within an apocalyptic temporality. Radical feminism's deployment of the idea of genocide to describe both the conditions that frame women's lives and the process by which the feminist revolution should proceed, blurred the distinction between legitimate and illegitimate violence that is fundamental to modern social order. In highlighting the arbitrariness of this distinction, radical feminists drew attention to the way the organization of everyday life is premised on the circulation of terror.

Finally, Chapter Seven interrogates the ways the category of gender works to structure US cultural and political responses to terrorism; by focusing on the SLA's 1974 kidnapping and "conversion" of Patricia Campbell Hearst. Mainstream culture constructed Hearst's abduction as both a terrorist and a feminist attack on the modern institution of the family. The abduction resonated with both the generic concern about the resilience of the family within modernity and historically specific anxieties about the (in)stability of the family. These fears were inspired by the New Left's challenge to traditional modes of social organization centering on the nuclear family, but also by the explicitly stated challenge to (patriarchal) social order posed by radical feminism. Thus, the SLA was commonly positioned within dominant discourse as a feminist terrorist organization. The state's response to the "Patty Hearst event" as well as its representation in popular culture operated to reassert the importance of the nuclear family and, in so doing, attempted to contain and annul the (feminist) terrorist threat of the SLA. However, despite these attempts, Hearst remains a fundamentally unsettling figure.

A crucial thread connects the discourses of femininity and terrorism. Indeed, within the US cultural imaginary in the late 1960s and early 1970s, the dual threats of (radical) feminism and terrorism were "crosswired" upon the site of the female terrorist. The female terrorist is a figure that marks the gendering of both terrorism and feminist political agency; indeed, she betrays the gendering of the political. Our understanding of terrorism today, then, necessarily passes through an interrogation of femininity, and vice versa. Situated at the borderlines of sexuality, threat, and abjection, the figure of the female terrorist compels a re-examination of the project of radical politics and the limits of gendered (post)modernity.

CHAPTER 1

Conceptualizing Terrorism

Terrorism is terrorism when some (but which?) people think that it is terrorism.

Chalmers Johnson[1]

In 1981, Irving Louis Horowitz claimed that, over the course of the 1970s, a shift had taken place within the United States in the grammar of official politics that saw terrorism become "front and center in the political stage."[2] Indeed, this decade saw the US government recognize that terrorism was not the distant problem of foreign nations but one that increasingly threatened close to home. Anthony C. Quainton argues that in this very same period "terrorism" "became part of America's popular political vocabulary,"[3] highlighting that terrorism's arrival in the vernacular occurred as the US government began to perceive itself as the victim of terrorism and mobilized the force of its institutional powers to contain the threat. A central premise of this chapter is that the ideas about terrorism that circulate in dominant culture in the Western world are largely the product of such *institutional knowledges*, formed in relation to the perceived threat of terrorism and the need for its "containment."

The 1970s mark an important moment in the history of the West's conceptualization of the practice of terrorism because, during this era, the new discipline of "terrorism studies" institutionalized the study of this "novel" and "menacing" political phenomenon. The ways terrorism is currently understood, in both academic analyses and popular culture, are the legacy, then, of a discourse on terrorism that emerged in the late 1960s and early 1970s. The proponents of terrorism studies shaped this discourse in a profound manner. Despite the proliferating literature on the subject of terrorism in the wake of recent so-called Islamic terrorist attacks on the West, however, a sustained analysis of the impact of terrorism studies' conceptualizations of Western popular representations of terrorism is yet to emerge.

This chapter analyzes the formative texts of terrorism studies, foregrounding the ways the institution of terrorism studies delimits the meanings of terrorism that circulate within dominant culture and, in turn, conditions the responses mobilized to quash its threat.[4] In so doing, this critique questions how dominant understandings of terrorism (re)produce the boundaries between illegitimate and legitimate forms of violence that have historically enabled social order, further considering the implications for Western culture's renderings of the political as the terrain of lawful political engagement and activity.

Since the inception of terrorism studies in the early 1970s, its exponents have offered a variety of pseudo-scientific definitions and theoretical frameworks for delineating terrorism as a discrete and knowable political phenomenon. The majority of these approaches cannot account for terrorism's success in generating *affective* responses in its audiences. Terrorism articulates with deeply embedded Western cultural anxieties about the stability of social order, particularly as it is inflected by gender. In the first instance, I turn to communication and cultural studies scholarship to situate terrorism in relation to the cultural milieu in which it operates and, in particular, its primary targets—namely, its audiences.

Terrorism: A Nebulous Term?

"Terrorism," as many commentators have pointed out, is a highly loaded term.[5] Debates over the definition and "correct" usage of the term have been tirelessly rehearsed within the literature of terrorism studies and, despite a vigorous debate over more than 35 years, the definitional problem still plagues academic, government, and security industry scholarship. In the context of this debate, it is often suggested that terrorism is a term with multiple, and frequently disparate, meanings. Philip Jenkins, a longstanding commentator on terrorism, has expressed concern that the word "terrorism" has been used "indiscriminately" in a variety of contexts to describe a wide range of "violent" actions. He notes that, while some commentators refuse to label the Irish Republicans terrorists, others "expand the description to fit groups and actions that would not normally be categorized by such a damning term."[6] Jenkins appears particularly concerned about the ways activists—specifically those on the political left—have appropriated the term to denounce their opposition "by applying the most harmful label possible."[7] As evidence, he cites UNICEF's claim that the commercial sexual exploitation of children is a "form of terrorism"; the "feminist militant" claim that rape is an act of "gender terrorism"; and union activists' claims that the deaths and injuries arising from unsafe working conditions, especially in the Third World, are a form of "corporate terrorism."[8] But he reserves his greatest criticism for the way "the use of the 'terrorism' card has become quite commonplace in radical denunciations of US foreign policy."[9]

The seemingly myriad uses of the term "terrorism" have given rise to a general concern, articulated most often within but also outside the academic discipline of terrorism studies, that the term can mean "whatever anyone wants it to mean at any given time."[10] This anxiety over "perverted" meanings betrays an ideological investment in the term. As Chalmers Johnson alludes to in the epigraph to this chapter, "terrorism" is a term that is imbricated in struggles for power and legitimacy within dominant culture, a site for the contest of meaning. This concern over the multiple meanings of terrorism arises in relation to the ways the term circulates not only within the academy, but also within the spaces of public culture more generally. In 1978, Walter Laqueur, a professor of modern history and an expert commentator on international politics, argued that misconceptions about terrorism frequently stem from the "vagueness—indeed, the utter carelessness—with which the term is used, not only in the media but also in government announcements and by academic students of the subject."[11] Naming a range of activities for which terrorism is used as a synonym—"rebellion, street battles, civil strife, insurrection, rural guerrilla war, coups d'état, and a dozen other things"—he cites this "indiscriminate" use as the reason for inflated statistics on terrorism, the obfuscated nature of its character, and the difficulties these things present for finding strategies to deal with it.[12] Laqueur is also concerned with delineating terrorism as a discrete political phenomenon—terrorism as *politically motivated* violence. More recently, Ghassan Hage has argued that, "through its intensive strategic use on the political market by the media and politicians, [the word 'terrorism'] has become further loaded with ideological assumptions."[13] Certainly, a wide variety of agents with diverse political agendas have tapped into the rhetorical power of "terrorism," and in the process have invested the term with their own particular ideological biases. However, it does not necessarily hold that the term has simultaneously become more confused, at least not at the level of dominant culture. Nor is it necessarily the case that counter-discursive uses of the term (such as the left's appropriation of the term to denounce the practices of Western democratic states) undermines the cohesion of the term as it circulates in mainstream Western cultures. While the applications of the term "terrorism" are often disputed, "terrorism" nonetheless signifies in a very particular set of ways.

For example, commenting on the attacks on the Twin Towers and the Pentagon in 2001, Jenkins argues on the one hand that "even within the United States, the term 'terrorism' means very different things to different people."[14] On the other hand, he suggests that terrorism's meanings are also at least partially fixed in the popular imagination: "most people would agree that certain actions indisputably represent terrorism (the horrors of September 11 being an obvious example)."[15] Here Jenkins invites his audience to unquestioningly accept September 11, 2001 as an "obvious" and "indisputable" act of terrorism, raising the question of how "we" come to "know" as a culture what terrorism is. Like Giovanna Borradori, I would "deny that terrorism has any stable meaning, agenda, and political content";[16] indeed, I take issue here with the ways that terrorism *presents* as a narrowly defined and self-evident category in the cultural imagination.[17]

This task necessitates a different approach from that provided by terrorism studies. Terrorism's meanings are produced in relation to the bodies of knowledge—institutional or otherwise—that circumscribe the term's usage within the sphere of the everyday. That is, terrorism is a discursive construct called into being in the complex negotiations among terrorists, audiences, sites of institutional power, and texts—it is *the discursive effect* of a communication process.

Terrorism as Communication

As an academic discipline with strong links to governments and security industries, terrorism studies has been primarily concerned with generating solutions to the "problem" of terrorism. It has attempted to objectify and classify terrorism in "scientific" terms, resulting in limited analysis of why terrorism can so powerfully capture the public's imagination.

One of the key defining features of terrorism is that it mobilizes a relationship with its multiple audiences. Terrorism can only be an effective, meaningful communication through the ways audiences perceive its incursions. It is a thinkable tactic precisely because of the modes of representation and meaning prevalent in Western societies. If we are concerned with understanding and negotiating the threat of terrorism, rather than focusing primarily on solutions that objectify, criminalize, and "contain" particular kinds of individuals and sets of practices, we must address the valencies of terrorism as a signifying practice.

For many commentators, it is terrorism's desired outcome of affecting audiences—of conveying a message to a wider public—that marks it as distinct from other forms of violence. For Lawrence Zelic Freedman, terrorism is "the use of violence when its most important result is not the physical and mental damage of the direct victim *but the psychological effect produced on someone else*."[18] For terrorism studies, then, audiences are of key importance to the terrorist project, but this remains largely unexamined. In this respect, critical cultural and communication theory has much to offer to the analysis of terrorism.

A few terrorism studies texts engage with the idea of terrorism as a communicative practice, mostly concerned with the role of the media as a facilitator of terrorism.[19] In an important 1982 book titled *Violence as Communication: Insurgent Terrorism and the Western Media*, Alex P. Schmid and Janny de Graaf famously suggested that "without communication there can be no terrorism."[20] Like many other commentators on terrorism, Schmid and de Graaf argue that terrorism's motives are primarily publicity-centered and that their victims function merely as vehicles for terrorists to potentially proselytize large audiences to their cause. Unlike the majority of their terrorism studies counterparts, Schmid and de Graaf take this argument one step further. They argue that terrorism is violence deployed for the purposes of propaganda and, as such, must be understood first and foremost as a communication practice: "For the terrorist the message matters, not the victim."[21] Schmid and de Graaf make an important conceptual shift with potentially far-reaching implications for our understandings of terrorism, offering a conceptualization through which we can unpack terrorism's significatory power, though, not without some qualification.

Schmid and de Graaf conceive of terrorism as a "violent communication strategy" that requires "a sender, the terrorist, a message generator, the victim, and a receiver, the enemy and/or the public."[22] The power of the terrorist message derives from "the nature of the terrorist act, its atrocity, its location and the identity of its victim."[23] Schmid and de Graaf explain terrorism's communicative dimensions in terms of the relatively straightforward transmission of information from senders to receivers—a conceptualization that falls within the theoretical frame of the "transmission" or "process" model of communication.[24] In this model, audiences feature as the passive recipients of messages, and are affected in predictable and quantifiable ways, emphasizing an understanding of communication in which the sender and the message are the determinants of meaning.[25]

Schmid and de Graaf's preoccupation lies primarily with explicating the role of the news media in disseminating terrorist messages to audiences. As Denis McQuail says of *Violence as Communication* in his foreword to the text, "Schmid and de Graaf focus on a conception of terrorism as . . . a way of ensuring public attention and even of channelling particular messages to chosen targets."[26] The body of Schmid and de Graaf's text revolves around unraveling the "symbiotic relationship" between terrorists and the media—namely, the nexus of their complementary interest in audience maximization. Because Schmid and de Graaf privilege an understanding of communication as the conveyance of messages to an audience configured as passive recipients, their analysis can only tangentially address how audiences experience, and make sense of, terrorism.

Much has taken place in media and communication theory since *Violence as Communication* was published. In recent years, the field of communication studies has embraced the insights of the "cultural turn" toward understanding communication as a culturally embedded process of meaning making. In this context, there has been a concerted effort to address the limitations of the transmission model of communication. This has sparked a revaluation of qualitative methods of communication research directed toward the conditions and possibilities of audience reception.[27] The analysis of terrorism formulated as a communication practice needs to take account of these developments.

Desperately Seeking an Audience

As Schmid and de Graaf point out, albeit without elaboration, an act of terrorism seeks to mobilize a relationship between terrorists and their audiences: "Through his violent act, the terrorist seeks to activate a relationship between victims and enemy, whereby the latter is made responsible for the former before a public."[28] That is, terrorism seeks to construct a relationship of accountability that sets up the public as the arbiter of justice. This relationship needs to be scrutinized if we are to understand the valencies of terrorism as a signifying practice. Not only does terrorism work to construct a relationship between terrorists and their audiences, but, perhaps more importantly, the audience becomes an important site through which terrorism comes to be produced as meaningful.[29] It is in the audience's consumption of the terrorist act—informed by its intersections with a cumulative historicity of meaning—that terrorism acquires the capacity to generate affect and, therefore, political effect. In this moment, the audience is constitutive of terrorism; complicit, unwilling or otherwise, in the production of terrorism's "successes."

Indeed, for Suman Gupta, writing in the aftermath of the terrorist attacks of September 11, 2001 in the United States, the principal achievement of al Qaeda's terrorist ploy was exposing the complicity of global media audiences in the production of terrorism. The global media's packaging of commodified images of terror for consumption by audiences constituted a kind of symbolic doubling back on the audiences of terrorism. In cannibalistic fashion, the deaths of "our own" civilians and the destruction of the household icons of Western capitalism were fed back to us. Gupta writes:

> The attacks did violence to the most potent symbols of a consumer society, striking at the very heart of the institutions that valorise and protect consumerism. The fact is that that violence itself got converted at the selfsame moment, despite our resistance and horror, into consumable images following the

irresistible logic of mass-media representation; the violence crudely aimed at the consumer society became food to that consumer society.[30]

This, Gupta suggests, was al Qaeda's most powerful comment on Western society and a source of major discomfort for Western audiences. He continues:

> This terrorist attack, by its enormity and by the context in which it occurred, had managed to turn the attention of the media and its relation to extreme violence (an unavoidable reality) upon itself. *Media consumers had now, I think inevitably, an inkling of their complicity in the* production *of media violence, had faced their discomfort with this complicity, and had ultimately surrendered to it.*[31]

In this reading, terrorism is not just about terrorists exploiting the institutional structures of Western society to advance their political goals, a formulation that permeates more traditional analyses of terrorism studies. "Terrorism" is also a commodity that feeds a late capitalist desire for spectacle. Terrorism both shocks and titillates. Audiences are simultaneously horrified and spellbound. Ironically, because of the centrality of media spectacle to the order of Western consumption capitalism, terrorism's "targets"—its audiences—in participating in an obsessive cycle of image consumption, actively engage in the production of terrorism as a meaningful event.

Jean Baudrillard, gesturing toward the work of Guy Debord, suggests that "the spectacle of terrorism forces the terrorism of spectacle upon us."[32] For him, the events of September 11 could, in the first instance, be thinkable, and, in the second instance, have a very powerful impact on the Western cultural imaginary, because of a Western cultural complicity with the publicity aims of terrorism.[33]

Writing in 1979, terrorism commentator H. H. A. Cooper stated that "few, if any, seem to have captured in words the essence of terrorism . . . it is to be comprehended through the senses rather than by way of erudite debate."[34] Cooper signals, however inadvertently, the affective dimensions of terrorism; terrorism as a threat that we *feel*. For Jacques Derrida, if "'terrorist' acts try to produce psychic effects (conscious or unconscious) and symbolic or symptomatic reactions," then "the *quality or intensity* of the emotions provoked (whether conscious or unconscious) is not always proportionate to the number of victims or the amount of damage."[35] Borradori, commenting on her discussion with Derrida, contends that we need to think about terrorism "as a psychological and metaphysical state as well as . . . a political category."[36] Terrorism is not an inherently objective and knowable category of political action. Terrorism cannot ultimately be quantified. As Derrida suggests, we must search for "meaningful and *qualitative* explanations."[37] It is necessary to move beyond traditional understandings of terrorism toward a more nuanced understanding of terrorism as "symbolic violence"—a form of communication embedded in a representational economy, and a practice that implicates audiences in the generation of *affect*.[38] Only by doing so can we explain how and why terrorism resonates so acutely with audiences.

Not only are audiences a crucial component in terrorist communication, but also terrorism is embedded in cultural processes of meaning. Again, Baudrillard is insightful, arguing that the events of September 11 could fascinate audiences to the degree that they did because they tapped into the unwitting "terroristic imagination which dwells in all of us."[39] Baudrillard alludes to the fact that terrorism operates in a Western symbolic economy that routinely works to call terrorism into being, as both a political practice and a spectacular effect:

> The fact that we have dreamt of this event, that everyone without exception has dreamt of it—because no one can avoid dreaming of the destruction of any power that has become hegemonic to this degree—is unacceptable to the Western moral conscience. Yet it is a fact, and one which can be measured by the emotive violence of all that has been said and written in the efforts to dispel it. At a pinch, we can say that they *did it*, but we *wished for* it.[40]

Baudrillard understands terrorism as a process that mobilizes a representational economy in whose reproduction its audiences are complicit—it plays into the "terroristic imagination" of the Western world. He suggests that, through our symbolic imaginings, "we" conjure terrorism into being, and that terrorism is constitutive of the political.

Borradori gives this idea a more explicit and material basis, writing that, for some time before September 11, 2001, "technocinematic culture"—films, video games, and so on—"had been anticipating the gutting (*éventrement*) and collapse (*effondrement*) of the two immense towers in downtown Manhattan."[41] A terrorist attack is always fundamentally intertextual, gaining its meanings in relation to ideas that circulate in the spaces of official and popular culture, through both "factual" and "fictional" texts. "Terrorism" is the representational effect of exchanges between terrorists and their audiences that take place *in and through the texts* that mediate them. As such, it is through an analysis of texts that we can unpack the meanings and significatory power of terrorism.

What "we" "know" about terrorism—the "knowledges" that are produced in the context of this relationship of exchange—constitutes what Michel Foucault calls "discourse." Both the relationship between terrorists and their audiences, and the range of textual representations this relationship generates, are embedded in discourse—they are produced and consumed in the context of "a culture's determined and determining structures of representation and practice."[42] "Terrorism," that embodiment of "absolute evil" that we know intimately without necessarily experiencing it as an immediate victim, is thus produced in and through discourse, and it is only in relation to discourse that terrorism can menace, while simultaneously assuming the appearance of an objective political "truth." Apprehending the meanings of terrorism and comprehending its significatory power requires an understanding of terrorism that addresses the symbolic economy in which terrorism's "senseless" violence nonetheless "makes sense," and consequently takes on the power to shake the "rational" and "moral" foundations of modern society.

A Note on Discourse

One of Foucault's key insights was that, while knowledge assumes the form of authority and "truth," and as such presents as natural, transparent, and untainted by the workings of power, it is in fact constituted in power relations.[43] For Foucault, all bodies of knowledge entail the production of discourse.

Discourse is "the social process of making and reproducing sense."[44] It constitutes the objects of our knowledge, defining what can be meaningfully said about a particular subject, who can say it, and in what context it can be said. Likewise, it also "rules out" or limits "ways of talking . . . or constructing knowledge about"[45] a topic. If discourse shapes how things are put into language, it also shapes the range of practices that are performable and regulates the conduct of individual and collective subjects. Foucault uses the idea of "discursive practices" to describe this aspect of discourse: "Discursive practices are not purely and simply ways of producing discourse, they are embodied in technical processes, in institutions, in patterns for general behaviour, in forms for transmission and diffusion, and in pedagogical forms which, at once, impose and maintain them."[46] For Foucault, discourse frequently has an institutional basis.

Discourse is also historically specific: the product of particular constellations of historical circumstances, it is marked by the times. Because discourse is constantly under negotiation, objects of knowledge get constructed differently at different moments in history. In this sense, discourse articulates the historicity of meaning. At any given point in history, multiple discourses pertaining to a particular topic coexist and compete for dominance. As such, discourse constitutes a site for the struggle over meaning, legitimacy, and the power of domination.[47] However, in every era, certain discourses, particular modes of representing and making sense, gain supremacy. These discourses are granted the legitimacy of institutional knowledge and support and are sanctioned by the general culture. Richard Terdiman describes this as "dominant discourse."[48]

For Terdiman, dominant discourse's "presence is defined by *the social impossibility of its absence*"; it is that which "goes without saying" and "whose content is always already performable by the general member of the population."[49] In Terdiman's formulation, dominant discourse is elusive. Being naturalized, it appears as self-evident and commonsensical and therefore evades perception. Hence, "to it is granted the structural privilege of appearing to be unaware of the very question of its own legitimacy . . . In modern societies, it is by this transparency that the 'ruling ideas' rule."[50]

Discourse is implicated in the reproduction of the power relations underpinning dominant culture, perpetuated at the level of "grand, overall strategies" and also in the "many, localized circuits, tactics, mechanisms and effects through which power operates—what Foucault calls the . . . 'microphysics' of power."[51] Against the horizon of competing discourses, dominant discourse "is always totalitarian by implication,"[52] seeking "to ensure that *all* are brought within the dominant's field of force so that its naturalized pervasiveness comes to define the limits of subjectivity and of autonomy."[53] Dominant discourse, then, is both constitutive of, and constituted by, dominant power relations. In the case of terrorism, dominant discourse is grounded in the institutional articulations of what Edward Herman and Gerry O'Sullivan call the "terrorism industry."

The Emergence of the "Terrorism Industry"

In the 1970s, as the US government began to perceive itself as the target of terrorism and marshaled its institutional energies to combat it, a new discourse on terrorism emerged and gained dominance within US culture. This same discourse, articulated only slightly differently, structures our present-day understandings of the practice of terrorism. Many of the key scholars of terrorism studies that contributed to the production of 1970s discourse on terrorism have also contributed to recent literature deployed to make sense of the events of September 11, 2001.[54] These scholars have further played an important role in advising governments about how to respond to terrorism in the new millennium.

In *The 'Terrorism' Industry*, Herman and O'Sullivan make a political economy argument about the ways "terrorism" has been mythologized and managed in the Western world and, in particular, in the United States since the 1970s.[55] They claim the ways terrorism articulates in the US imagination are the product of a government public relations agenda that sells the nation's foreign policy activities to citizens of the United States and other Western nations alike. The terrorism industry is a constellation of government bodies, research institutes, and intelligence and security organizations that cross public and private sector institutions, which "manufactures, refines, and packages for distribution information, analysis, and opinion on a topic called 'terrorism.'"[56] Together, the organizations comprising the terrorism industry "establish policy and provide opinions and selected facts about official acts and plans on terrorist activity in speeches, press conferences, press releases, hearings, reports, and interviews. [They also provide] risk analysis, personal and property protection, and training, and a body of terrorism 'experts.'"[57] While Herman and O'Sullivan do not make the claim explicitly, we can understand them as signaling that the terrorism industry is a key site in the production of dominant discourse on terrorism. As a set of institutions that collaborate in the production of "scientific" knowledge about terrorism, it produces the object of "terrorism," governing the way that terrorism is meaningfully talked and reasoned about.

Gilda Zwerman makes a similar argument, specifically locating the rise of "terrorism studies" in relation to the moral panic—"the antiterrorist hysteria of the political climate"[58]—that saw the consolidation of both the apparent threat of terrorism and government counter-terrorism responses in the United States in the mid-1970s. Zwerman identifies the key proponents of this field as "neoconservative intellectuals . . . from a variety of traditional academic disciplines" including "political science, criminology, and psychology" who have successfully advanced "'terrorist studies' into a recognized field of scholarship" through the generation of "expert" literature and tertiary curricula.[59]

The framework of understanding provided by the terrorism industry works overwhelmingly in consonance with the interests of the state. Herman and O'Sullivan write that "the analysts supplied by the private sector of industry, along with those working in government, constitute the 'experts' who establish and expound the terms and agenda demanded by the state."[60] This idea is echoed by Zwerman who, writing about the literature on terrorism of the 1970s and 1980s, suggests that the terrorism studies literature presents a picture of terrorism that aligns neatly with establishment priorities:

> Most of the research cited in these texts is funded by government and law enforcement agencies and relies primarily on information from secondary and biased sources including intelligence and media agencies . . . The field of terrorist studies may be regarded as an extension of counterinsurgency thought, which borrows its formulations from politically reactionary . . . ideological paradigms within traditional academic disciplines, providing a "scientific" rationale for the repressive apparatus of the state.[61]

The high level of knowledge exchange between institutional powers means the information made available to the public is tightly controlled, narrow in focus, and echoes the interpretations of terrorism expounded by terrorism studies scholarship. In this context, Zwerman argues, "conservative ideologues . . . in the government, the courts, and the mainstream media" determine "what is 'known' about recent incidents of political violence and the background and motives of the individuals involved in these actions."[62]

The news media are an important source of information about terrorism for public consumption and a crucial site for the reproduction of dominant discourse on terrorism. As Jenkins outlines, the news media rely heavily on "expert" opinion in their reporting of terrorist incidents, legitimizing the "official" line on terrorism:

> Most materials that appear in the media can be traced to a small number of official agencies . . . which enjoy a very high degree of credibility . . . The news media generally treat this kind of official information as authoritative . . . The media often seem content to serve as the mouthpieces of the law enforcement bureaucracy.[63]

The reproduction of dominant discourse on terrorism, however, is not restricted to news media representations. Public perceptions of terrorism are formed in audiences' interactions with a variety of representations of terrorism that circulate in both "fictional"—films, television, novels—and "nonfictional"—historical and "true crime"—texts. These texts, while they may be configured as forms of "entertainment," reproduce stereotypical understandings of politically motivated violence and thus are equally important in shaping popular understandings of terrorism.[64] Jenkins claims the products of the "media-entertainment" industries, like the news media, are heavily implicated in the production and circulation of discourses on terrorism. Interestingly, he argues that the majority of these texts tend to reproduce terrorism in the "safe" terms of dominant discourse, reinscribing the understandings of terrorism that emanate from the terrorism industry.

Characteristics of the Discourse on Terrorism

The term "terrorism" operates within a highly emotive register. Within Western cultures, it circulates as a signifier of *terrible*, *unpredictable*, and *illegitimate* violence. As US President George Bush Junior's addresses to the nation in the aftermath of the attacks of September 11, 2001 repeatedly demonstrated, terrorism has come to signify in the Western imagination as one of the most, if not *the* most, heinous of "crimes against humanity."

It is, in popular speak, the abysmal expression of extreme and senseless violence, of violence at its abhorrent and unspeakable worst. As Jenkins notes, terrorism "is perceived as a kind of ultimate evil."[65]

As a form of political currency, it seems, terrorism has the capacity to mobilize (excessive) collective anxiety and moral outrage. As Eileen MacDonald contends, "our reaction to the term 'terrorist' is Pavlovian. We know what sort of brutes they are, and nothing more really needs to be said on the subject."[66] Indeed, Charles Townshend argues that terrorism "seems to go straight off the chart of 'common sense'—to be not only unjustifiable, but atrocious, mad, or 'mindless.'"[67] And Hage contends that the term inspires us to abandon all critical perception.[68] The construction of terrorism as "senseless" and abhorrent violence has been particularly pronounced in the context of so-called Islamic terrorist attacks on the West such as those that unfolded on September 11, 2001. However, the West has repeatedly expressed a disproportionate fear of that which is labeled terrorism since at least as far back as the early 1970s, when both "home-grown terrorism" and "international terrorism" first became prominent political preoccupations for Western nations.[69]

Within the literature of terrorism studies, notwithstanding an abiding concern about the mutability of the term, terrorism has come to signify in a very specific set of ways. In an overview of the various definitions deployed within the terrorism studies literature over its 35-year history, Jenkins claims that "the word terrorism has commonly come to mean violent acts carried out randomly against nonmilitary, civilian targets, with the aim of inspiring fear in the wider population. Also, the acts are intended to promote some kind of political goals."[70] Drawing attention to the political motivations of terrorism simultaneously disavows the fact that all violence is political and overlays a classificatory framework that establishes a distinction between legitimate forms of violence and illegitimate forms of "political" violence (which are frequently read as "fanatical"). While Jenkins does not explicitly rule out the possibility of state terrorism, his definition works within an economy of meaning in which terrorism most usually signifies as the activities of small clandestine groups directed at overthrowing established government. Jenkins' definition is typical of dominant discourse on terrorism in its assumption that terrorism comprises the activities of groups positioned outside the formal structures of power within the societies they attack—that it is a tactic of violent and *subaltern* resistance. Laqueur's influential definition of terrorism explicitly couches terrorism in these terms:

> Terrorism, interpreted here as the use of covert violence by a group for political ends, is usually directed against a government, less frequently against another

group, class, or party. The ends may vary from the redress of specific "grievances" to the overthrow of a government and the taking over of power, or to the liberation of a country from foreign rule. Terrorists seek to cause political, social and economic disruption, and for this purpose frequently engage in planned or indiscriminate murder. It may appear in conjunction with a political campaign of guerrilla war, but also in a "pure" form.[71]

Here Laqueur emphasizes an understanding of terrorism as a covert practice that typically operates against established regimes with the specific objective of disrupting the ostensibly seamless operation of power. Laqueur's definition also implies a moral judgment. By defining terrorism as a form of violence that is used to achieve "political ends," he implicitly draws the distinction between legitimate and illegitimate violence in a way that is typical of terrorism studies definitions. Further, his description of terrorist violence as "planned or indiscriminate murder" mobilizes the discourses of criminality to construct terrorism as a form of demonized and illegitimate deviance. Terrorism, then, is a term embedded within power relations, which, in its operations, betrays the limits of the workings of power within the discursive economy of dominant Western culture.

This fact does not escape the protagonists of terrorism studies, who commonly note that "one man's terrorist is another man's freedom fighter." There is tacit acknowledgment among the "expert" literature that labeling an act "terrorist" is the semantic effect of a structure of power relations. Conor Cruise O'Brien states this idea concisely:

The words "terrorism" and "terrorist" are not terms of scientific classification. They are imprecise and emotive. We do not apply them to all acts of politically motivated violence nor to all people who commit such acts. We reserve their use, in practice, for politically motivated violence *of which we disapprove.*[72]

What Cruise O'Brien draws attention to here is that issues of power and legitimacy are fundamentally at stake in the application of the term "terrorism." As Jenkins suggests, *"any group labeled as terrorist is denied any legitimacy,* and the public tends to feel that no measures are too severe to deal with it. It is almost as if the group has been read out of the human race."[73]

What the literature on terrorism implicitly acknowledges, then, is that labeling an act of violence "terrorism" defines an "enemy," and in so doing, reinscribes the ideological boundary between legitimate and illegitimate violence. As such, the appellation "terrorism" operates within an economy of legitimacy to mark the limits of "lawful" opposition to the status quo, delineating the distinction between so-called criminal forms of violence and state-sanctioned coercive measures. "Terrorism" thus operates asymmetrically to define certain political actions as "illegitimate" violence. In this sense, within democratic societies, the use of the word "terrorism" marks the limits of the workings of power within dominant culture. As Hage contends, "the most important aspect of the classification 'terrorist' [is that] it involves a form of symbolic violence that forces us to normalise certain forms of violence and pathologise others."[74] Within dominant discourse, terrorism signifies primarily as the violence of clandestine, politically estranged extremist groups directed at institutional and legitimized power. Constructing terrorism in this way facilitates the normalization of the coercive dimensions of the state—it produces violence used to sustain the status quo as "natural" and "normal." This is the mark of dominant discourse.

However, just as the literature on terrorism commonly pays no more than passing homage to the idea that audiences are fundamental to the success of terrorism, so too is it with the acknowledgment of the power relations implicit in labeling an act of "terrorism." Terrorism studies typically reasserts the legitimacy of the structures of power that underpin dominant culture by characterizing terrorism as an attack on the state.

Attacking the State

Historically in Western culture, terrorism has commonly materialized as an attack on the political institution of the state, executed by "nonstate" actors. In more sophisticated analyses of terrorism, "the state" describes the bureaucratic apparatus that sustains and supports processes of government—what Anthony Giddens usefully describes as "a set of institutional forms of governance maintaining an administrative monopoly over a territory with demarcated boundaries (borders), its rule being sanctioned by law and direct control of internal and external violence."[75] In dominant discourse, however, the terrorist challenge to the state is primarily articulated in terms of a straightforward attack on the government of the day. As Herman and O'Sullivan, recounting the ways terrorism has been represented in Western official discourse, suggest, "terrorists were evidently those who used violence in *opposing governments*, like the Red Brigades, the Baader–Meinhof gang, and national liberation movements."[76] That is, terrorism gets constituted as a violent and criminalized form of contesting the institutions of government in Western cultures.

In particular, terrorism is often described as a form of violence afflicting modern Western democracies. For example, Yehezkel Dror defines it as "the use of selective intense violence by small groups *to undermine democratic government*,"[77] and Horowitz claims that democracy is "the structural victim of terrorism."[78] Describing the Western model and semantics of terrorism,

Herman and O'Sullivan claim the Western world propagates the idea that "democracies are especially hated by and vulnerable to terrorism."[79]

This perception is reinforced by claims that terrorism in the Western world first appeared simultaneously with the foundation of modern democratic states. For example, Laqueur claims, "it is generally believed that systematic political terrorism is a recent phenomenon dating back to the last century,"[80] going on to argue that the rise of terrorism is imbricated with the historical rise of democracy and nationalism. He posits the failure of modern democratic regimes to live up to expectations as a catalyst for terrorism,[81] highlighting that the democratic preclusion of the state's violent repression of oppositional groups makes them, paradoxically, a target for terrorism.[82] Laqueur thus contributes to a discourse in which terrorism is a negative by-product of modern democracy. Indeed, he implies, as does much of the terrorism studies literature, that terrorism exploits the very virtues of democratic political organization to assail democratic regimes.[83] In this discourse, the tolerance of political diversity that is considered a touchstone of democracy is constructed as one of the conditions rendering democratic societies vulnerable to terrorism. As Herman and O'Sullivan, critiquing the Western model of terrorism, suggest, "one of the merits of this approach from the standpoint of the Western establishment is its rooting of terrorism in Western freedom itself, with the West portrayed as an unfair victim of its own virtues."[84] Terrorism, this discourse would have us believe, singles out democracies. As Herman and O'Sullivan claim, it is "part of the myth structure of the Western model [for understanding terrorism] that, whereas the West is continuously under siege from terrorism, the East is free from this scourge."[85]

Formulating terrorism in these terms presumes that it is practiced by small, clandestine groups against democratic governments.[86] As I have outlined, this conceptualization of terrorism circulates widely within official discourse on terrorism, and, in constructing it in opposition to the democratic state, simultaneously demonizes it and reproduces the legitimacy of the modern democratic state. Thus, within the literature on terrorism, while the acknowledgment that terrorism is an ideological construction often makes an appearance, this idea is rarely pursued. Indeed, many analyses highlight the limitations of the labeling as problematic while simultaneously advocating the adoption of a definition of terrorism that reproduces its blindnesses. For example, on the one hand, Jenkins avows the difficulties implicit in "drawing a neat line between terrorism and the horrors of modern warfare as conducted by states"[87]—a designation, we should note, that turns on the construction of "legitimate" violence. On the other hand, he advocates the US State Department definition of terrorism as "a solid working basis for discussion."[88] This definition describes terrorism as "premeditated, politically motivated violence perpetrated against noncombatant targets by sub-national groups or clandestine agents, usually intended to influence an audience."[89] In effect, Jenkins grants no more than superficial credence to the power relations implicit in the application of the term terrorism.

Similarly, for Martha Crenshaw, the editor of an important collection on terrorism published in 1983, both left- and right-wing terrorism ultimately invoke the question of legitimacy.[90] For Crenshaw, however, the key questions revolve around how democratic states should deal with the terrorist challenge to their legitimacy. As such, she contributes to the discursive reproduction of the democratic state as the authorized expression of popular political will—as pure and beyond "terrorism." Commentators such as Crenshaw and Jenkins thus acknowledge that terrorism brings the legitimacy of the state under scrutiny, but in the broader context of their respective arguments, they disavow the possibility, to which terrorism potentially draws attention, of the illegitimacy of the state and of democratic state violence.[91] They acknowledge the power relations implicit in the terrorist label and then proceed to implicitly claim the power of delineation for themselves.

Presenting as transparent, commonsensical, inevitable, and authoritative, "dominant discourse appears within the social formation like the unmarked case in linguistics—*noticed only in its violation.*"[92] Dominant discourse seeks to totalize the field of significatory practices, to naturalize particular modes of representation, and to exclude alternatives. In so doing, it "defines the social field as an ideological preserve."[93] In Western culture, "terrorism," that "worst possible kind of violence," is constituted within the framework of a dominant discourse that subtends dominant power formations. Nonetheless, the operation of discourse never entirely precludes the production of alternative modes of meaning, or what Terdiman calls "counter-discourses." These counter-discourses vampirize and redeploy dominant modes of representation to construct alternative meanings that challenge naturalized modes of thought and practice. In their violation of dominant discourse, counter-discourses "point up the coherent social interests which [dominant discourses] further, and those which they tend, most often quietly and subtly, to subordinate."[94]

It is little surprise then that the advocates of terrorism studies are so vociferous about the need to define terrorism in precise terms and to apply the term with discretion. Nor is it surprising that they object so strongly to radical groups deploying the term to describe practices that fall outside the terrorism studies definition of terrorism. The circulation of counter-discursive constructions of terrorism—for example, the appropriation of the term by radical groups to describe US foreign policy initiatives or the description by some feminists of rape as a form of gender terrorism—makes visible the existence of a dominant discourse on terrorism, potentially deconstructing its "common sense" and exposing its ideological investments.

Dominant discourse is sustained by a paradox. On the one hand, it appears as timeless and authoritative; on the other hand, this appearance must be continually and closely regulated—its assertions must be ceaselessly reaffirmed. The effort required to police the reproduction of dominant discourse evidences its contingency.[95] We can thus read the terrorism studies anxiety around the definition and correct usage of the term "terrorism" as a marker of both the existence and limitations of dominant discourse. This intense and sometimes obsessive preoccupation with policing the boundaries of dominant discourse on terrorism undercuts the confidence with which terrorism studies so often seeks to assert itself. So too, concern over the routine "misuse" of the trope of "terrorism" within the spaces of official and popular culture alike betrays an ideological commitment to particular understandings of terrorism: understandings that align themselves with dominant order, and, not least, reveal an awareness of the contingencies that circumscribe this "truth production."

CHAPTER 2

Constructing the Terrorist: The Threat from Within

Domestic terrorism is the unlawful use, or threatened use, of force or violence by a group or individual based and operating entirely within the United States or its territories without foreign direction committed against persons or property to intimidate or coerce a government, the civilian population, or any segment thereof, in furtherance of political or social objectives.

1999 FBI report on terrorism[1]

In its descriptions of the practice of terrorism and the delineation of the threat it apparently poses to social order, dominant discourse tends to focus attention on the individual terrorist as causative of terrorism. This conflation of *terrorism* with *terrorists* has two important consequences for the construction of terrorism within Western cultures.

First, focusing discussions of terrorism on the terrorist has a dehistoricizing and depoliticizing effect that facilitates the demonization of the terrorist and, consequently, of terrorism. Further, Western popular understandings of terrorism continually produce the problem of terrorism as "new" and "unprecedented," eliding prior histories of "political violence." How does this "historical amnesia" structure the domain of the political in ways that underline the apparent resilience of dominant order? And how does this process of forgetting compel a particular understanding of whence the terrorist threat to the status quo derives?

Second, constructing terrorism in terms of the propensities of certain individuals constitutes one mechanism by which the gendering of terrorism operates. The inscription of terrorism on the individual terrorist works to reproduce terrorism as a political practice that is, in dominant discourse, the prerogative primarily of men. What are the implications of this gendering of terrorism for the construction of female terrorist subjectivity? How does the female terrorist operate in relation to the cultural category of femininity?

In an economy of meaning in which terrorism is gendered masculine, the female terrorist's femininity sets her apart from the male terrorist and conjures her as a particularly aberrant and demonic threat to social order. She is perceived as *hyperterrorist* in that she is regarded as highly subversive, extraordinarily violent, viciously deceptive, and difficult (if not impossible) to rehabilitate. Feminist analyses have typically claimed that the female terrorist constitutes an excessive threat because she disrupts deeply embedded cultural assumptions about femininity, destabilizing the naturalized gender relations that structure and organize Western culture.[2] But is her disruption of Western reified femininity the only source of the (excessive) anxiety the female terrorist inspires? Why does her "violence" present as "disintegrative, anomalous, threatening"?[3] Might the figure of the female terrorist also activate a Western cultural anxiety that Woman always exceeds the boundaries that patriarchy establishes to contain her?

Terrorism = Terrorists: The Emphasis on Perpetrators

Writing in the late 1970s, Paul Wilkinson suggested that the "new" phenomenon of revolutionary terrorism plaguing the Western world "implies the invention of a new profession, the professional terrorist."[4] Delineating the individual terrorist subject—whether cataloguing the specific historical protagonists of terrorism or providing a more generic profile of the "typical" terrorist—has been a major concern for scholars of terrorism studies. The figure of the terrorist is a product of these institutional knowledges and their modes of representation.[5] They actively call the terrorist into being.

More than this, since the late 1960s, terrorism scholars and law enforcement agencies have characteristically sought to define terrorism primarily in terms of its perpetrators, and by extension, the organizational structures in which they operate, the range of tactics they deploy, and their targets (human or otherwise). For instance, the US legal definition of terrorism classifies terrorism as a specific kind of violence executed by *particular kinds of groups and/or individuals.*[6] Further, most existing analyses of terrorism proceed by describing the historical incidence of terrorist organizations and their attacks. Walter Laqueur's important book, *Terrorism,*[7] is still the most thorough analysis of the phenomenon. It provides a catalogue, interspersed with political analysis, of terrorist groups that have operated in different locations throughout the world at various historical moments. For Laqueur, terrorism—the abstract political concept—manifests in, or is typified by, the actions of particular groups of terrorists. In this context, terrorism, the practice, gets conflated with its agents. Indeed, Ghassan Hage claims that "no author . . . has made it clear whether he or she is undertaking an analysis of terrorism as such or of terrorist organisations."[8] Terrorism thus comes to be synonymous with its perpetrators.

Within the scholarship on terrorism, the terrorist emerges as causative of terrorism. In Wilkinson's analysis, for example, "activist personalities prepared to initiate terror" provide the necessary link between the "erosion of shared democratic values, a state of anomie, or a crisis of democratic institutions" and the occurrence of terrorism.[9] The terrorist personality is thus positioned as *translating* disillusionment into political violence. The terrorist is constructed as the embodiment of terrorism.

Dehistoricizing and Depoliticizing Terrorism

Positioning the terrorist at the center of discursive projections of terrorism constructs terrorism as operating in a historical vacuum. Seen as the effect of individual psychologies, terrorism is excised from its social, cultural, political, economic, and historical contexts and therefore always presents discursively as a novel affliction of the contemporary world.

The conflation of the terrorist with terrorism leads some commentators to define terrorism in terms of terrorist motivations. For example, Chalmers Johnson, reporting on a US Department of State conference in 1976, concludes that "terrorism is, like criminality, a matter of behavior *and* intent."[10] Similarly, Lawrence Zelic Freedman, elaborating his definition of terrorism, claims that "terrorism also involves, in addition to the act, the *emotion and the motivation of the terrorist.*"[11] Inasmuch as terrorism gets defined as the end result of the projection of terrorist psychology, then both terrorism and the terrorist come to be pathologized. In this logic, the search for solutions to the problem of terrorism rests upon unlocking the secrets of terrorist pathology.

Terrorism studies thus frequently overrides systemic factors that might explain the rise of terrorism—such as the breakdown in democratic institutions that Wilkinson alludes to—and foregrounds accounts that position the terrorist as aberrant. Many accounts dehumanize the terrorist, frequently in highly condemnatory terms, feeding into the pathologization of the terrorist. For example, Laqueur, in a consideration of "the motivation of the political terrorist," argues that "political terror . . . tends to be less humane than the variety practiced by 'ordinary' criminals . . . It is the terrorists' aim not just to kill their opponents but to spread confusion and fear. It is part of the terrorist indoctrination to kill the humanity of the terrorist."[12]

The terrorist that emerges in Laqueur's analysis is dehumanized, cruel, and sadistic. He—for the terrorist is male in Laqueur's formulation—operates outside the moral economy that underpins "civilized" society. He is not just criminal, he is excessively so. Laqueur writes that "the 'ordinary' criminal, unlike the terrorist, does not believe in indiscriminate killing. He may torture a victim, but this will be the exception, not the rule, for he is motivated by material gain and not by fanaticism."[13] In his claim that "terrorists are fanatics,"[14] Laqueur characterizes the terrorist as marked by extreme and uncritical zeal. The terrorist is constructed as mentally unhinged, possessed by a form of sinister political fever, an acutely dangerous—because "political"—madness.

The equation of terrorism with its perpetrators constructs terrorism primarily in terms of deviance, reiterating a traditional criminological definition of criminal behavior as the effect of "deviant personalities." This dehistoricizes and depoliticizes terrorism. Terrorism studies scholars also frequently distinguish terrorism from other forms of "criminal" activity by emphasizing the "political" nature of terrorism. However, the ways they construct their object of study divert discussion from the political challenge terrorism poses to dominant order, privileging instead the psychology of deviance. Similarly, a focus on individual terrorists at the expense of a critical analysis of the historical contexts in which terrorism operates enables the construction of terrorism as a form of madness: a madness compounded by the fact that the terrorist appears to operate in a historical vacuum. By dehumanizing, pathologizing, depoliticizing, and dehistoricizing the terrorist, terrorism is criminalized, and the terrorist is produced as a site for rehearsing the boundaries of power and legitimacy, in effect reproducing the state's priorities of law enforcement and social control.

These ideas about terrorists, and consequently, terrorism, are reproduced at the level of popular culture, in an often exaggerated form, and "imbued with extraordinary levels of fantasy."[15] As with the terrorism studies literature, both fictional and nonfictional popular cultural texts typically pit terrorists against democracies,[16] and personify terrorism such that the demonized terrorist operates as shorthand for the demonization of terrorism more generally. Further, the terrorist is constructed quite narrowly and ahistorically as the origin of terrorism. As Philip Jenkins suggests:

> The message from popular culture is that the problem [of terrorism] is chiefly *the work of a handful of very evil individuals* and understanding this menace is perhaps less difficult than comprehending the diverse factors (political, social, economic, spiritual) which drive the faceless terrorists of real life. Terrorism can thus be personalized in the form of Carlos, Colonel Qaddafi, or Osama bin Laden.[17]

The terrorist icons that Jenkins identifies here are all male. Further, Jenkins suggests that the personification of terrorism that we see in popular cultural texts simplifies terrorism for public consumption, disavowing the situatedness of terrorism, and fundamentally dehistoricizing and depoliticizing the terrorist. Writing about news media representations of terrorism, in particular, Aida Hozic explains that reportage others the terrorist by depriving them of their human face and presenting terrorists out of context, such that their actions seem "as distant and devoid of reason as a natural catastrophe."[18] Such coverage amalgamates "all terrorist acts into one formula," elides the political contexts and aspirations motivating terrorism, and effects "the separation of terrorists from 'ordinary' and sane people."[19]

The spectacularization of terrorism within popular culture grants terrorists publicity, and as such, appears to fulfill their aims. Hozic comments that "the whole spectacular machinery gives terrorists . . . publicity which they on their own could never dream of acquiring,"[20] ultimately underlining the legitimacy of state power by "present[ing] terrorism in such a way that it start[s] working for and not against society."[21]

This tendency of both the "expert" literature and popular cultural texts to interpret terrorism through a dehistoricizing and depoliticizing frame positions each wave of terrorism that strikes on home soil as a *new and unprecedented phenomenon.* In the face of terrorism, nations such as the United States frequently suffer from what Richard E. Rubenstein terms "historical amnesia,"[22] constructing political violence and upheaval as the exception to the norm. The outbreak of terrorist violence in the late 1960s and early 1970s in the United States was commonly perceived in this way. Because terrorism circulates as novel and unprecedented, it is imagined as a practice that always takes place "elsewhere," so when it strikes "at home" we are always taken by surprise. As Jenny Hocking argues, in the absence of knowledge concerning historical precedents of terrorism in the host nation, terrorism is thus often deemed to warrant the introduction of special legislation entailing the increase of state powers.[23] In this relationship between the cultural imagining of the terrorist/terrorism and the exercise of law and order, we can see the material effects of dominant discourse on terrorism in operation.

The 1970s "New Breed of Terrorism"

As Laqueur pointed out in 1978, one of the popular myths prescribing the understanding of terrorism is that "terrorism is a new, unprecedented phenomenon. For this reason, its antecedents (if any) are [regarded as] of little interest."[24] Our understandings of terrorism are always predicated upon a disavowal of the past, a process of burying history, of sending it underground. Terrorism, in this context, registers as a fundamental breach, an "extraordinary" rupture of social relations. However, "terrorism," of course, is not unprecedented in Western cultures. Rather, this forgetting is an absence that structures political memory.

As previously noted, Rubenstein claims that US culture has a particular proclivity for historical amnesia:

> Stormier eras fade in the imagination; we are easily led to believe that the lull which surrounds us is the norm, and lightning flashes of violence the rare exception. Thus, in the late 1970s, the dramatic disorders of the recent past already seem *frozen in time*, stock footage for a television documentary on "The Turbulent Sixties."[25]

Writing in the late 1970s, Rubenstein is referring to the terrorism of left-wing insurgent groups with predominantly "white", middle-class constituents. In Rubenstein's account, the terrorism that plagued the United States in the preceding decade had already been mythologized as a feature of a distanced and disconnected past. Only a few years earlier, though, it had been perceived as a new form of terrorism that posed a serious threat to social order in the United States. As a 1999 Federal Bureau of Investigation report attests, "from the 1960s to the 1980s, leftist-oriented extremist groups posed the most serious domestic threat to the United States."[26] Indeed, "the Weather Underground alone was responsible for some 800 bombings from 1969–72, including explosions at the University of Wisconsin Center for Mathematical Sciences, a US Senate office building and the Pentagon."[27] The report continues:

> Approximately 641 terrorist incidents occurred in the United States between 1971 and June 1975. Among these attacks were 166 bombings, 120 fire bomb-ings, and 118 shootings . . . The vast majority were attributed to left-wing/ anti-war extremists, many operating within such organizations as the Weather Underground, Armed Forces of Puerto Rican Liberation (FALN), the Black Liberation Army, and the Symbionese Liberation Army.[28]

Contemporary discourse on terrorism commonly constituted the terrorism that surfaced in the United States in the late 1960s and 1970s as a "new breed of terrorism" that broke violently with the US tradition of relatively peaceful consensus politics. Rubenstein notes that leading scholars viewed the United States as "a pluralistic society characterized by shared social and political values and a 'genius' for compromise" and that "the conclusion drawn by many was that the United States, having mastered the art of peaceful change, could in good conscience presume to lead the world."[29] In this context, the left-wing political violence experienced by the United States in this era was interpreted as rupturing a history of postwar harmony.

One of the key distinctions of this "new breed of terrorism" was the perception that it was "home-grown"—a threat coming from, and attacking *within*, US society. This "new" terrorism was perceived as coming from "within" in two senses.

First, evidence suggests that the rise of the terrorism of the late 1960s and early 1970s marked the first moment when groups of young, educated, predominantly middle-class US citizens, advocating violent revolution, orchestrated attacks against what they configured as a conservative and corrupt political culture that served only the interests of the US elite.[30] Like its European counterparts—for example, the *Brigate Rosse* in Italy and the *Rote Armee Fraktion* in Germany—this terrorism hailed a new kind of participant: the so-called alienated youths,[31] who, although claiming to operate on behalf of subaltern interests, were drawn predominantly from within the dominant classes.[32]

Further, this was the first time in living memory that the United States had experienced a systematic campaign of *left-wing* political violence.[33] A large number of participants in the terrorist violence of the era had been influenced by key left-wing philosophers of armed revolution and by the left-wing student protest movement on university campuses in the late 1960s. As Gilda Zwerman notes:

> Virtually all of those imprisoned [for actions of political violence in the United States in the 1970s] . . . were active in militant sectors of the protest movements in the 1960s and eventually became part of a small segment of the "anti-imperialist" tendency of the Left . . . Most would define themselves as socialists or communists.[34]

In the context of the Cold War, the fact that this "new breed of terrorism" was affiliated with left-wing political traditions gave it a particularly sinister dimension.

Second, this was also a terrorism that threatened US society *on its own soil*. Previously, terrorism had been configured as a threat manifesting outside the boundaries of the US state. Now, contemporary discourse suggested, the United States was faced with a threat from within its own borders. This dominant cultural construction of left-wing insurgent terrorism as "new" thus positioned it in opposition to a perceived terrorist threat from "outside." It simultaneously elided a history of right-wing political violence within the United States.

As Ted Robert Gurr notes, throughout its short history, the United States has witnessed numerous instances of what can be defined as "political violence" on its own soil. Notably, throughout the nineteenth century and into the twentieth century, the United States was home to lengthy programs of

> Terror in defense of the status quo . . . by self-appointed Regulators, Vigilantes, Klansmen, White Cappers, and others who sought to establish or re-establish social order when it was threatened by desperados, freed slaves, non-Anglo-Saxons, and the lazy and licentious . . . They were grass-roots organizations, usually led by men of substance in their communities; their purposes were widely supported; and they made calculated use of intimidation backed by violence to achieve these purposes.[35]

Like the left-wing political violence of the 1970s, this kind of right-wing political violence could be understood as a terrorist threat from within. However, at this juncture in history, the record of right-wing political violence was disavowed, producing a significatory medium in which left-wing political violence was routinely constructed as a menacing form of terrorism, whereas right-wing political violence was not labeled, nor understood, as terrorism.[36]

In the claim to be fighting for a revolution on the basis of liberal notions of the equality of all individuals, regardless of race, creed, or class, left-wing terrorism signified the threat of subalterneity—the rise of subaltern classes to power.[37] While these groups claimed to be struggling to annihilate dominant culture's structures of power in order to instate an egalitarian structure that would grant subjects autonomy, this was not the full extent of the perceived threat. It was not only equality per se that terrorized, but also the *reversal of order*: the threat that those who had historically enjoyed the benefits of membership of the dominant class, who had traditionally had access to power, might find themselves subjugated to the will of the subaltern classes.[38]

Left-wing groups enacted a radical critique of US culture that argued for the overturning of dominant order and the instatement of a new, egalitarian order. Left-wing political violence was aimed at both the material mechanisms of the state and the cultural apparatus that reproduced a logic of dominance and subordination. It targeted society as a whole. Designed to expose the inadequacies of "the system," left-wing terrorism thus presented in the cultural imaginary as the deconstructive moment of dominant culture, earning itself the label of terrorism.[39] The 1970s labeling of certain acts of political violence as terrorism thus followed a defensive logic. It sought to contain the "terrorism" of groups that, at the level of discourse, threatened the set of cultural ideas and practices that reproduced and legitimized dominant order.[40]

A "Man's Game"

The normative understandings of terrorism generated by the "expert" analyses of the terrorism industry and reproduced in popular discourse construct the standard terrorist as male. This construction of the terrorist as male is sometimes explicit. For example, Freedman writes that the terrorist "in the United States has been a young adult white man; physically he has been slight and small but not unattractive."[41] However, it is more often implicit. As noted above, in Laqueur's analysis, the terrorist is almost exclusively a "he," constituting an example of what Elizabeth Grosz describes as the more generalized invisibility of masculinity in Western culture, the unspoken of the male body.[42]

In Laqueur's use of the male pronoun to represent the universal terrorist, then, there is a slippage between the general ("he" as representative of the nongender-specific terrorist) and the specific (constructing the maleness of the terrorist), resulting in the taken-for-grantedness of the masculinity of the typical terrorist. Indeed, while Laqueur acknowledges the presence of women in the terrorist organizations of the Western world in the late 1960s and early 1970s, he does so only in passing and, for him, the female terrorist is both an exception to the norm and "a phenomenon of recent date."[43]

At the level of popular culture, the terrorist is personified by a range of masculine figures including Carlos the Jackal, Colonel Qaddafi, and Osama bin Laden.[44] As Susanne Greenhalgh notes, the qualities associated with terrorism are those that are generally associated with masculinity. Within popular culture in the Western world, she writes, "violent activism, aggression, and willingness to make use of others all constitute terrorism as an extreme expression of militant *machismo*."[45] In this sense, terrorism signifies not only violent resistance to established regimes of power by small clandestine operatives, but also a form of (albeit contested) *masculinity*.

Terrorism thus circulates in the popular imagination as the mechanism of disputes that are fundamentally *between men*. By emphasizing the masculinity and the youth of the typical terrorist, dominant discourse suggests that terrorism constitutes what Greenhalgh labels "a dialogue with fathers," or perhaps more precisely, the failure of the dialogue with fathers that traditionally underpins patriarchal order in Western cultures.[46] Zwerman claims that the United States' "home-grown" terrorists of the late 1960s and early 1970s cited male political icons Frantz Fanon, Regis Debray, Malcolm X, and Che Guevara as key inspirations for their participation in violent political actions.[47] In this context, terrorism is constituted as the marker of a contest between, on the one hand, benevolent fathers, and, on the other, young men misguided by contemporary revolutionary male thinkers and political leaders.

As such, within dominant discourse, terrorism frequently features as the symptom of the incomplete socialization of young men into the patriarchal order of Western modernity. This is best articulated by Freedman, who explains terrorism in terms of the dysfunctional family and the "absent father":

> [The terrorist] has experienced during his earlier development severe impediments to his achievement of an integrated, relatively homogenous acceptance of himself as an adult male . . . [and in particular the] psychically prepotent deprivation of an appropriate adult male, whether biological father or father substitute, who could provide the boy with a model whom he could imitate.[48]

The terrorist in this formulation represents the result of a glitch in the transferral of patriarchal power from one generation to the next. In this way, terrorism is constructed as "a man's game."[49]

The majority of representations of terrorism that circulate in both counterterrorist and popular cultural forms thus work with a gendered understanding of what constitutes terrorism. Given that the terrorist, and by extension, terrorism, signifies as masculine, the female terrorist is positioned as a highly ambiguous figure. The informational dependency of popular cultural and media institutions in the Western world on the key proponents of terrorism studies for the provision of "expert" opinion on terrorism means that popular cultural representations of the female terrorist tend to replicate those that circulate within the literature of terrorism studies. So, given the gendering of its discourse, how does terrorism studies represent the female terrorist?

"Shoot the Women First": Constructing the Female Terrorist Threat

A small body of terrorism studies literature deals specifically with the problematic of the female terrorist. Historically, the emergence of this literature is bound up with the rise of the "terrorism industry" in the late 1960s and early 1970s. Writing toward the end of the 1970s, H. H. A. Cooper pointed to the then-recent "discovery" of the excessively vengeant female terrorist as the source of a proliferation of academic analyses of the female terrorist, emotively adding that "through the actions of a few extremely vicious examples, the world has come to the shocking, and almost certainly correct, realization that, after all, the female of the species may well be deadlier than the male."[50] In his reference to the outpouring of "analyses, investigations, explanations and the like," we can understand Cooper as describing the emergence of a new discourse on female terrorism—the institutional production of the female terrorist as an object of knowledge.

This discourse on female terrorism, which originated in the 1970s and continues to shape dominant understandings of the female terrorist today,[51] situates the female terrorist within the broader criminological paradigm of female criminality[52] and, in so doing, typically reproduces its gendered limitations.[53] Alison Young has argued that the discipline of criminology is largely gender-blind and that "gender is only re-marked when femininity is in question."[54] And Ngaire Naffine has argued that, when orthodox criminology pays attention to gender, it treats it as a "'specialist topic' (rather than integral to the analysis of crime)," and it does so to speak about *women's* crime.[55] Just as traditional criminology privileges the male criminal as the unmarked case, within terrorism studies, the masculinity of the male terrorist is largely invisible, and the significance of the category of gender goes largely ignored. Except, that is, when terrorism studies turns its attention to the specialized study of the female terrorist. When the terrorism studies' gaze comes to rest on the female terrorist, she is always already positioned in relation to her gender. In other words, within counter-insurgency literature, the female terrorist is always precisely that—a *female* terrorist. In this sense, she is constructed as qualitatively distinct from the generic (male) terrorist.

Terrorism studies is not traditionally concerned with understanding the ways terrorism as a practice might be gendered but, rather, with identifying, categorizing, and demonizing the female terrorist subject. It does not usually fix on the female terrorist to undertake an analysis that engages critically with feminist theory. Ultimately, the terrorism studies literature is underpinned by, and reproduces, conservative understandings of gender identity. As Zwerman notes, "when the dimension of gender is considered, the knowledge base in terrorist studies is broadened, although its political bias remains, combining counterinsurgency thought with antifeminist formulations of female criminality."[56]

The tendency to treat the female terrorist as a special case, combined with the gender conservatism of the terrorism studies literature, plays out in ambiguous ways, resulting in contradictory claims about both the frequency of women's involvement in terrorism and the kinds of subjectivities women inhabit within terrorist organizations. On the one hand, there is an assumption, as Cooper expresses it, that "terrorism is simply not women's work."[57] In counter-terrorist and popular culture texts alike, this idea takes expression in the assertion that, apart from a small number of "notable exceptions," women have been remarkably absent from the domain of terrorism. A corollary of this logic is that women take on secondary roles within terrorist organizations, implying that men do the "real work" of terrorism while the women play support roles for their male counterparts.[58]

On the other hand, and more frequently, we can detect an exaggerated concern with what are perceived to be growing numbers of women, not just participating in, but leading, terrorist violence. Proponents of early terrorism studies who discuss the female terrorist frequently cite a documented rise in numbers of women in Western nations engaging in acts deemed terrorist and highlight women's efficiency as terrorist operatives.[59] Laqueur, writing in 1977, expresses anxiety about the so-called rise of the female terrorist threat when, commenting on the terrorist organizations of the Western world, he suggests that women are not only more numerous than men but also more zealous than their male counterparts. Noting the "growing role played by women in Europe and America," he writes that, "in the United States, there were apparently more women than men in their ranks and the women were the more fanatic."[60] Laqueur refers here to the "new breed of terrorism"—the phenomenon he calls "urban terrorism"—of the Western world in the late 1960s and early 1970s. As with the more generic constructions of the era's left-wing terrorism discussed above, female political violence is constructed as a "new" phenomenon that has made a sudden entrance onto the contemporary cultural and political landscape. For example, Cooper claims that this era gave rise not just to a "new breed of terrorism" but, more precisely, to a "new breed of *female* terrorist."[61] The claim that the female terrorist was a new phenomenon fed into, and was fed by, dominant discourse on terrorism that positioned the "home-grown" terrorism of the 1960s and 1970s as a new feature of political life in the United States. The rise of the female terrorist was itself thought to be one of the novelties that characterized the "new breed of terrorism."

In the terrorism studies literature, this "new breed of female terrorist" frequently features as a strikingly dangerous phenomenon. As Greenhalgh contends, the female terrorist is generally "regarded as potentially monstrous, an uncontrollable Fury who will devour all in her path, engulfing everything in rivers of blood."[62] As outlined in the introduction to this book, Cooper invokes none other than the monstrous-feminine threat of the Greek mythological figure, the Gorgon, to characterize the novel and threatening force of the female terrorist.[63] Barbara Creed notes that the Gorgon represents the castrating threat of the *vagina dentata*, which symbolizes "male fears and phantasies about the female genitals as a trap, a black hole which threatens to swallow them up and cut them into pieces . . . The *vagina dentata* also points to the duplicitous nature of woman, who promises paradise in order to ensnare her victims."[64] In Greek mythology, the Gorgon can only be conquered by slaying her. By association then, Cooper implies that the female terrorist represents a highly deviant, dangerous, and beguiling figure of excess that must be dealt with by mobilizing the full weight of the state's law and order apparatus, including its "special" powers to "shoot to kill."

Summarizing the terrorism studies literature, Zwerman states that the female terrorist "is considered more dangerous and incorrigible than most other types of female criminals as well as the men who engage in the same activities."[65] For example, Cooper writes that "women terrorists have consistently proved themselves more ferocious and more intractable . . . than their male counterparts. There is a cold rage about some of them that even the most alienated of men seem quite incapable of emulating."[66] However, this sentiment was perhaps best articulated by Christian Lochte, director of Germany's intelligence-gathering network on subversives in the 1970s, who advised his counter-terrorist squads that

> For anyone who loves his life, it is a very good idea to shoot the women first. From my experience, female terrorists have much stronger characters, more power, more energy. There are some examples where men waited a moment before they fired and women shot at once. This is a general phenomenon with terrorists.[67]

Lochte's intimation, that men's attitudes toward women have hindered their ability to deal efficiently with the female terrorist enemy, articulates a concern about the ways men's preconceived notions of femininity have the potential to veil the violent threat the female terrorist poses.

Further, Deborah Galvin suggests that male victims of female terrorists are profoundly affected by encounters with terrorist women and that, while they may at first appear to have survived a female terrorist attack unscathed, they are likely to suffer "delayed reactions" and severe long-term effects. She contends:

> The male victim may be unable, personally, to cope with the degrading fact that he was overpowered by a woman. This can be a very traumatic experience, especially if the male holds a position of authority . . . [He] may find his self-concept as powerful, dominant, masculine challenged to the extent that it damages present and future relationships with wife/lover, peers and other daily relationships.[68]

Galvin implies that, in her refusal to behave like a "normal woman," the female terrorist undermines her male victim's sense of masculinity. For Galvin, the female terrorist's most severe and damaging quality is not her terrorism per se, but her transgression of the culturally ascribed meanings of femininity. In short, dominant discourse suggests that men should not be fooled by the feminine exterior of the female terrorist. It is a disguise, and she will play it to her advantage. In this sense, the female terrorist is constructed as fundamentally deceptive.

Some feminist scholars claim that female terrorists are positioned within dominant discourse as doubly deviant in that they not only challenge the structures of dominant order by violent and "illegitimate"' means (as do male terrorists), but they also threaten the naturalized order of femininity. Eileen MacDonald argues that "in taking up arms [female terrorists] commit a double atrocity: using violence, and in the process, destroying our safe traditional view of women."[69] Zwerman suggests that "when the protagonists [of terrorism] are women . . . it triggers not only fears and anxieties about 'terrorism' in general, but about the motivations of the women who *defy deeply held notions of female behavior.*"[70] And Luisella de Cataldo Neuberger and Tiziana Valentini argue that "the meaning of violence for women is unclear and the meaning of actions that do not fall into established behavioural schemes eludes us."[71] It can be argued that the female terrorist—the woman who actively engages in a violent politics of opposition—trespasses into the domain of masculinity, and, in so doing, transgresses legitimized forms of femininity. That is, she operates to disrupt the idealized version of femininity traded in Western culture; a reified femininity that constitutes women as passive, maternal and/or nurturing, peace-loving, and often pious. In this context, the female terrorist signifies as an excessively deviant woman, and this is thought to produce the range of extreme responses to female terrorists that characterize dominant discourse.

However, the female terrorist does not just disrupt normative assumptions about femininity; she also gives expression to deeply embedded fears about women that haunt the edges of the Western cultural imagination and ratifies the justness of a historical tradition of treating women with deep mistrust. She confirms the Western cultural suspicion that women are only ever just "under control" and that the boundaries of femininity need constant and rigorous policing. The female terrorist constitutes one crucial site where the fundamental elusiveness of Woman is reiterated—where femininity itself is revealed as a dissembling force, as fundamentally unknowable and therefore sinister and threatening. In her simultaneous rupture of idealized Woman and affirmation of subversive femininity, the female terrorist represents one site where the multiple and conflicting meanings of femininity intersect.

How, then, does the cultural construct of the female terrorist operate as a boundary marker of gender identity in Western culture? To show why the female terrorist—the figure that undermines steadfast gender determinations—is regarded with such trepidation, I turn to the concept of the "symptom."

The Female Terrorist as Radical Other

As numerous feminist scholars have argued, Western culture is founded upon an economy of gender relations in which femininity circulates as the negation of masculinity. In this context, the figure of Woman is constituted as fundamentally Other.[72] As Luce Irigaray expresses it, "the 'feminine' is always described in terms of deficiency or atrophy, as the other side of the sex that alone holds a monopoly on value: the male sex."[73] Constructed as the inversion of masculinity, in most contexts, femininity is not only accorded an inferior position in the gendered hierarchies of Western thinking, but is at the same time absolutely necessary to the structural privileging of masculinity, providing it with "an unfailingly phallic self-representation."[74] The symbolic economy that subtends Western culture is structured around a "sexual indifference"[75] that positions masculinity as the standard by which all else is measured. As such, Woman presents as Man's necessary (inferior and/or deviant) Other.

In her astute analysis of the gendering of crime, Young points to this simultaneous prohibition and necessity of femininity in Western culture, both "deviant" and essential to "its structuring of sexual difference."[76] She argues that the female criminal subject inverts both the interpellation of the normative (male) subject's relation to the law and the gendering of normalized (male) deviance, and, as such, she presents in the cultural imagination as "the inversion of an inversion."[77] Young's claim that the female criminal marks an inversion of an inversion differs from the claim that the female criminal is doubly deviant. Young's model reads masculinity as the standard against which both "normality" and "criminality" are measured. In Young's analysis, women are always already deviant—criminal or otherwise. By contrast, the idea that the female criminal is doubly deviant understands the female criminal as disrupting normative understandings of both the law-abiding subject (configured as nongendered) and an idealized and abstracted femininity. Thus, the idea that the criminal woman is doubly deviant does not always account for the structural privileging of masculinity that underpins dominant cultural understandings of the "normal" subject. Young's analysis shows how the female terrorist disrupts not just an idealized femininity, but also the construction of masculinity as a coherent category.

The female terrorist also manifests the more general threat of feminine deviance, of femininity as excess—or what Carole Pateman has termed, borrowing from Rousseau, "the disorder of women."[78] She represents the materialization of the ever-present, generalized potential of women's subversion, their rupture of the reified category of Woman around which the gender relations underpinning Western cultural order are structured. As Teresa de Lauretis argues, "gender, like the real, is not only the effect of representation but also its excess, what remains outside discourse as a potential trauma which can rupture or destabilise, if not contained, any representation."[79] The female terrorist, as a figure of feminine excess, thus exposes the fragility of gendered order.

Her positioning at the borders of gendered subjectivity means that, at the level of representation, the female terrorist is constructed ambivalently. She manifests paradoxically as simultaneously hyperterrorist (and therefore not properly feminine) and hyperfeminine (and therefore not properly terrorist). It is possible to understand this paradox as an effect of the female terrorist's operation as what Lynda Hart, following Lacan, calls the "symptom." For Hart, the symptom is a representational construct that marks the limits of any particular system, in this case the system of gender identity that underpins Western patriarchal order. As Hart describes it, the symptom is

> Constitutively paradoxical, for it is an element at once necessary to any system's ability to constitute itself as a totality *and* the site that marks the system's instability. [It] both manifests and corrupts . . . [It] gives support to being; it is what allows a signifying system to appear consistent, and yet it is always in excess in that system, for it cannot be fully circumscribed within it.[80]

As symptom, the female terrorist demarcates the category of femininity. She both enables the production of femininity as a relatively stable and coherent category and, situated as Other to legitimized femininity, marks the limits of the system of gender identity. However, simultaneously "outside" and necessary to ("within") the significatory system of gender, she threatens from the borders and reminds the system of its fragility. She represents the system's excess, thus signifying as a site of instability and potential subversion.[81] Indeed, her positioning at the limits undermines the very possibility of representation.

Echoing Young's analysis of the generic female criminal as the inversion of the inversion, Hart describes how, as a transgressor of positively coded femininity, the female criminal approximates masculinity, thereby threatening to usurp masculine privilege:

> If the "normal" woman was man's opposite, the invert of the normal woman became man's double. Imagining the female invert as inhabiting *his* sexual subject position enacted a rupture in sexual difference that also established her as a powerful threat to his exclusive claim to masculinity.[82]

Or, the female criminal, in her illegal occupation of the terrain of masculine subjectivity, posits the fallibility of, in Irigaray's terms, masculinity's "unfailingly phallic self-representation,"[83] "the blind spot of an old dream of symmetry."[84] In so doing, the representational construct of the female criminal operates with the subversive force of what Jonathan Dollimore describes as "the proximate." As Dollimore outlines:

> First . . . "proximates" will permanently remind the dominant of its actual instability . . . as well as produce a paranoid fear of impending subversion. So there will be both a justified fear as well as an excess of fear; second . . . proximity will become the means enabling displacement and projection, while the justified/paranoid fears will be their motivation: proximity becomes a condition of displacement; which in turn marks the same/proximate as radically other.[85]

Reading the female criminal through Dollimore's concept of the proximate, she does not draw attention only to the fragility of the cultural renderings of sexual difference, nor merely give form to the fear of potential subversion. She also generates an *excess of fear*. Inasmuch as she reminds the system of the contingency of its limits, the female criminal represents a threat that must be obsessively contained. The dominant thus responds with a recuperative gesture that displaces this excess of fear onto the female criminal, banishing her to the hinterland of radical Otherness. Her proximity threatens and must therefore be paranoiacally differentiated. She is constituted not as Same, not as Other, but as *radically* (or excessively) Other. In this way, the unsettling figure of the female criminal is placed in service of the (patriarchal) dominant. As the inversion of an inversion, her radical Otherness constitutes her as a site of containment and control.

Dollimore's concept of the proximate plays out in relation to the specific case of the female terrorist. As we have seen, dominant discourse on the female terrorist is characterized by an (often irrational) excess of fear. The female terrorist is constructed as an acutely violent and potent threat to social order—more radical, more subversive, and more violent than her male counterparts. Female terrorists are routinely constructed as highly motivated, excessively emotional beings with the capacity to commit the most heinous of crimes and show no remorse, and they are reportedly more difficult to rehabilitate.[86] The female terrorist is constructed, that is, as more terrorist than terrorist—as *hyperterrorist*.

As hyperterrorist, the female terrorist is inserted into the representational order as not properly feminine. For example, Daniel Georges-Abeyie has claimed that "contemporary female terrorists are likely to exhibit male personality or physical traits"[87] and are likely to display "aggression, unadorned faces and bodies, toughness, or other masculine qualities."[88] In this context, the female terrorist operates as a boundary marker that cordons off the "good" woman from her maligned sister. Simultaneously, however, exemplary of the nonfeminine, the female terrorist encroaches dangerously on the domain of masculinity. As such, her proximity is rigorously disavowed: it is claimed that the female terrorist is categorically distinct from the male terrorist in her unlimited capacity for violence, and she is constructed as the embodiment of unfettered evil. Or, in Dollimore's terms, the construction of the female terrorist as more terrorist than her male counterpart can be read as an instance of the radical othering, and thus containment, of the proximate.

The traces of a second, and contradictory, mechanism of radical othering of the female terrorist can be found in various claims that the female terrorist is *not a proper terrorist*. It is commonly suggested within dominant discourse that women do not turn to terrorism of their own free will, but that their engagement with terrorism is inseparable from their sexual and emotional affiliations with men.[89] For example, a 1985 study of Italian women terrorists indicated that husbands or brothers were responsible, more often than not, for their recruitment, and cited "romantic and affectional ties" as significant motivating factors.[90]

Indeed, MacDonald claims that society's standard response to the female terrorist is that she is a victim of male seduction: "The men are ultimately responsible for the violence; the women, victims of their own weakness, play a subordinate role."[91] Their passion, MacDonald continues, is construed not as a strength but as a weakness: "the women are seen as overly emotional rather than fiercely committed."[92] The female terrorist's engagement with terrorism, then, is thought to be founded upon trivial (hysterical and/or sexual) passions as opposed to the more legitimate political passions that inspire male terrorists. In this sense, she is always already pathologized and sexualized. Like the male terrorist, then, the female terrorist is thought to suffer from a form of madness. However, it is a madness that is coded peculiar to women— a kind of hormonally driven madness that is written into her biology.[93]

Failing the presence of a sexual or emotional motivation, it is often suggested that women are drugged or brainwashed into participating in terrorism.[94] First, these ideas about the female terrorist articulate with a long Western cultural tradition of essentializing women as emotional, malleable, irrational, and impulsive.[95] To thus construct the female terrorist operates to render her comprehensible within the range of culturally ascribed "typical" feminine behaviors. Indeed, she represents the "logical" limit of these behaviors: a manifestation of excessive femininity, she is *hyperfeminine*. Second, whether she is constructed as prey to her emotions, or as (coerced) victim of substance abuse, or pathologized as susceptible to "thought reform," importantly, the female terrorist is always already illegitimate, lacking "the justification of being male."[96] In this sense, the female terrorist can never be a *real* terrorist. She is always a fraud, a flawed and deviant version of her male equivalent, and the source of her illegitimacy is her excessive femininity.

The Female Terrorist as Feminine Excess

While the female terrorist is never quite considered a proper terrorist, *she nonetheless terrorizes*. As symptom, the female terrorist generates an *excess of fear*. This excessive fear is the terror of uncontainable femininity, which exceeds the value "imposed upon women by male systems of representation."[97] She terrorizes because she embodies the possibility of femininity as excess—she inspires the excess of fear associated with, to use Young's phrase, "femininity as inversion."

In Western culture's logocentricism, femininity gets idealized in terms of reified feminine "virtues" such as passivity, nurturance, compassion, gentleness, self-sacrifice, obedience, and so on. Despite the system's obsessive attempts to delineate the boundaries of femininity—to distinguish Man from Woman and the evil Fury from her benign counterpart—femininity stubbornly resists containment within these binary structures. For Irigaray, Woman always "also remains elsewhere."[98] Or, as Hart expresses it, "but 'Woman' is also 'not-all'; there is something in 'her' that exceeds the signifying system of the phallocentric symbolic."[99] Elusive and slippery, Woman constantly threatens to exceed the neatly defined boundaries that are set up to police her. Woman, in this sense, is enigma—"one doesn't know how to take (hold of) her . . . Woman always escapes: black continent, hole in the symbolic, breach in discourse."[100] The "truth" of Woman always remains submerged but ready at any moment to re-emerge with striking force.

In Western culture this fear of femininity as excess has taken expression in a history of constructing femininity as highly subversive and uncontainable. In the shadows of positively coded femininity lurks the specter of the vengeful, unstoppable, vicious Fury. This history stretches back as far as the biblical story of Eve's role in the "fall of man," but has assumed particular inflections in Western modernity. In *Idols of Perversity*, Bram Dijkstra argues that nineteenth-century Western modernity was marked by a cultural undercurrent of misogyny that culminated by the turn of the twentieth century in an unprecedented and widespread antifeminine sentiment. Women came to represent the embodiment of evil—a sexualized threat to the intellectual development of rational Man, and therefore an obstacle on the path of Man's progress to spiritual enlightenment.[101] In particular, Woman, as the personification of the sins of the flesh and signifier of the moment of original sin, presented a profound threat to Man's spiritual betterment. She exerted a constant downward pull on Man, a pull that, if he surrendered to it, would dash his chances of spiritual transcendence. Woman constantly beckons, threatening to undo him, a shadow from which he cannot separate himself and which threatens to engulf him.[102]

In contemporary Western culture, this positioning of women as evil and subversive continues to shape and regulate cultural understandings of femininity, albeit in slightly modified ways. As Stuart Hall has argued, "histories have their real, material and symbolic effects. The past continues to speak to us."[103]

In the context of this history, the feminist argument that the female terrorist is terrorizing because she disrupts culturally sanctioned understandings of femininity downplays the subversive aspects of femininity as they are constructed by Western culture. The female terrorist disrupts positively inscribed femininity, and simultaneously confirms femininity as subversive. She represents the threat of all women (being capable of) transgressing the limits of culturally sanctioned female subjectivity, drawing attention to the contingencies of the category of idealized femininity. She disinters the history of subversive femininity that dominant cultural proscriptions of Woman seek to disavow, problematizing the system of gender relations that underpins dominant order.

In a passage that strikingly parallels Dijkstra's description of nineteenth-century texts that testify to women's inherent corruptive capacities, J. K. Zawodny argues that women's presence in terrorist organizations intensifies the violence of their activities:

> Women's ability to manipulate the membership of the organization on an informal level is [a] problem . . . Men who compete for women try to "outdo" each other, often initiating violence first; looking for a formalized excuse afterward . . . The presence of women within a terrorist organization is a psychological inducement to violence that is constantly present on all organizational levels.[104]

In Zawodny's analysis, the roles women assume within terrorist organizations are of little consequence. Women's mere presence within these organizations is enough to exacerbate their propensity for evil. Woman, as such, is the (inadvertent) catalyst of malfeasance. Just as Woman as sexual being dragged the nineteenth-century male from the path to spiritual enlightenment and individual betterment, the female associated with the terrorist organization, coded as a malevolent sexual threat, corrupts and provokes the terrorist male. She represents the threat that femininity inevitably slides into criminality: "The fallen woman has not descended. She has ascended to the place that was already marked out for her by the patriarchal unconscious."[105] Discursively, she resonates as the disavowed but ever-present destructive potentiality of femininity.

The Threatening Woman: Unknowable Femininity

Young argues that criminology constructs femininity as a secret and "women as objects to be decoded."[106] Criminology, she argues, has gone to extraordinary lengths to objectify, classify, and describe femininity—to contain it within its taxonomical strictures—but despite these attempts, femininity emerges as an "identity that eludes detection, confounds discovery and is dangerously slippery and fluid."[107]

When the literature of terrorism studies directs its gaze toward the female terrorist, it too falters. In a manner that parallels Cesare Lombroso's attempts to describe and categorize the female criminal in the late nineteenth century, terrorism studies has sought to delineate, and thus contain, the threat of the female terrorist.[108] Terrorism studies discourse seeks to install clear-cut dimorphic boundaries, to categorize, name, and order, and, in so doing, to (re)inscribe the limits of lawful opposition. It seeks to distinguish between terrorists and their victims; between the legitimate violence of the state and the illegitimate violence of the terrorist; between terrorism's madness and the rationality of the state; and between forms of political resistance institutionalized as democratic rights (the right to protest, to freedom of speech, etc.) and violent and illegal forms of political opposition. However, these distinctions always operate on uncertain ground, and are always on the verge of collapsing. This is why terrorism studies must work so very hard, why its assertions often seem obsessive, and, at times, even paranoid. And when the issue of gender is introduced into the uncertain hierarchies of terrorism studies discourse, the limits of its categories are thrown into sharp relief.

Dominant representations of the female terrorist are constituted in and through a discursive *impossibility of evidence*, called into being by the discourse of terrorism studies itself. That is, terrorism studies begins with the assumption that the female terrorist, marked as she is by (albeit deviant) femininity, constitutes a secret to be discovered and unveiled—it posits the elusiveness of the female terrorist as its point of origin.[109] However, precisely because terrorism studies operates with an overarchingly conservative understanding of gender—a framework that constitutes and is constituted by the idea that femininity is obscure(d)—terrorism studies works to continually reproduce the female terrorist as elusive and unknowable.

The Impossible Body of Evidence

Terrorism studies discourse sets up the female terrorist as *a priori* unknowable, and then subjects her to the methods of "scientific" inquiry, only to find, all too predictably, that when confronted by the phenomenon of the female terrorist, its classificatory mechanisms are confounded. She stubbornly resists the taxonomic impulse of counter-terrorist efforts. Indeed, there is a sense in which, despite the feverish convictions about the illuminating potential of scientific analysis with which terrorism studies begins its quest for a typology of the female terrorist—despite the appearance of scrutinizing her in the name of unveiling her "truth"—terrorism studies always sets itself up to fail.

Terrorism studies has simultaneously been deeply fascinated by the female terrorist and generally disinterested in "knowing" her. For, when it comes to the study of the female terrorist, terrorism studies abandons all pretense at "scientific" methods in preference for abstractions. As Zwerman notes:

> The image of the female terrorist, as created by counterinsurgency experts, is rooted in the horror of the crime she has committed (or the action with which she has been associated): it does not explore the subject beyond this reality. There are no interviews with these women and few data sources. These experts rely primarily on sensationalized media accounts of the infamous events, FBI files, and "incriminating" communiqués of the group.[110]

Here Zwerman highlights a *lack of evidence* at the heart of terrorism studies knowledge about the female terrorist, a kind of willful ignorance of her. More than this, though, terrorism studies systematically operates to construct an *impossibility of evidence* in relation to the female terrorist. Zwerman continues, "indeed, the terrorist experts' description of these women implies that obtaining first-hand knowledge could endanger the life of the researcher."[111] The female terrorist is thus constructed as untouchable and unknowable, called into being across a body of impossible evidence. Gender preconceptions preclude the results of investigation, ultimately confirming that the female terrorist is elusive, unpredictable, and therefore highly threatening.

These half-hearted attempts to study the female terrorist betray the gendering of the ideological investments of terrorism studies. Constituted by, and constitutive of, a representational economy in which femininity circulates as the negation of masculinity, terrorism studies is not interested in knowing her. As Zwerman notes, "the field of terrorist studies is more concerned with generating antipathy towards its subject than with theory or scholarship."[112] Terrorism studies, concerned as it is with demonizing and othering the female terrorist, insists on locating her at the extreme end of a spectrum of female deviance as a highly dangerous and subversive force that must be contained at all costs.

As a *female* terrorist, she is always already constructed as excessively deviant. Having established her excessive deviance, there is no apparent need to qualify the threat she poses in any further detail. All that is required is that the threat she poses be continually reproduced within the cultural imagination. Indeed, this image of her as a monstrous and inhuman threat is, in some aspects, oddly consoling. In the first instance, this is because she confirms a deeply embedded Western cultural suspicion of women. Further, the "masked, quasi-military figure with cold killer eyes, cradling a Kalashnikov"[113] has us convinced that, if she was circulating among us, we would be able to identify her and weed her out. In demonizing her, the dominant cultural construction of the female terrorist propagates the idea that, as an excessively aberrant female, she is readily identifiable, either physically or emotionally, and therefore able to be fixed within the frame of deviance and hence contained. This idea is borne out by the terrorism studies research. Some commentators claim to be able to read the marks of a terrorist written onto her body or into her psyche.[114] The female terrorist is thus thought to be marked by detectable (physical and/or emotional) difference from "ordinary" women, presenting physically as nonfeminine, and/or exhibiting the discernible symptoms of a psychopathology. In that these "symptoms" are constructed as reliable indicators of the likely manifestation of a female terrorist, women who deviate from the normative ideals of feminine physicality and/or disposition, whether "terrorist" or otherwise, are brought under scrutiny. Nonnormative forms of femininity thus register as (potentially) terrorist, mobilizing the figure of the female terrorist to regulate and reinforce the boundaries of acceptable femininity.

However, dominant discourse's construction of the female terrorist as a threat identifiable via a range of physical and/or emotional markers rests on a fundamental disavowal of what the researcher might logically conclude when coming into contact with the female terrorist in more than a superficial way. Namely, that she appears, both physically and emotionally, "normal." Beyond terrorism studies' surface claim that the female terrorist represents an excessively pernicious threat to social order, a small number of analysts have dared to delve into the "depths of the unknown" to know the female terrorist better. What these analysts claim is that "these 'monsters' often look and speak much like the next-door neighbour or the woman behind you in the queue at the check-out"[115]—that they are "disturbingly normal."[116] Similarly, and not surprisingly, "scientific" studies have been unable to produce conclusive evidence that female terrorists differ from their "normal" counterparts. For example, a neurological study in which Ulrike Meinhof, notorious leadership member of the German Baader-Meinhof Gang,[117] was brought under the knife posthumously failed to ascertain differences in brain function that might explain the phenomenon of the female terrorist. In 2002, it came to light that, when Meinhof died in prison at the age of 41 in 1976, her brain was removed and "preserved in formaldehyde for secret study," unbeknownst to her family.[118]

However, the *Washington Post* reported that "scientists apparently came up with no physiological explanation for the leader's political violence."[119] Thus, the female terrorist confounds science. Unable to be demarcated from the rest of the female species, she prevails as a secret—perennially unknowable and intangible.[120] Indistinguishable from other women, she haunts, her presence acutely felt but indefinable.

Thus, terrorism studies' claim that the female terrorist is both excessively threatening and marked by discernible difference disavows evidence to the contrary. The idea that little, if anything, separates the terrorist woman from the average woman everywhere permeates terrorism studies discourse in the form of a paranoia. Terrorism studies is characterized by a deep anxiety that the boundaries between the good woman and her antithesis—the highly deceptive and demonic female terrorist—are at best blurred, and at worst, nonexistent.[121] The female terrorist evidences the insidious—because not necessarily visibly discernible—threat of femininity more generally. Femininity, obscured and obscuring, exceeds the boundaries that structure terrorism studies' taxonomies. As such, not only the female terrorist but also the "good" woman are sources of anxiety and dread within the popular imagination. For example, Zwerman notes how, in the "climate of the growing antiterrorist hysteria of the early 1980s," the US government implemented new legislation to enhance domestic law enforcement, security, and intelligence powers in dealing with terrorism.[122] In this context, she claims, the lines between political activism and terrorism as well as those between terrorists and their supporters became highly blurred; targets of domestic counter-terrorism programs could now include "associates," "supporters," or "those engaged in forms of 'pre-violent' political protest."[123]

How does this blurring of boundaries impact on politically active women? In a context in which a culture of political activism purportedly provides an environment in which terrorism can take root, both male and female political activists come under increased suspicion. However, men and women are positioned differently within this milieu of mistrust. Because femininity is configured by counter-terrorism discourse in conservative ways that privilege an understanding of women as "naturally" nurturing and supportive and easily seduced by charismatic (terrorist male) types, women are positioned by the discourse as much more likely to be supporters of terrorism, however it comes to be defined. Men, meanwhile, are not constructed as predisposed to supporting terrorism in this way. Not surprisingly then, the pliancy of the distinction between political activism and terrorism that Zwerman identifies has had a more profound effect on women than men.[124] Indeed, in the context of concerns about increasing numbers of women associated with terrorist organizations—whether as leaders and/or active terrorists, or as members in secondary roles—women's presence on the 1960s and 1970s landscape of political resistance rendered possible the blurred distinction between political activism and terrorism. Standing at the threshold between legal and illegal opposition, women always (threaten to) exceed the neatly defined categories that are set up to police political behavior. The politically active woman is thus always already marginal and therefore problematic. She is liminal, a condition that Victor Turner describes as "ambiguous."[125]

When the female terrorist appears on the horizon, the category of Woman itself becomes highly problematized and problematic. Within the literature of terrorism studies, much attention is paid to the potential for terrorist women to exploit dominant culture's assumptions about "the weaker sex" to strike when it is least suspected. Charles A. Russell and Captain Bowman H. Miller suggest that "'posing as wives and mothers,' female terrorists 'can enter restricted areas without arousing suspicion and gather intelligence for their male comrades.'"[126] And Maxwell Taylor uses the urban myth of the "bomb in the baby carriage" to illustrate how terrorist organizations exploit cultural assumptions about women to their strategic advantage, claiming that a mother's baby carriage offers terrorists "an almost perfect opportunity to move materials and weapons around" because "all the cues of passivity possible—caring, presence of children and loving behavior" render unlikely its search by security forces.[127]

Femininity itself thus presents as dissimulating and subversive, as a site of fundamental deception. As Zwerman notes, the counter-terrorism literature posits that "one of the requisites for survival in clandestinity is to 'blend in' and maintain a low profile in the neighborhood, workplace, school, and so forth."[128] The monotony of women's quotidian experience, demanded by a culture structured by a gendered division of labor, is thus constituted as the space of (potential) transgression.[129] In this sense, femininity circulates as a dissembling force, a threat to (patriarchal) order, generalizing the threat of the female terrorist. The problem becomes one of predicting which women are terrorists. Fears about the female terrorist are displaced onto all women, and femininity itself is posited as (potentially) terrorist. Ultimately, this suspicion operates to legitimize the policing of women's behavior. The "extraordinary" threat of the female terrorist thus represents the very "ordinary" threat of femininity as the subversive excess that troubles gendered order in the Western world.

Called into being across a set of contradictory claims, the female terrorist is constructed ambiguously, but is always perceived as a highly unsettling figure. She is at once exemplary of the absence of femininity where it should rightfully appear and a manifestation of the excesses of (deviant) femininity, taken to its "logically" destructive limits. She is both extraordinary in defying the laws of femininity and disturbingly ordinary in that she represents the Western cultural fear that femininity inevitably slides into criminality. Although highly ambiguous, she is nonetheless a *necessary* figure: an identifiable site onto which Western cultural anxieties about feminine excess can be projected and thereby contained.[130] Even so, she is only ever *just* under control. Whether configured as the hyperterrorist who disrupts prescriptive femininity or as the manifestation of excessive hyperfemininity, the figure of the female terrorist destabilizes the rigid structure of gender that underpins social and cultural order. As the hyperterrorist, marked by her "proximity" to Man, she threatens the neat boundaries between Man and Woman. As the hyperfeminine figure, as excessive femininity, she menaces the idealized category of Woman that is so fundamental to the reproduction of social order through time.

Whereas the generic (male) terrorist of the late 1960s and early 1970s represented a threat *from within* the dominant class, the female terrorist represents a terrorizing threat that derives *from within* in a different sense. Namely, she menaces the gendered, symbolic economy that underpins Western social and cultural order, representing the ever-present seed of destruction that lies (latent) at the heart of Western modernity.

The threat of the female terrorist is precisely the threat of the unbound symptom—the dissembling manifestation of the excess of meaning that threatens to undo the systems of representation through which dominant order—its politics of exclusion and its concomitant "common sense"—is constituted. As Hart notes, citing Slavoj Žižek, "if the symptom were to become unbound, it would mean 'literally "the end of the world"' . . . the total destruction of the symbolic universe.'"[131] At stake here is the implosion of meaning. This is the reason the female terrorist invokes such acute anxiety and why the continual attempts to contain her are rehearsed with the force of zeal. Importantly, Žižek invokes the end of the world, the apocalypse. As will become evident in subsequent chapters, the female terrorist is frequently positioned by dominant discourse as poised on the precipice of the apocalypse. Her actions are interpreted as operating within an eschatological temporality, and she manifests as end-time personified.

CHAPTER 3

Feminist Terrorists and Terrorist Feminists: The Crosswiring of Feminism with Terrorism

> I recognize there is dynamite in this and I'm scared shitless.
> Carol Hanisch speaking about her radical feminist awakening[1]

The Religious Right, Feminism, and Terrorism

In a *Washington Post* article of September 14, 2001, the icon of the North American religious right,[2] Reverend Jerry Falwell, is reported as having seized the moment of al Qaeda's September 11 attacks on the United States as an opportunity to reprimand feminists, along with "the pagans, and the abortionists, and . . . the gays and the lesbians" for their indirect hand in turning "God's wrath" against America.[3]

Since at least as far back as the emergence of radical feminism in the late 1960s, "feminism," in its various guises, has been a thorn in the side of the North American Christian political right. As outrageous as Falwell's remarks may be, what is significant is the explicit connection they draw between the occurrence of terrorism on US soil and the influence of feminism within dominant US culture. In Falwell's formulation, feminism is, however indirectly, causally connected to, and responsible for, terrorism.

Indeed, for the vanguard of the religious right, feminism is not just a *catalyst* of the kind of terrorism the global community witnessed in September 2001. As a form of subaltern politics that threatens both the state and society, *feminism is itself "terrorist."*[4] Like terrorists, feminists are understood to endanger the very fabric of a democratic United States whose touchstones are the values of life, liberty, and the pursuit of happiness. In a newsletter article entitled "Feminism Meets Terrorism," "sweetheart of the silent majority,"

Phyllis Schlafly, applauds the efforts of the firefighters who bravely scaled the staircases of the World Trade Centre in a courageous attempt to free those trapped in the "towers of inferno" and then unleashes a litany of accusations against feminists.[5] Claiming that feminists have "*intimidated* our military," Schlafly warns that "the feminist *battalions* are on the *warpath*," wielding their constitutional rights as "a *machete to destroy*." Their "*attacks*," she claims, are designed to "*wipe out* masculine men" and in the process "*eliminate* gentlemen, the kind of men who would defend and protect a lady." Schlafly's millenarian logic turns on the assumption that "out there" in middle America there is a terrorist army of women who must be resisted and ultimately defeated if the United States is to ensure its own preservation.

In a newsletter to members of his community of fundamentalist Christians, Falwell's televangelist colleague, Reverend Pat Robertson, writes: "The feminist agenda is not about equal rights for women. It is about a socialist, anti-family political movement that encourages women to leave their husbands, kill their children, practice witchcraft, destroy capitalism, and become lesbians."[6] Feminism is pictured here as a violent, destructive, "antidemocratic," sexually deplorable, regressive, pagan, and amoral movement that attacks the underpinnings of a US "democracy" that serves Christian, heterosexual consumers living within the structure of the nuclear family. In Robertson's formulation, feminists are the ultimate modern-day Infidels who menace the good work done by "God's men." Feminism, *like terrorism*, threatens the political, social, fiscal, and sexual economies of dominant order.

This discursive crosswiring of feminism with terrorism has not been confined to the commentary of the US religious right. On the contrary, since the 1970s, it has characterized both academic accounts of women's involvement in terrorism and popular cultural constructions of feminism and terrorism. So what are the conditions that produced this discursive nexus between feminism and terrorism?

The female terrorist becomes a preoccupation within the specific criminological field of (counter)terrorism studies, and within dominant culture more generally, at the precise moment when "home-grown terrorism"—terrorism carried out by US citizens on US soil—begins to be perceived as a threat to dominant order. This moment is simultaneous with the rise in strength and consolidation of women's liberation in the United States. In the period under question, proponents of (counter)terrorism studies repeatedly draw attention to the coincidence of the rise of second-wave feminism (also known as "women's emancipation" or "women's liberation") and a seemingly dramatic increase in numbers of women participating in terrorism.[7] In so doing, they establish an explicit connection between the rise of feminist politics and the occurrence of terrorism in the United States. Indeed, a number of these "experts" construct a commitment to feminism, however loosely defined, as a necessary precondition for women's participation in so-called revolutionary terrorism. To what extent, then, does the identified discursive equivalence between feminism and terrorism finds its origins in the particular constellation of forces informing the rise and representation of second-wave feminism? How does the coincidence of the rise of feminism and the perceived increase in female terrorism inform the construction of the novelty of the female terrorist? And what are the effects on feminism, and political activism more generally, of a discourse that privileges the crosswiring of feminism and terrorism to establish and secure the Otherness of both the female terrorist and the feminist, within the representational economy of late 1960s and early 1970s US culture?

Terrorist Radicals and Radical Terrorists: A Politics of Blame

The meanings of terrorism are always in dispute. What is clear, however, is that the discursive significance of the variety of urban terrorism that occurred in the United States in the aftermath of 1968 must be understood in the context of the contemporary upsurge in radical activism of the New Left and the ways these actions were coded into dominant discourse.[8] A belief in the interconnectedness of the organized left and the rise of terrorism characterized the discourse of terrorism, particularly as it was (re)produced in the counter-terrorist texts of the era.

To leap forward for a moment to the 1980s, Gilda Zwerman notes that, "during the first and second terms of the Reagan administration, antiterrorism became a central concern for many federal bureaucracies,"[9] which sought to extend state powers. According to Zwerman, such changes blurred the lines drawn by establishment institutions between "radical" and "criminal" and/or "terrorist" activity, and betrayed a governmental preoccupation with radical organizations as the breeding ground of terrorists.[10] Organizations including the Weather Underground, Black Panthers, Black Liberation Army, Republic of New Africa, Armed Forces of National Liberation (FALN), May 19th Communist Organization, United Freedom Front, and the Jonathan Jackson–Sam Melville Unit[11] came to occupy an increasingly ambiguous position on the spectrum of political dissidence, amid speculation that such organizations had direct links to "foreign and transnational supporters of terrorist activity including the Soviet KGB, Cuban DGI, Libyan government and Palestinian Liberation Organization."[12] Zwerman argues that the legislative changes that occurred in the 1980s were a direct response to the continuing perceived threat of terrorism stemming from the US experience of the radical challenge—posed by organizations working for "peaceful" social transformation and "terrorists" alike—to dominant order in the late 1960s and early 1970s.

For Walter Laqueur, who in 1977 wrote what is still considered by many as the most comprehensive study of terrorism, the occurrence of terrorism "always assumes the protective colouring of certain features of the *Zeitgeist*" that are "populist, frequently nationalist, intense in character but vague and confused."[13] Laqueur expands upon this idea to address the specificities of the terrorism of the late 1960s and early 1970s, suggesting that the rise of urban terrorism in the Western world during this period was deeply imbricated with the activities of the organized left. Noting the importance of "Communist and Arab" financing to the terrorism of the West, he argues that "the inspiration for the last upsurge of terrorism in the Western World came from a very different source," namely the influence of the New Left, which, in Laqueur's view, mobilized "millions of students . . . [whose] radicalisation was bound to have political consequences."[14]

Laqueur was not alone in making connections between the occurrence of widespread radical activism and terrorism. In 1970, sociologist Ted Robert Gurr advanced a highly influential general theory of political violence that posited it as "the predictable outcome of a widening gap between a group's 'value expectations' and the political system's 'value capabilities.'"[15] Gurr's theory implies the importance of the New Left in raising—in this logic to an unreasonable extent—the expectations of disenfranchised groups within US society as a necessary precondition for the advent of terrorism. Here, terrorism results when the demands of radicals cannot be met, either materially or symbolically, within the existing system. In this assertion, a politics of blame is discernible. Underpinning his analysis is a narrative that suggests both the "failure of the system" and the New Left's ignition of the expectations of "oppressed minorities" contributed to an environment in which terrorism could flourish. Like Laqueur, Gurr establishes a *causal* connection between radicalism and terrorism.

A corollary to this kind of theorizing suggested that, if radicals had not agitated among the "oppressed" classes, the United States, and indeed the Western world, might never have experienced the terrorism of the late 1960s and early 1970s. This idea is succinctly expressed by Frederick J. Hacker, who writes

The root causes of terrorism are not deprivation or oppression as such, but the perception and experience of injustice and the belief that such injustice is . . . arbitrary, and unnecessary, and remediable . . . Unfulfilled promises of abundance, equality, independence, and sovereignty, provoke bitter frustration and a spreading feeling of needlessly suffered injustice that can and should be terminated by violence.[16]

For Hacker, who works here with a neoliberal understanding of individual agency, the responsibility for terrorism lies explicitly with the dispossessed and with those who agitate to inspire false hopes for the amelioration of their adverse circumstances.

This view circulated beyond the perimeters of the academic (counter)terrorism debate. For example, responding to the 1974 Symbionese Liberation Army (SLA) kidnapping of Patricia Campbell Hearst, an article in the left-wing journal, *Ramparts*, blamed the SLA's emergence on the organized left's collapse and "failure to regroup," condemning left-wing terrorism as "acts of desperate violence . . . often conceived as protests against inaction itself."[17] In the mid-1970s, then, some sections of the flailing New Left drew conclusions that echoed those of the conservative texts of counter-terrorism. However, whereas Laqueur attributes the rise of terrorism to the *presence* of the New Left, the *Ramparts* article focuses on its *decline* and the (perceived) closing down of spaces for political critique within dominant culture.[18] Evident here is a medium of commentary in which terrorism is the comprehensible, if not logical, outcome of radical left-wing activism in the Western world.[19] In conservative counter-terrorist analyses, the New Left figures as the fertile ground in which terrorism can, under certain circumstances, take root.

As outlined in Chapter Two, the terrorism of the late 1960s and early 1970s in North America was constructed by dominant discourse as a "new" phenomenon, eliding a history of systematic campaigns of terror in the United States and enabling a causal link between urban terrorism and the New Left to be established within dominant discourse. In the cultural imagination, both urban terrorism and the New Left were configured as *novel* features of the contemporary political landscape—phenomena whose emergence was not only coincidental but mutually constitutive. This discursive link circumscribed the crosswiring of feminism and terrorism.

From the Coffeemaker to the Molotov Cocktail: The Claim That Feminism Leads to Female Terrorism

Representations of the female terrorist circulating in both the counter-terrorist literature and popular cultural forms in the late 1960s and early 1970s produced the female terrorist as a new feature of Western politics. Female terrorists were thought to be increasingly prevalent and particularly lethal. H. H. A. Cooper's 1979 description illustrates this point:

> The female terrorist has not been content just to praise the Lord and pass the ammunition; she has been, as often as not, the finger on the trigger . . . This *new* woman revolutionary is no Madame Defarge patiently, if ghoulishly,

knitting beside the guillotine while waiting for heads to roll. The *new* breed of female terrorist not only must have its hands firmly on the lever but must be instrumental in the capture of the victim and in the process of judgment, as well as in dragging the unfortunate death instrument.[20]

Aside from its concern with the "new" female terrorist, discernible here is a preoccupation with the shift in the balance of gendered power relations produced by the struggle for women's liberation in the late 1960s and early 1970s. Cooper alludes to the influence of feminist ideals of equality and emancipation on women's roles in the left-wing terrorist organizations of the era. The assumption is that the actions of female terrorists are informed by feminist "ways of being."

Such assertions underpin the logic of much of the literature on female terrorism as well as popular cultural representations.[21] Eileen MacDonald observes that mass media representations of female terrorists invariably ask: "'How could a woman do this?' The answer . . . seemed to be that *they were all lesbians; or, if not quite that, then feminists gone mad.*"[22] Leaving aside for a moment the idea that female terrorists are lesbians, female protagonists of terrorism are typically represented as out-of-control feminists. Daniel Georges-Abeyie summarizes key findings of the scholarship dealing with women's motivations for engaging in terrorism.[23] Among the 13 explanations he notes, more than half invoke a connection between feminism and terrorism,[24] ranging from the explicit claim that female terrorism is a logical progression of "extreme" feminism, to the more coded claim that the excesses of "sexual liberation" produce hormonal imbalances in women that lead to female terrorism. Most point subtly to the transformation in women's roles taking place in the late 1960s and early 1970s as a result of the demands of women's movements in the United States. They do not necessarily name feminism as a causal factor of women's involvement in terrorism, but their references to women's desire for greater equality and their denunciation of patriarchal values nonetheless conjure the specter of women's liberation. Terrorism, so the mythology goes, is the refuge of women with feminist-informed aspirations for self-determination, and terrorist organizations provide a commodious environment for the avid—or perhaps more precisely, the extreme—feminist.

This discourse, as with the New Right's rhetoric today, positions feminism as leading in a manifestly direct manner to women's involvement in terrorism. Many counter-insurgency analyses of female terrorism focus almost exclusively upon the problematic of *motivation*,[25] signaling a desire to establish a *causal context* for women's involvement in terrorism and to hold something accountable. This search for "root causes" is also a process by which to negotiate a politics of blame. Within counter-insurgency discourse, feminism is responsible for female terrorism.

This view is supported by contemporary criminological accounts of female criminality. Freda Adler argues that women's participation in violent political crime was on the increase at this time.[26] In 1977, writing about the "politicized female"—a category whose most threatening representative, we can presume, is the female terrorist—she noted: "No longer satisfied with their traditional limitation to the typewriter, the mimeograph machine, and the coffee-maker, they are increasingly taking a more active role in the turbulent confrontations."[27] Adler's discussion of "politicized women" proceeds via a criminological concern with "a changing breed of female offender,"[28] whose appearance can be attributed to the rise and prominence of feminism:

> By the decade's end [1960s], large numbers of American women in all walks of life had begun to see themselves as Betty Friedan had portrayed them in *The Feminine Mystique*: a systematically and subtly suppressed majority whose real security lay in the strength of their own right arm, and whose time of delivery had arrived.[29]

This criminological narrative runs parallel to the New Right's logic of blame, in which it is systematically argued that feminism has led to an increase in female criminality. By extension, as the counter-terrorist literature argues, the most acute expression of this—its most "out-of-control" manifestation—is the rise of female terrorism. The female terrorist thus represents "one of the excesses of women's lib"[30]—the unsettling threat of feminism.

Backlash

Zwerman, one of few scholars to critically analyze law enforcement representations of female terrorists in the United States, claims that "critical scholars have paid little attention to the . . . relationship between the image of the 'female terrorist' as constructed in counter-insurgency literature, and the growing backlash to American feminism."[31] Zwerman identifies an unexplored connection between an excessive establishment preoccupation with female terrorists since the 1970s and the concurrent perceived need to contain the forces of women's liberation. What is constructed discursively as an increase in female terrorism is rendered intelligible through its coincidence with the rise of feminism.

In *Backlash: The Undeclared War Against American Women*, Susan Faludi expresses concern about the prevalence of reasoning that links "rising female independence to rising female pathology," and hence to rising rates of female crime.[32] In Faludi's analysis, the logic that positions female terrorism as a nasty side effect of feminism is symptomatic of yet another wave of antifeminist backlash in the United States.[33] For Faludi, a "backlash" is "a powerful counterassault on women's rights . . . an attempt to retract the handful of small and hard-won victories that the feminist movement did manage to win for women."[34] Backlash is engendered "not by women's achievement of full equality," rather "it is a pre-emptive strike that stops women long before they reach the finish line."[35] The emergence of an antifeminist backlash signals the perception of feminism as a threat. Dominant culture responds by rewriting feminism in its own language as a calamitous affliction, in order to discredit it and annul its threat. Feminist psychologist, Dr Jean Baker Miller concurs: "backlashes occur when advances have been small, before changes are sufficient to help many people."[36] Antifeminist backlash is thus a counter-offensive launched in order to prevent the perceived threat of women's liberation from materializing. Rosalind Petchesky describes the second-wave feminist threat in the following manner:

> The women's liberation movement in the 1970s had become the most dynamic force for social change in the country, the one most directly threatening not only to conservative values and interests, but also to significant groups whose "way of life" is challenged by ideas of sexual liberation.[37]

In the backlash imagination then, feminism inspires fear, paranoia—even *terror*.

Faludi notes, "the most recent round of backlash first gained full momentum in the late '70s on the fringes, among the evangelical right,"[38] but its emergence coincided with the substantial gains of the second-wave feminist movement, namely "Congress' approval of the ERA [Equal Rights Amendment] in 1972 and the US Supreme Court's legalization of abortion in 1973."[39] It is at this precise point that "home-grown terrorism" emerges on the political landscape, and the figure of the female terrorist becomes a preoccupation for law enforcement agencies. Faludi gestures to the dimensions of the feminist threat as constructed by the New Right:

> The American Christian Cause's fundraising newsletter warned, "Satan has taken the reins of the 'women's liberation' movement and will stop at nothing" . . . *Feminists are a deadly force*, as the commentators on the evangelical 700 Club explained it, precisely because they threatened a transfer of gender power; they "would turn the country over to women." *That the New Right fastened on feminism, not communism or race, was in itself a testament to the strength and standing of the women's movement in the last decade.*[40]

If the New Right's commentary is the (superlative) expression of the desire to preserve the status quo, its proclamations can be read as (albeit extreme) expressions of the anxieties that underpin dominant culture more generally. Feminism lurks in the imagination of the New Right, as well as that of dominant culture, as the potential for the wholesale destruction of a safe, secure, and structured patriarchal social order. *Feminism terrorizes*. This is audible in the New Right's claims that feminists are a "deadly force" and the "enemies of every decent society."[41] In the New Right's logic, feminism, like terrorism, haunts the borders of the self-proclaimed "rational" society.

While in the rhetoric of the New Right feminism is derogated with no holds barred, in the (sometimes) more measured forum of counter-terrorism literature, the expression of the feminist threat takes a more circuitous route. Aside from a handful of ultraconservative analyses that address the problem of female terrorism and its connection with feminism in vitriolic terms, the threat of feminism appears most often in the form of allusion, and on the odd occasion, in the accidental form of a Freudian slip. For example, to illustrate his argument that terrorism arises not from oppression per se but from *a political awareness of the injustice of oppression*, Hacker uses the following case in point. Note that he is discussing terrorism as a *general phenomenon*, not female terrorism specifically:

> First, an individual, or a small or large group becomes aware of either real or imaginary oppression . . . Second, oppression is no longer regarded as natural, biological, and unavoidable. For instance, as long as women believed that they were an inferior breed, confined in their activities to the kitchen, the church and the children, their awareness of their oppression did not matter because they accepted the fact that their peculiar status was the result of immutable biology . . . The next step then is characterized by the realization that alleged inferiority is not biologically ordained but socially prescribed, which means that this status may be socially changed.[42]

In the third step of Hacker's ontology of terrorism, the "oppressed" call for action and demand concessions. Finally, if society does not respond in a timely and adequate manner, terrorism, configured in Hacker's analysis as a form of "violent self-help," becomes conceivable, if not inevitable.[43]

Hacker's use of the example of women's liberation to illustrate his argument about the causes of terrorism in general (a phenomenon which is usually gendered male) betrays the experience of a sublimated threat, namely feminism in its extreme form—*female terrorism*. Implicit here is a warning about the need to respond early to women's liberation in order to thwart the potential unleashing of women's fury. As in the rhetoric of the New Right, feminism terrorizes, and "we" must respond in order to contain it.

US Urban Terrorism = Female/Feminist Terrorism

The underlying assumption in the literature dealing with female terrorism of the late 1960s and early 1970s—which often takes explicit expression—is that *female terrorism is also always already feminist terrorism*, the threat of feminism taken to its extreme. This equation is symptomatic of the broader discursive crosswiring of feminism with terrorism. More than this, the urban terrorist groups active in North America in the late 1960s and early 1970s were understood as predominantly female organizations, attracting large numbers of female members and entrusting women with leadership roles. Given the discursive positioning of female terrorists as feminist terrorists, these apparently female-dominated, white, urban terrorist groups were understood as *feminist* terrorist organizations. Home-grown "urban" terrorism, at this juncture in history in the United States, came to mean white, middle class, female and feminist terrorism—what I designate as "(female) terrorism."

In *Shoot the Women First*, MacDonald argues that the terrorist women she interviewed expressed a "key awareness . . . of being a *double* victim, with oppression having to be fought on two fronts . . . They see themselves as victims not only of what their male comrades would call 'political oppression' but also of male oppression."[44] In this narrative, remembering that MacDonald claims to analyze these women's modes of self-representation—their own understandings of their aims and their "terrorist" actions—the actions of MacDonald's female terrorist subjects are informed by a feminist sensibility. Like Hacker, MacDonald constructs the female terrorist as a *feminist* terrorist, exposing the workings of a discourse of female terrorism in which feminism not only leads to (female) terrorism, but also produces feminist terrorists. One way this discourse plays out in dominant culture is in the counter-insurgency construction of terrorist organizations as hotbeds of feminist revolution that are supportive and/or incendiary of feminist ideals. For example, Georges-Abeyie argues that terrorist organizations that "champion feminist and socialistic objectives"[45] do not randomly attract women, they specifically lure women with feminist-informed aspirations for equality and self-determination.[46]

Explicating the role of women in a variety of Western revolutionary terrorist groups, Cooper's description of the female terrorist echoes the New Right's damning portrayal of feminists as a "deadly force" precisely, and in so doing, reproduces the discursive alignment of feminism and terrorism: "*Woman as terrorist is now a deadly force* to be reckoned with, and her activities have altered many preconceptions, prejudice, and patterns of response . . . Chivalry has no place or meaning in this deadly struggle."[47] For Cooper, the urban terrorist organization takes feminist principles to new levels. He implies that women working within urban terrorist groups gain a degree of independence and responsibility not available to them in the "legitimate" and "chivalrous" context of broader society. The terrorist organization is thus constructed as a feminist space.

This view is not supported by the accounts of women who became involved in terrorist organizations. On the contrary, their personal feminist principles rarely translated into practice within the context of the terrorist organization.[48] While these groups often claimed to strive for a utopian society in which egalitarian principles could find full and proper expression, available anecdotal evidence suggests that the implementation of a feminist gender politics within terrorist organizations was at best partial, and at worst non-existent.[49] Nonetheless, the assumption that terrorist organizations with a high participation of women are also, in one sense or another, feminist organizations is one that endures.

Embryonic US second-wave feminism was widely understood as a white women's movement,[50] so it is not surprising that the equation of feminism with terrorism took place most obviously in relation to white, urban terrorism. This equation is most audible in relation to the terrorism of white groups such as the SLA and the Weathermen (later known as the Weather Underground).[51] These organizations feature in counter-insurgency literature as female-dominated groups *and* feminist terrorist groups.

Remarkably, Cooper asserts that both the self-determination accorded women and the centrality of their roles within terrorist organizations provide clues to these organizations' political aspirations. He illustrates his point, in highly condemnatory terms, with reference to the SLA:

> Although its titular leader was a black man, a majority of its active members were women. Its theoretical underpinnings . . . were the creation of women, and its operations were executed by a majority of female participants. Indeed, this deadly bunch of amateurs seems to have had its own affirmative action program, with the real power and policy-making functions deliberately consigned to women . . . What remains as an abiding impression is the fanaticism of its female members.[52]

Adler also expresses surprise at "the fact that women had organized and staged"[53] the SLA's kidnapping and conversion of Patricia Campbell Hearst, an event that became a nationwide terrorist media spectacle. Despite the fact that the group was ostensibly led by a black male ex-prisoner, Cinque (Donald DeFreeze), women, claims Adler, were the masterminds and the executors of the group's plan.[54] In this logic of blame, the SLA, thought to be a group both dominated and coordinated by women, was a feminist terrorist organization.

With regards to the Weather Underground, Georges-Abeyie notes that women's factions—and we can take him to mean "feminist" women's factions—had a powerful influence over the group's agenda.[55] Indeed, the Weather Underground was initially known as the Weathermen, taking its name from a line in Bob Dylan's "Subterranean Homesick Blues."[56] The name change was reportedly the direct outcome of female members' demands for a gender-neutral title for the organization. Interpreted as the group's self-conscious gesturing of the importance of feminist principles to their terrorist agenda, this only further contributed to a popular mythology that positioned the Weather Underground as a feminist terrorist organization.

Laqueur has noted that "terrorism is not merely a technique. Those practicing it have certain basic beliefs in common."[57] In the discourses outlined above, it would seem that *all white female urban terrorists*, especially those operating within US society, have in common a (fanatical) belief in the philosophy of *feminism*. For Cooper and Georges-Abeyie, the strong presence of women within terrorist organizations catalyzes those organizations' feminist political agendas. Inasmuch as these texts configure feminism as a threat—a threat materializing as the female terrorist—they can be understood as backlash texts.

In Cooper's narrative, the feminism of the SLA appears as a form of madness. Describing the SLA as a "bizarre band" of "alienated, questing women," he asserts that

> Everything about this pathetic, self-styled army had a *strange, fantasy-like quality, utterly divorced from any social or political reality* . . . Their words and actions ring with an *unreasoning, demented, religious zeal* . . . Whatever it was they were seeking . . . —power, respect, sexual liberation—they clearly did not find it.[58]

In Western modernity, it has become customary to construct that which threatens social order most as madness.[59] Madness operates here to simultaneously identify a threat and insert it into the representational order in such a way as to secure its containment.[60] It is the same threat implied in Hacker's analysis of the "root causes" of terrorism, namely the need to respond to the demands of feminists lest feminism evolve into female terrorism. Cooper extrapolates this threat in explicit terms: "The practical consequences are predictable. The women move away to form their own collective, excluding the men on the grounds that they are superfluous or expendable."[61] What underlies Cooper's narrative is the threat of women's (feminist) separatism. It is the threat of feminism taken to its extreme, the rise of *a vengeful, separatist and autonomous feminist terrorism* aimed at, and beyond the control of, men/male society. As MacDonald expresses it, "the whole basis of society might crumble as a result of these dangerously unleashed women running amok."[62] The demonized threat of feminism taken to its "logical" limits thus attaches itself to the female terrorist. Hence, then, we see the discrediting of feminism Faludi claims is characteristic of backlash culture.

Sexualizing the Deviancy of the Female Terrorist

The association of the female terrorist with the feminist constructs them both as fundamentally Other. This configuration is compounded by the construction of the female terrorist (and the feminist, for that matter) as lesbian. In the discourse on female terrorism, the female terrorist is, simply put, not a proper woman. Indeed, she fundamentally threatens the naturalized order of femininity. Georges-Abeyie, proffering an embryonic "theory of female terrorism," writes:

> Women who lack the characteristics and traits that society considers appropriate—gentleness, passivity, non-violent personalities, seductiveness, physically attractive faces and figures—may seek success in some non-feminine realm, by displaying aggression, unadorned faces and bodies, toughness, or other masculine qualities.[63]

Just as Cooper resorts to the language of madness in a reflex action of defending the patriarchal status quo, so too Georges-Abeyie's construction posits a nonfeminine Otherness popularly, if erroneously, associated with lesbians, that serves to recuperate the threat of the female terrorist.

Georges-Abeyie argues that, some "notable exceptions" aside, women have historically played a very small role in terrorist enterprises. In his investigation of these female anomalies—found, he argues, in their largest numbers in white, urban terrorist groups—he draws particular attention to their counter-hegemonic sexual practices: "North American and Western European terrorist organizations with female leadership or sizeable numbers of female cadres proselytized female homosexuality and bisexuality as well as pansexualism and feminist ideology."[64] Georges-Abeyie is deeply concerned by "the *homosexual/feminist* orientation common within American white terrorist groups."[65] In his slashed descriptor, "homosexual/feminist orientation," the slash signals the conjoining of the concept of "deviant" sexuality with feminism. In this discourse, feminism, homosexuality, and female terrorism are "natural" and othered allies.

Singling out the SLA for special attention in this regard, Georges-Abeyie identifies Patricia Soltysik (also known as Mizmoon or Zoya) as "the theoretician [of the SLA] and homosexual lover"[66] of another female SLA member, Camilla Hall, constructing the lesbian feminist as the organization's mastermind and its most threatening member. The impetus for (female) terrorism is seen to derive from the combination of feminism and lesbianism, which he also argues with reference to the Weather Underground:

> The WU . . . espoused the need for the decline of the nuclear family and for homosexual love—both physical and emotional—to free women from male psychic and physical domination. *The Weather Underground, like the SLA, espoused and practiced a program of extreme feminism, homosexuality-bisexuality,* gay rights and socialism.[67]

For Georges-Abeyie then, as for many other analysts of his ilk, the terrorism of white, North American (feminist) terrorist groups not only threatens dominant order via a systematic campaign of political violence, it also threatens the libidinal economy of exchange that structures the everyday.[68]

In the late 1960s and early 1970s, certain varieties of feminism advocating for the sexual revolution, as well as groups within the New Left more generally, promoted counter-hegemonic sexual practices as a tactic for subverting dominant order. As Todd Gitlin observes, for these groups, "sex was not simply a pleasure but a statement."[69] In the New Left's framework, sexual practices were bound up with the moral, social, capitalist economic, and political network of domination extant in North America. Through experimenting with alternative forms of the family and living arrangements, perhaps most notably in the form of the "commune," as well as advocating a more "adventurous" exploration of the potentialities of sex, the New Left sought to intervene into the structural organization of dominant culture's sexual economy. They pursued, that is, a program of *politicizing* sex, and sexual experimentation became a political practice *du jour*.

To what extent "sexual liberation" was a successful alternative is highly debatable. Many women argued, for example, that "sexual liberation" was not at all liberating for women, and in effect merely consummated the relationships between male activists through their sharing of women.[70] Gitlin, retroactively analyzing the ways sex operated within the Movement, claims that "sex was less a motive than a cement . . . The vulgar way to say it was that the clan was consolidated through the exchange of women."[71] Women became more and more dissatisfied with their place within the Movement—and with what they increasingly identified as their sexual exploitation by Movement men—such that, when they began to organize autonomously to address their "oppression" as women, sex and its related social and cultural practices were among their stated concerns.[72] Everywhere within the Movement, however, women who embraced the ideals of women's liberation struggled with the problem of devising strategies for resisting their positioning as subordinate, including their own often-subtle incorporation of aspects of the patriarchal worldview. Marge Piercy, for example, analyzing her involvement with the Movement, wrote, "I began to see how many male structures I took into my head in order to make it in the male-dominated world [of the Movement, resulting in] co-operation in my own manipulation."[73] Women thus began to search for alternative "ways of being" that would allow them to develop and apply feminist principles less hindered by the totalizing tendencies of patriarchal ways of thinking.

In this context, "political lesbianism" presented itself as a viable strategy for avoiding collaboration with the "enemy."[74] For example, the radical feminist group, Radicalesbians, theorized lesbianism as a political choice, arguing that it was only through nurturing women's relationships with other women that women could escape male definitions of femininity and build a way of being around women's priorities.[75] Similarly, Martha Shelley suggested in "Notes of a Radical Lesbian" in 1969, that "lesbianism is one road to freedom— freedom from oppression by men."[76]

Ultimately, within dominant culture, lesbians were perceived as, quite literally, "out of control" in that they operated outside the boundaries of male authority. Not only did they refuse the performance of hegemonic femininity, they also undermined the sexual economy of dominant culture, based, as Luce Irigaray has argued, on the exchange of women.[77] As such, they were perceived as establishing a new economy of sex in which men were both unnecessary and excluded from participation and control. That is, the woman-centered philosophy of lesbianism conjured the same threat that Cooper identifies in relation to the female terrorist—that of *feminist separatism.*

Independence from men defined the lesbian, for dominant culture, as the threatening Other. Lesbianism was interpreted in terms of "deviance," a moral and psychological illness. Despite lesbian groups' claims to the contrary,[78] their desire to separate from men was constructed as symptomatic of man-hating, which, again, was understood as a sign of illness.[79] It is possible to see how these constructions articulate with that of feminism as a form of madness. Indeed, the terms "feminism" and "lesbian" were strongly linked in the popular imagination. Both feminists and lesbians were constructed as man-haters and both were understood as demanding independence from men. In many instances, the meanings of the two terms were conflated, as we saw earlier in Georges-Abeyie's preoccupation with the "homosexual/feminist orientation" of white, urban terrorist groups. There was an assumption within dominant culture that just as the female terrorist is always already feminist,

so too is the lesbian. It was also commonly assumed that the reverse applied—
that all feminists were lesbians. To quote Radicalesbians:

> Lesbian is a label invested by the Man to throw at any woman who dares . . .
> to challenge his prerogatives . . . To have the label applied to people active in
> women's liberation is just the most recent instance of a long history.[80]

The idea that feminists are lesbians still has currency today, as is evidenced by
Pat Robertson's claim that feminism is about, among myriad other "terrible"
things, turning women into lesbians.

Within dominant culture, the application of the label "lesbian" simultaneously identified the threat of feminism and operated to contain it.[81] "Lesbian"
was a technology for policing the boundaries of femininity as defined by
dominant (patriarchal) culture, a way of defining the feminist as fundamentally Other. It is not surprising, then, that lesbianism gets attached to the
figure of the female terrorist. Constructed as nonheterosexual women within
a culture that privileges heterosexuality, both feminists and female terrorists
were positioned as mutually constitutive Others, discrediting both by representing them as external to the range of socially sanctioned female behaviors.
Female terrorists, feminists, and lesbians inhabit the territory of the nonfeminine, signifying in a closed circuit of Otherness. In this context, the feminism
and/or the lesbianism of female terrorists helps to construct their abnormal-
ity, their excessive aberrance. In thus containing the threat of the female terrorist, who signifies as *feminist* terrorist, the threat of the feminist (who always
threatens to metamorphose into the feminist terrorist) is also recuperated.

* * *

If urban terrorism of the late 1960s and early 1970s was constructed in terms
of its "novelty," what is "new" about the female terrorist of the same era is not
just that she fights her *left-wing* guerrilla war *on American soil*; nor that she is,
more often than not, an educated member of white, middle-class society and
therefore a threat from *within*. She is also "new" in that she is understood as
a product of another phenomenon, itself "new": women's liberation.

Constructing the problem of the female terrorist as a new one enabled the
establishment of a conceptual link between the "rise" of female terrorism and
the rise of women's liberation. Importantly though, the discourse that crosswired "feminism" with "terrorism" failed to define the feminism against
which it railed, operating in a homogenizing, essentializing, and reductive
manner to produce *a generic feminist Other* that incorporated all manner of
feminisms, regardless of their political underpinnings, their programs of

action, or the character of the challenge they posed to patriarchal order. This lack of specificity around the meanings of feminism and women's liberation within the discourse that proscribed the female terrorist enabled the wholesale demonization of feminism and women's liberation.

While dominant discourse suggests that feminism in general is responsible for (female) terrorism, the threat of feminism to which these texts respond is in fact quite specifically that of *radical feminism*. So what are the particularized codings of radical feminism that enable the cultural approximation of feminism and terrorism? Across what shared discursive terrain do radical feminism and terrorism manifest and disrupt Western logocentrism? In order to account for their alignment, I turn now to terrorism's relationship to the linear and routine time of Western modernity.

CHAPTER 4

Terrorist Time: Terrorism's Disruption of Modernity

> In terrorism are found the same elements of self-sacrifice, the attempt to burn and obliterate the present body, the rebirth of new life from the ashes of the old, and the promise of a messianic future that we associate with the legend of the phoenix.
>
> Moshe Amon[1]

Ghassan Hage has argued that within the Western imagination, "terrorism" marks "the worst possible kind of violence."[2] Similarly, Philip Jenkins claims that terrorism "is perceived as a kind of ultimate evil."[3] What are the structural conditions and processes through which terrorism can signify as deadly and catastrophic—as both the epitome of evil and the scourge of modern political life?

Jacques Derrida has suggested, in relation to the attacks of September 11, 2001, that terrorism presents in the cultural imagination as a "major event." In making this claim, he draws upon Heidegger's notion of the event as "a happenstance that resists appropriation and understanding."[4] For Derrida, a major event is

> That which in the undergoing or in the ordeal *at once opens itself up to and resists experience* . . . a certain *unappropriability* of what comes or happens . . . The event is first of all *that which* I do not first of all comprehend. Better, the event is first of all *that* I do not comprehend.[5]

Derrida argues that an act of terrorism presents with the quality of immediacy, manifesting as momentous, unforeseeable, and *ultimately unassimilable.* He suggests that terrorism produces a fundamental incomprehension, which in turn produces attempts to bring the experience of terrorism within the realm of the knowable, to produce the terrorist act in ways that will contain the threat it poses.[6] However, this attempt at appropriation always "falters at some border or frontier."[7] For Derrida, then, terrorism's affect derives not just from its attack on "a 'what' or a 'who,' buildings, strategic urban structures, symbols of political, military, or capitalist power, or a considerable number of people of many different origins living on the body of a national territory."[8] Rather, there is simultaneously always something more fundamental at stake. I argue here that terrorism manifests as the dissembling of modernity itself.

Perceived as an attack on the (democratic) state, terrorism is configured as the nasty side effect of a political system that provides for diverse political opinions and practices. Terrorism is thought to be particularly pernicious (and illegitimate) because it exploits the very freedoms guaranteed by democratic governance. While this understanding of terrorism is commonly accepted within both Western popular culture and the more specific field of counter-terrorism, it is something of a category mistake—a fundamental "misrecognition" in the Baudrillardian sense—to conceptualize terrorism *as a consequence of* the existence of modern states—democratic or otherwise.[9] Similarly, the idea that terrorism assaults the state—in the sense of the government and its institutions—per se is problematic. Rather, terrorism only attacks the state inasmuch as the state is a manifestation of the organizational drive of modernity, a symptom of the modern organization of power.

Derrida claims that understanding the impact of terrorism requires paying attention to its chronology, to "the thought and order of temporalization it seems to imply."[10] To make sense of the affect generated by terrorism, I use the concept of "terrorist time" to signal, on the one hand, the time of modernity, and on the other hand, the temporal framework within which terrorism articulates. Jean-François Lyotard and Zygmunt Bauman have argued that modern social order and its legitimizing discourses are based on a concept of linear, developmental time, of time as trajectory. Modernity turns upon a notion of time as structured, ordered, and imbued with historical purpose, and the passing of time comes to be conflated with progress and evolution, with processes of amelioration, and the gradual perfection of society. In the modern imagination, history culminates in the eventual achievement of the liberatory promise of modernity—the arrival of utopia. Following Henri Lefebvre, this conceptualization of linear time becomes possible because of the routinization of time that occurs in and through the mechanisms of the "everyday"—the structure that enables the ongoing "march of progress."

What I call "modern time" is simultaneously a condition of terrorism's opposition to dominant order—the terrain upon which it operates—and the abstract representative of "the enemy"—that which it seeks to dissemble. By disrupting the quotidian flow of time, terrorism radically deconstructs the order imposed by the everyday in modernity. In this context, terrorism conjures the apocalyptic end of modern linear time, and by extension, the apocalyptic end of modernity. Registering as a transgression that conjures the radical end of modern social order, terrorism articulates within the cultural imagination as the moment of end-time. As discursive equivalents, both terrorism and radical feminism, as subaltern modes of resistance, find their epistemological foundations in apocalyptic thought and this produces them, at the level of discourse, as geminate practices. It is thus through an analysis of the eschatological logic of both radical feminism and terrorism that the cultural approximation of feminism and terrorism can be understood.[11]

Joseph Conrad's 1907 novel, *The Secret Agent*, provides a starting point from which to consider the significatory power of terrorism, particularly in relation to the temporality of modernity.

The Secret Agent

The Secret Agent paints a deeply ironic portrait of modern English society. The storyline revolves around the planning and execution of an anarchist bombing designed to undermine the complacency of the "imbecile bourgeoisie"[12] and pave the way for the "Future of the Proletariat," the anarchist society at the center of the novel's plot.[13] A secret agent, Mr. Verloc is charged by Mr. Vladimir with carrying out this attack on behalf of an undisclosed foreign power, but entrusts the planting of the explosives to his dim-witted brother-in-law, Stevie. As Stevie approaches the chosen target, however, he trips, detonating the bomb prematurely and killing himself. Importantly, the chosen site for this anarchist bombing is the first meridian at the Royal Observatory in Greenwich Park.

It is significant that Conrad sets his novel in 1886. At this time, for over 200 years, Greenwich had been a significant maritime site and home to the internationally renowned Royal Observatory, which measured "stellar transit times" and produced "almanacs and astronomical predictions."[14] In the nineteenth century, Greenwich gained prominence for British citizens as the source of their first experiences of a national, standardized time system.[15] However, in October 1884, amid heated debate, the International Meridian Conference, held in Washington DC, and attended by 41 delegates from 25 nations, officially established Greenwich as the location of the first meridian—longitude 0°—and the standard for the calculation and implementation of the first globally integrated system of time zones. From this point onward, time would operate as a mechanism of an increasingly globally coordinated process of routinization and integrated scheduling. Thus, at the historical moment in which Conrad's novel is set, Greenwich had established an international profile as, quite literally, the origin of modern linear and calculable time. As Vladimir suggests, "the whole civilised world has heard of Greenwich. The very boot blacks in the basement of Charing Cross Station know something of it."[16] As such, we can understand the anarchists' attack in *The Secret Agent* as an assault on modern time.

While by all reports Conrad was somewhat reluctant to admit it, the terrorist bombing described in *The Secret Agent* is based on an actual incident that took place in 1894 and was popularly known as the "Greenwich Bomb Outrage."[17] While the objectives of the attack remain unclear, it was commonly reported as an anarchist terrorist attack on the first meridian at Greenwich. Taking place in the year of the tenth anniversary of the International Meridian Conference of 1884, this "real-world" attack might thus also be read as a political statement relating to the global prominence of Greenwich as the center of modern timekeeping. It too can be read as an attack on time itself.

Both the fictional and the "real-world" conceptualizing of a terrorist attack on the first meridian can be understood *as a literalization of the dominant Western cultural reading of terrorism—namely, terrorism as the disruption of time*. Modernity is underpinned by two different but mutually constitutive conceptions of time—linear time and the time of routine. In terrorism, both come under attack, marking terrorism with its political power.

Linear Time and Modernity

Scholars of terrorism frequently trace the historical roots of the word "terrorism" back to the immediate aftermath of the French Revolution when Robespierre implemented a systematic campaign of terror to secure the gains of the newly established democratic regime.[18] The etymology of the term highlights that both terrorism and modern democracy are coeval, that terrorism is first named simultaneous with the rise of modern democracy. Dominant discourse frequently constructs terrorism as a negative by-product of modern Western democracy. However, given the historical coincidence of the rise of modern democracy and terrorism, one can think of them not as causally related—democracy giving rise to terrorism—but as systemic features of what critical theorists have described as *modernity*. Both terrorism and the modern (democratic) state can be read as consequences of the structural transformation of the economic, social, cultural, and political fabric of Western society that is characteristic of the shift to modernity.

For Bauman, modernity is not simply "reducible to the technological explosion"; it also encompasses "momentous changes in the social system as well as in the set of conditions in which human action takes place."[19]

Bauman insists upon modernity as a moment in Western history in which social relations, and the ideologies that underpin them, undergo a paradigmatic shift. Alongside industrialization, those factors impacting upon the social and psychological dimensions of, and characterizing, modernity might include the rise of industrial capitalism, the rise of the modern nation-state, urbanization, the separation of Church and State, and the spread of Enlightenment values. However, while it might be understood as a periodization, following Lyotard, modernity is not only an epoch but also a "mode within thought, speech and sensibility"; a way of apprehending, constructing, and inhabiting the time and space of the social, characterized first and foremost by the privileging of "grand narratives."[20]

For Bauman, modernity's chief characteristic is an "'Apollonian' effort to construct a logical, rational, and harmonious world order."[21] Similarly, Peter Beilharz argues that "modernity is a project, and not only a period, and it is, or was, a project of control, the rational mastery over nature, [leading] to planomania and technocracy."[22] Modernity sets itself the impossible duty of creating "a fully designed, fully contained world."[23] As Bauman puts it:

> Among the multitude of impossible tasks that modernity set itself and that made modernity into what it is, the task of order (more precisely and most importantly, of *order as task*) stands out . . . as the archetype for all other tasks, one that renders all other tasks mere metaphors of itself.[24]

While it is sometimes suggested that modernity marks a descent into chaos, in Bauman's analysis, modernity is characterized by an organizational drive, a ceaseless quest for social order. Order is the product of human agency, indeed its ultimate goal. The construction of order becomes a responsibility of modern individuals and collectivities that must be obsessively pursued: what Bauman describes as "a conscious practice . . . wary of the void it would leave were it to halt or merely relent."[25] Order, in the modern imagination, becomes synonymous with progress. Like order, progress "consists of applying human reason (rationalizing) to the task of making the world better geared to serve human needs."[26]

Both the organizational modality of modernity and the modern notion of progress are underwritten by a linear unfolding of time as the trajectory of historical meaning and purpose. As Lyotard states, "the idea of a linear chronology is itself perfectly 'modern.' It is at once part of Christianity, Cartesianism and Jacobinism."[27] Similarly for Bauman, "the history of time began with modernity. Indeed, modernity is, apart from [and] perhaps . . . more than anything else . . . the time when time has a history."[28] Both Bauman and Lyotard posit linear ontological time as a key feature of the modern land-scape, enabling the processes of order to be imagined and enacted.

In modernity, one of the key sites where the notions of order and linear time converge is that of the modern state. Thought to embody Reason, the state manifests as a naturalized and ideal form of modern sociopolitical organization, imposing order over the irrational forces of nature.[29] As numerous theorists have argued, the state becomes a naturalized site of linear time in modernity.[30] Further, the experience of the state in modernity is structured by a teleology—a history and a destiny couched in the terms of linear time. History, as the linear and ontological expression of national destiny, constitutes the gradual unveiling of the blueprint of the utopian society; the passage of time marks the path to amelioration and the emancipation of the modern citizen.[31] Indeed, in some circumstances, the establishment of new states has been accompanied by the turning of the clock back to Year Zero, signaling the imbrication of the new order with the linear time of history.[32] In this sense, the nexus of linear time and order manifests in the modern state.

As Bauman suggests, in modernity, time becomes increasingly abstracted—reified and "liberated" from its traditional grounding in space.[33] Linear time becomes a self-referential system whose points of fixity depend upon time as calculable and ordered by the imagining of a linear and causal relationship among past, present, and future. Linear time, that is, becomes a technology of order and control, a medium for the organizational force of modernity. Bauman claims that the early phase of modernity is based on

> [the k]ind of time that could be cut into slices of similar thickness fit to be arranged in monotonous and unalterable sequences. Space was truly "possessed" when controlled—and control meant first and foremost the "taming of time."[34]

Bauman privileges linear time, over space, as the primary ordering principle of modernity. For Bauman, in modernity, time is (endlessly) manipulable—its mutability is limited only by the technologies available to quantify it and tame it into subservience: "Unlike space, [time] could be changed and manipulated; it has become . . . the dynamic partner in the time-space wedlock."[35] In the modern imagination, time thus presents not only as a structuring and organizing force, but also as one to be conquered and corralled into the service of the organizational imperative of modernity. Paul Virilio extends this idea, positing modernity as the history of *acceleration*. For Virilio, modernity represents the ceaseless effort to control, indeed to discipline and "overtake," modern time,[36] culminating in the vanquishing of time as obstacle. Modernity, claims Virilio, ultimately aspires to *uchronia*.[37]

Terrorism and Apocalyptic Time

On the one hand, then, terrorism disrupts modern linear notions of time as historical development and progress, enabling it to present as unique and special. In this sense, it operates on the temporal plane, presenting as *extraordinary*: as outside the realm of "ordinary" experience. Derrida writes, emphasizing how audiences *experience* terrorism, that terrorism's disruption is "always what's most striking, the very impact of what is at least *felt*, in an apparently immediate way, to be an event that truly marks . . . a singular and . . . 'unprecedented' event."[38] For Derrida, terrorism assumes the appearance (and it is *only an appearance*) both of novelty and of historical rupture within Western cultures, defying Western notions of history as a cumulative project framed by the uncompromising advance of linear time. Terrorism thus resonates for Western audiences as singular and disturbing because it is always framed by the before-and-after of linear time.

On the other hand, terrorism does not simply *disrupt* ordinary time; it fundamentally threatens modernity itself, forcing upon its audiences a different temporal *logic* that challenges the seamlessness of ordinary linear time and the order it implies. For Derrida, terrorism produces a trauma that stems not from present or past events, but from "the precursory signs of what threatens to happen . . . which will be *worse than anything that has ever taken place*."[39] The future determines the event's unappropriability:

> A weapon wounds and leaves forever open an unconscious scar; but this weapon is terrifying because it comes from the to-come, from the future, a future so radically to come that it resists even the grammar of the future anterior.[40]

Terrorism brings the future to bear upon the present, it *irrupts the present*. In the same gesture, the past gets forgotten. Each wave of terrorism presents as "new," arriving on the scene of the present out of "nowhere." In our apprehension of terrorism, *the past disappears*. If, as Virilio has argued, modernity ultimately strives for uchronia, terrorism enacts *heterochronia* in the present. While modernity posits a linear and causal relationship between past, present, and future—a concept of time epitomized in the modern state—terrorism inhabits the space of present and future simultaneously, erasing the past. Terrorism thus registers (albeit momentarily) as the end of modern linear time, and, consequently, the (apocalyptic) end of modern social order per se.

Whereas in its traditional religious formulation, the apocalypse signifies as a moment of simultaneous destruction and renewal, in modernity, the emphasis is on destruction. In transporting the future into the present, terrorism articulates according to the temporality of the secular apocalypse, the destructive moment that entails the radical overthrow of the "old order."[41] As H. H. Rowley has explained, apocalyptic narratives foretell "the future that should break into the present."[42] Terrorism thus threatens in eschatological terms, speaking in the language of "final solutions" and manifesting as the destructive end of society "as we know it." Terrorists, whether state or non-state actors, practice the politics of endgame, seeking to suspend and ulti-mately to stop time, however partial, incomplete, or fragmentary that may be in effect. It is this quality that generates terrorism's significatory power. And thus, terrorism is perceived not just in terms of a temporal disruption but as the temporal moment of "the last days."

This is most acutely expressed by Moshe Amon, who discusses terrorism through the prism of the legend of the phoenix. For Amon, terrorism is symptomatic of twentieth-century thinking that "is rife with apocalyptic pre-monitions."[43] Indeed, it represents the conclusion of "the age of revolution which strives to clear the way from everything inhibiting the disclosure of the perfect order at the end of the road, or the rainbow."[44] He continues: "The old phoenix reaches his *pre-destined end:* he is ready for *self-destruction . . .* Terrorism is just . . . the last step in a trend towards *social and cultural nega-tion.*"[45] Here Amon constructs terrorism in a way that renders it as the apoca-lyptic end of modernity. Terrorism represents, for Amon, end-time itself, a form of cultural suicide.

Inasmuch as it operates according to an apocalyptic logic that disrupts the mechanism of time at the heart of modernity, *terrorism thus registers, always already, as an attack on modernity itself.* If the concept of the modern linear time of progress postulates an evolutionary history of amelioration and the arrival of utopia, in signifying the apocalypse, terrorism constitutes a funda-mental denial of the liberatory promise of modernity.[46] It conjures the much feared but disavowed *failure* of modernity.

To return to Bauman, what grounds modernity's abstracted notions of linear time in the "real world" is the concept of *routine*: "*it was the routiniza-tion of time that held the place whole, compact and subject to homogeneous logic.*"[47] The timetable is equally as important as the calendar to the experi-ence of modernity. However, it is precisely in this relationship to linear and routinized time that modernity experiences itself as vulnerable, confronting the possibility of disruption. As Bauman suggests, "a train running ahead of schedule or automobile parts arriving on the assembly line ahead of other parts were heavy modernity's most gruesome nightmares."[48] In this descrip-tion, Bauman affirms the terror associated with the potential rupturing of modern order based on the conception of routinized time. This is one aspect of the "terroristic imagination" that Baudrillard claims, "dwells in all of us."[49] It is precisely this terror that the practice of terrorism engages and mobilizes.

Terrorism thus threatens not only at the level of *linear* time, but perhaps more fundamentally, it disrupts notions of *routine*. Derrida states that terrorism as "an event always inflicts a wound in the everyday course of history, in the ordinary repetition and anticipation of all experience."[50] Terrorism subverts the regularity of the everyday.

The Everyday of Modernity

Michel de Certeau's *The Practice of Everyday Life* is fundamentally concerned with the politics and practice of opposition inhering in Western modernity. In his analysis of the subversive potentialities implicit in dominant culture, de Certeau distinguishes between "tactics" and "strategy."[51] Like Bauman, de Certeau understands modernity as characterized by *organization*. He uses the term "strategy" to refer to the organizational force of modernity, which organizes the general population according to the interests of the dominant class. As de Certeau explains it, strategy "postulates a *place* that can be delimited as its *own* and serve as the base from which relations with an *exteriority* composed of targets or threats . . . can be managed . . . A Cartesian attitude, if you wish: it is an effort to delimit one's own place in a world bewitched by the invisible powers of the Other."[52] By establishing control of space, strategy simultaneously subordinates time to its agenda: strategy marks "a triumph of place over time . . . a mastery of time through the foundation of an autonomous place."[53] Whereas Bauman privileges time as the fundamental organizing principle of modernity, de Certeau argues that time comes to be ordered via the ordering of space. Nevertheless, the outcome is the same: the ordering of time operates as an instrument of the order of modernity.

Like Bauman, de Certeau is preoccupied with the routinization of the social experience of time as an effect of governance in modernity. He conceptualizes time's materialization as a set of repetitive practices in terms of "the everyday." In de Certeau's formulation, the everyday is both underpinned by, and enables, modern time. Strategy—the organizational "attitude" of modernity—thus takes expression in the *spatial and temporal ordering of the everyday*.

Alongside de Certeau, Lefebvre has been an influential theorist of the everyday. He defines the everyday as

> what is humble and solid, what is taken for granted and that of which all the parts follow each other in such a regular, unvarying succession that those concerned have no call to question their sequence; thus it is undated and (apparently) insignificant; though it occupies and preoccupies it is practically untellable, and it is the ethics underlying routine and the aesthetics of familiar settings.[54]

Lefebvre notes that the everyday is an effect of modernity—"the modern." He describes it as that which remains after all that is extraordinary has been removed from quotidian experience; it is the set of routines we perform, the spaces we inhabit, and the routes we traverse. Its temporal expression is that of repetition.[55] The routine of time supplements and sustains the ordering of space. That is, the everyday is a *spatial and temporal framework*, a template that governs the ways individuals perform the rituals of everyday life, locking subjects into particular modes of operating and ensuring their compliance with the laws of social order. The everyday has its own momentum. It propels us forward; it guides us through the performance of life in ways that safeguard and perpetuate the stability of dominant order, implicating us in the modern project of progress and binding us in modern time.

The everyday is naturalized, evading detection, and as such, critique. Not just a set of practices, it is also the sets of ideas that legitimize the routinized organization of time and space. Importantly, the everyday is also totalizing in reach, consisting of

> pressures and repressions at all levels, at all times and in every sphere of experience including sexual and emotional experience, private and family life, childhood, adolescence and maturity—in short, that which would seem to elude social repression because it is spontaneous and "natural."[56]

In this context, time thus becomes a force of compulsion, a tool of modern hegemony. Indeed, time thus postulated is itself terrorist.

The everyday is theorized as simultaneously a mechanism of dominant order—a tool of repression—and a vehicle for the transgression and deconstruction of that order. As Lefebvre suggests, "it is the point of delicate balance and that where imbalance threatens."[57] In the moment of recognition that the everyday is both repressive and vulnerable, de Certeau's notion of the "tactical" comes into play: de Certeau argues that, against the totalizing organizational schema of the everyday, political opposition assumes the form of "tactics." Whereas strategy represents the organizational force of modernity that operates in line with dominant interests, tactics are the arsenal of the subaltern deployed in the guerrilla war on the totalizing hegemony of the everyday.[58] Unlike strategy, tactics have no enduring claim to the spatial realm of dominant order. Rather, tactics borrow these spaces and make them function temporarily in a different register.[59] As de Certeau suggests,

> By contrast with a strategy . . . a *tactic* is a calculated action determined by the absence of a proper locus . . . The space of a tactic is the space of the other . . . It is a maneuver "within the enemy's field of vision," as von Bülow put it, and

within enemy territory. It does not, therefore, have the options of planning general strategy and viewing the adversary as a whole within a dist[inct], visible and objectifiable space. It operates in isolated actions, blow by blow . . . Being without any base where it could stockpile its winnings . . . what it wins it cannot keep. It must vigilantly make use of the cracks that particular conjunctions open in the surveillance of the proprietary powers. It poaches in them. It creates surprises in them. It can be where it is least expected. It is a guileful ruse.[60]

Tactics *surprise*, radically intervening into the temporal order of modernity held in place by the routine of the everyday—indeed, subverting the terrorist time of the everyday. Whereas modernity operates according to the principle of linear routinized time, tactics mobilize the principle of apocalyptic time. Tactics exploit the inevitable fissures that open up in the time-space of the totalizing order of the everyday. They seize opportunistic moments to strike, momentarily exposing the system's vulnerabilities, and then disappear as quickly as they appeared. Although tactics operate on the principle of speed, and while they cannot make a permanent claim to strategic space, they can nonetheless have permanent effects. In the moment of disruption, tactics force a confrontation with the conceptual limits of the everyday in modernity, exposing the assumptions on which modern order is based. Tactics operate by stealth, turning dominant order upon itself, and in so doing, problematize the very notion of modern order.

Terrorist Tactics

As a tactic, terrorism takes us by surprise and then "disappears."[61] If modern time constitutes the abstract mechanism of order in modernity, for terrorism, it marks the terrain of opposition, the space of potential disruption of order. It is in relation to notions of modern time, the kind of time that Greenwich itself symbolizes, that we experience terrorism. Modern time is simultaneously the terrain upon which terrorism operates and the abstract target of its attack. In this sense, terrorism operates on the ground of the enemy, precisely to attack the enemy. As Jean Baudrillard has written of the terrorists who carried out the attacks of September 11, 2001, "they have assimilated everything of modernity and globalism, without changing their goal, which is to destroy that power."[62]

Significantly, terrorism opportunistically exploits the potential for political action that is ever-present in the fabric of everyday life, precisely because the routinized order implied by the everyday is so pervasive and unquestioned. As Baudrillard has observed, again, in relation to the attacks of September 11, 2001,

> They have even . . . used the banality of American everyday life as cover and
> camouflage. Sleeping in their suburbs, reading and studying with their fami-
> lies, before activating themselves suddenly like time bombs . . . [This] casts
> suspicion on any and every individual. Might not any inoffensive person be a
> potential terrorist? If *they* could pass unnoticed, then each of us is a criminal
> going unnoticed.[63]

In its generalization of the threat of terrorism onto "any and every individual," Baudrillard's narrative echoes the idea that any *woman* might potentially be a female terrorist. He also notes that the terrorists' exploitation of
the routinized schemata of the everyday in fact operates to *undermine* the
everyday itself, resulting in "an even more subtle mental terrorism."[64] Or,
in de Certeau's terms, terrorism operates tactically to expose the logic of the
everyday.

As Derrida has suggested, beyond the immediacy of the attack in the
material world, terrorism defeats familiar and accepted ways of making sense
of the world: "the system of interpretation, the axiomatic, logic, rhetoric,
concepts, and evaluations that are supposed to allow one to *comprehend* and
to explain."[65] In particular, it trounces the everyday and its reproduction of
notions of modern time. Indeed, if modernity is a structure of thinking, and
if the everyday is the structure through which ideology—that which is "taken
for granted"—plays out, then terrorism vampirizes the everyday to undermine modernity itself. Indeed, the everyday order to which modernity aspires
becomes the stage of its potential downfall. In disrupting the linear and routinized time of modernity, terrorism announces modern order as the seed of
its own destruction.

In this sense, terrorism presents in the popular imagination as a symptom
of what Derrida has termed "suicidal autoimmunity."[66] This is perhaps what
Amon refers to when he suggests that terrorism is "the last step in a trend
towards social and cultural negation."[67] Terrorism represents, that is, the
moment of cultural implosion, modernity's *dénouement*. However, there is a
further dimension to terrorism's power of dissimulation. What does terrorism
problematize when it ostensibly attacks the (democratic) state?

The State and Terror

Social contract theory has traditionally provided an important conceptual
narrative for the rise of the modern state and society. For Thomas Hobbes,
the first key thinker of social contract theory, the "state of nature" precedes
"society" and the "state;" it represents presocial "man" at his most basic.
Hobbes describes the state of nature in the following way:

Whatsoever therefore is consequent to a time of Warre, where every man is Enemy to every man, the same is consequent to the time, wherein men live without other security, than what their own strength, and their own intention shall furnish them with all.[68]

Characterized by violence and lawlessness, the state of nature pits individuals against one another in the struggle to survive both the forces of nature and death at the hands of another, constituting a world in which people live "worst of all [in] continual fear and danger of violent death"[69]—a world characterized and ruled by terror. For Hobbes, the state of nature is eventually supervened by the social contract, a pact between individuals to bond together for protection, surrendering a degree of individual freedom in exchange for the protection of the state. Thus, both the state and society—coterminous in Hobbes' work—are born. What is noteworthy about this narrative is that the state intervenes in, and imposes order upon, a "reign of terror." Indeed, social contract theory suggests that the state, and the social organization it implies, holds terror at bay, that it sublimates terror.

A similar conceptualization of the state as founded on terror underpins accounts of the etymology of terrorism. As noted earlier, the term "terrorism" first comes into popular usage in the West in the context of the French Revolution's so-called Reign of Terror, which aimed to eradicate the last vestiges of the ancien régime and consolidate modern democracy. As Derrida notes, this was "a terror that was carried out in the name of the state and that in fact presupposed a legal monopoly on violence."[70]

Elaborating on the historical roots of terrorism, Walter Laqueur explicitly acknowledges the role of terrorism in the establishment of the modern democratic state.[71] However, he elides the issue of how a term that originally designated a generalized "reign of terror"—"a system of coercive intimidation"[72]—came to signify much more specifically as a challenge to (democratic) government. Laqueur's work fits within what Edward Herman and Gerry O'Sullivan have called the "Western model of terrorism" that privileges an understanding of terrorism as attacking democratic states.[73] It is thus not surprising that Laqueur skims over this transformation in the meaning of the term terrorism.[74] Indeed, a closer analysis of this history suggests that terrorism cannot be understood as originating in an opposition to the modern (democratic) state, and further, that terrorism and the modern (democratic) state are neither mutually distinct, nor necessarily diametrically opposed. Rather, terrorism's historical grounding in the defense of modern democracy points to the fact that the modern democratic state is *founded in terror*, upon the same fault line along which terrorism operates. This history posits terrorism not as alien to the democratic state but as foundational to—indeed, constitutive of the political. Further, in Western discourse, the French Revolution is frequently constructed as marking the historical moment when peaceful cooperation and the rule of mass consensus supplant the violence and terror of tyrannical regimes. In this sense, modern democracy, as with the state in social contract theory, supervenes the reign of terror.

Like terrorism, then, both the modern state and modern democracy are products of the constellation of forces prescribing the transition to modernity, marking historical moments in which the process of the sublimation of terror can be witnessed. In both instances, order superimposes terror. Therefore, it might be said that *the sublimation of terror is not restricted to the political institutions of modernity but, beyond this, is a key structural feature of the experience of modernity more generally*. Terrorism, then, is the desublimation of the terror underpinning modernity. In this context, terrorism problematizes not just the state but, more fundamentally, the organization of power in modernity and, as such, should be understood as an attack on modernity itself that is in fact implicit in the project of modernity. While terrorism often manifests as a challenge to the state, it does so because the state represents one manifestation of the organization of power in modernity.

The Terrorist Society

One of the key definitional categories used to distinguish certain forms of terrorism from others is that of "state terrorism." In the terrorism studies literature, and in Western discourse more generally, "state terrorism" frequently features as a synonym for the violent and persecutory practices used to enforce the agendas of communist or totalitarian states, and is a phenomenon primarily associated with "third world" or "Eastern bloc" nations.[75] These states are commonly referred to as "terrorist regimes" in dominant discourse, distancing Western democratic regimes from the practice of terrorism and, in turn, enabling the construction of Western democracies as the victims of terrorism. This can be read as a disavowal of the terror that underpins Western modernity.

For Lefebvre, terrorist societies are not those that are usually labeled as such in dominant discourse:

> A society where violence and bloodshed reign is not a "terrorist" society, for whether red or white, political terror is short-lived; it is a means used by a specific faction to establish and maintain dictatorship; political terror is localised, it cannot be imputed to the social "body," and such a society is terrorised rather than terrorist.[76]

Lefebvre argues that the "advanced" modern Western liberal democratic nation-state epitomizes the terrorist society. His description of such a society is couched in a historical narrative. For Lefebvre, the terrorist society is embedded in a *telos*; it evolves out of a particular historical formation; the gradual development, we might say even "refinement," of a specific set of historical circumstances. Lefebvre is centrally preoccupied with the ways the hegemony of Western modernity is (re)produced through time. The evolution of the terrorist society he describes culminates in its apocalyptic end. He writes, "a terrorist society . . . cannot maintain itself for long; it aims at stability, consolidation, at preserving its conditions and at its own survival, but *when it reaches its ends it explodes.*"[77] Like Derrida, Lefebvre can be construed here as articulating the idea of modernity's apocalyptic end. He is thus implicitly preoccupied with modernity as a finite project. For Lefebvre, the terrorist society is a sign of the beginning of the end.

Lefebvre claims that "a *terrorist* society is the logical and structural outcome of an *over-repressive* society,"[78] a society in which the overt mechanisms of repression are gradually replaced—indeed, rendered superfluous—by forms of self-repression. Such a society "holds violence in reserve and only makes use of it in emergencies; it relies more on the self-repression inherent in organised everyday life."[79] It is important to note here that, in the terrorist society, violence is not overt but rather circulates as a threat. By way of examples of over-repressive societies, Lefebvre cites societies in which capitalism, Protestantism, or both proliferate.[80] Indeed, he argues that an over-repressive society is one whose "outcome and materialisation would be a certain type of (liberal) democracy."[81] It is clear from Lefebvre's narrative and these examples that his *terrorist society is the refined form of the modern Western liberal democracy.* Indeed, given his preoccupation with "the modern," and bearing in mind that modernity marks not just a time frame but also a structure of thinking, Lefebvre's critique suggests that the terrorist society represents the culmination of the organizational forces of modernity, modernity's *end point.*

In Lefebvre's critique, the hegemony of Western modernity entails the subordination of the members of modern society to a general "strategy": a repression rendered possible by *the spatial and temporal organization of everyday life.* The everyday is fundamentally oppressive: Lefebvre laments "the misery of everyday life, its tedious tasks [and] humiliations."[82] De Certeau also emphasizes that everyday life is "what presses us, even oppresses us, because there does exist an oppression of the present."[83] For Lefebvre, what facilitates this oppression and sustains social organization, is *terror.* In a terrorist society, noncompliance is punished, not through the deployment of explicit violence but via the *threat of violence*, which compels individuals to submit to the everyday. As Lefebvre writes,

> In a terrorist society terror is diffuse, violence is always latent, pressure is
> exerted from all sides on its members, who can only avoid it and shift its weight
> by a super-human effort; each member is a terrorist because he wants to be in
> power (if only briefly); thus there is no need for a dictator; each member
> betrays and chastises himself; terror cannot be located, for it comes from every-
> where and from every specific thing; the "system" . . . has a hold on every
> member separately and submits every member to the whole, that is, to a strat-
> egy . . . unknown to all but those in power, and that no one questions.[84]

Lefebvre invokes Hobbes' description of the state of nature to argue that the
experience of premodern sociality was characterized by fear—"fear of want, of
disease, of the unknown, of woman, of the child, of sexuality, of death and the
dead . . . "[85] However, where traditional Enlightenment narratives construct
forms of modern social organization as the triumph of Reason over the forces
of nature, irrationality and terror, Lefebvre suggests that "the modern" instan-
tiates terror; "a deep-rooted irrationality that [is] an *extension of rationality*."[86]
Modern social organization does not banish fear, it compounds, magnifies,
and converts fear to terror: "not any longer the terror of nature but . . . the
terror of society."[87]

For Lefebvre, the terrorist society is one in which "compulsion and the
illusion of freedom converge."[88] That is, the terrorist society is enforced not
by coercion, but compulsion—a kind of compulsory compliance produced
through the ordering of the everyday and entailing the *cooperation* of each
and every member of society.[89] In a terrorist society, social order, maintained
through the totalizing organization of the everyday, is based upon the *democratization* of terror.

In a terrorist society, there is no outside from which to oppose the system.
Self-regulation is the chief mechanism of control. Control is not imposed by
an identifiable source, the terrorist society operates by displacing responsibility
onto individual members of society, each of whom lives in terror.[90] In modernity, power becomes invisible. The exercise of power appears to disappear, we
perceive ourselves as "free." Terror thus underwrites the everyday. In this context, modern time, practiced through the structure of the everyday, becomes
an instrument for the repression of terror and the regulation of the social body.

If the modern Western liberal democracy epitomizes Lefebvre's terrorist
society, then this helps explain why Western culture feels so besieged by terrorism—what terrorism problematizes, why terrorism resonates as an attack
on modern democracy, and why modern democracies perceive themselves so
acutely as the victims of terrorism. Terrorism, while ostensibly a political
practice that problematizes the modern democratic *state*, in fact *politicizes the
terror of the everyday in Western modernity.* By disrupting modern time and

problematizing the naturalized order of the everyday, terrorism draws attention to the terror *within*. This feature of terrorism—its politicization of the terror that circulates in and through the everyday—renders it, in Derrida's terms, fundamentally "unassimilable."[91]

Another way of thinking about this is that terrorism derives its affective power from its ability to undermine the distinction between legitimate and illegitimate violence that underpins Western liberal democratic social order; the normalization and democratization of terror implied and made possible by linear time and the organization of the everyday. As Hage suggests, terrorism marks a struggle, "first over the distribution of means of violence, and second, and more importantly, over the classification of the forms of violence in the world, particularly of what constitutes legitimate violence."[92] This is one of the reasons why we perceive terrorism as an attack on the state in Western modernity. As many critical theorists, beginning with Max Weber, have argued, the state assumes and represents a monopoly on violence.[93] This command on violence is legitimized by the construction of the state as the naturalized expression of linear time in modernity. Thus, as a practice that problematizes the organization of terror/violence in modernity, terrorism is perceived as a practice that articulates in relation to the state.

Terror, from this perspective, is simultaneously a tool for contesting power *and* a tool for reproducing the structures of power that underpin dominant order. In politicizing the terror of the everyday, terrorism problematizes the principle of freedom that is so fundamental to Western democracy. In this context, terrorism can be understood as an expression of the failure of the liberatory promise of modernity, *thus assailing modernity itself from within*.

And so it is that the subaltern practice of terrorism represents the apocalyptic moment when the terror that underpins the everyday threatens to engulf the modern project. It marks a moment of reversal in which the linear and routinized time of modernity is turned back in upon itself, subverting the processes by which modernity is able to function. It registers as the unleashing of the terror that is tamed by modernity, a terror that, once desublimated, is uncompromising. Terrorism gives expression to the terror of the loss of routine, the terror of the loss of order, the terror that is sublimated by modern forms of social organization. It thus presents as the terror of the end of society itself and the annihilation of modernity.

Mr. Vladimir's Philosophy of Bomb Throwing

In a critical scene in Conrad's *The Secret Agent*, the diplomat for an unnamed foreign power and darling of English high society, Mr. Vladimir, summons his secret agent, Mr. Verloc, to issue a set of instructions regarding the execution of an "anarchist outrage." Vladimir outlines his "philosophy of bomb throwing"

> The imbecile bourgeoisie of this country . . . are blinded by an idiotic vanity. What they want now is a jolly good scare . . . A series of outrages . . . executed here in this country . . . These outrages . . . must be sufficiently startling—effective.[94]

Vladimir envisages a form of terrorism that will achieve a startling effect and this requires an attack planned and executed in London, one that strikes *from within*. Derrida has argued that

> The most irreducible source of absolute terror . . . would be the one that comes from "within," from this zone where the worst "outside" lives with or within "me." My vulnerability is thus, by definition and by structure, by situation, without limit. Whence the terror. Terror is always, or always becomes, at least in part, "interior" . . . The worst, most effective "terrorism" . . . is the one that installs or recalls an interior threat, *at home*—and recalls that the enemy is *also always* lodged on the inside of the system it violates and terrorizes.[95]

Vladimir goes on to advocate an act of terrorism that attacks the very heart of bourgeois society: an "outrage" directed at something the bourgeoisie treasure, and which cannot be misread. The incident must be interpreted as an anarchist plot aimed at the *pure destruction* of the status quo:

> A bomb outrage to have any influence on public opinion now must go beyond the intention of vengeance . . . You anarchists should make it clear that you are perfectly determined to make a clean sweep of the whole social creation.[96]

This notion of complete destruction is a key component of the modern terrorist vision.

In order to attack the foundations of society in a way that resonates with the bourgeoisie, Vladimir promotes a departure from traditional political violence, which he deems no longer adequate:

> An attempt upon a crowned head or on a president is . . . almost conventional—especially since so many presidents have been assassinated. Now let us take an outrage upon—say, a church. Horrible enough at first sight, no doubt, and yet not so effective as a person of an ordinary mind might think. No matter how revolutionary and anarchist in inception, there would be fools enough to give such an outrage the character of a religious manifestation . . . But how to get that appallingly absurd notion [that of complete destruction] into the heads of the middle classes . . . By directing your blows at . . . learning—science. [S]

uch a demonstration will affect them more profoundly than the mangling of a whole street—or theatre—full of their own kind . . . [W]hat is one to say to an act of destructive ferocity so absurd as to be incomprehensible, inexplicable, almost unthinkable; in fact, mad? Madness alone is truly terrifying.[97]

Vladimir articulates a shift in the ways terrorism is conceptualized in the Western world, distinguishing between what can be termed "traditional" and "modern" terrorism. Traditional forms of terrorism such as assassination attack, to use Michel Foucault's expression, the *visibility of power* as represented, for example, by a head of state or a church.[98] By contrast, modern terrorist warfare concerns itself with reaching a significantly more abstracted audience. While its objectives might include that of sending a message to the representatives of institutional power, it is first and foremost concerned with producing a more generalized effect, with generating affect within a much wider audience. Vladimir describes his audience, in a sense his "real" target, as "the bourgeoisie." His attack is aimed, not just at the representatives of institutional power, but also at an entire class who, in the anarchist formulation, exploit the proletariat for their own gain and are thus responsible for perpetuating a society based on a fundamentally corrupt power structure. In this sense, Vladimir's "terrorist outrage" strikes not at the visibility of power but at the *invisibility of power*. As Crick claims, "in an age of bureaucrats, tyrannicide is plainly less useful than terror."[99] If the everyday renders the power structures of modernity invisible, and it is the everyday that terrorism attacks in order to enact its symbolic dissembling of modernity, then terrorism, by disrupting time and politicizing the terror of the everyday, attacks the "invisible" organization of power in modernity.

Vladimir proposes an attack on learning, and in particular on modern science. His desire is to disrupt the apparently seamless logic of Western modernity, the structures of thinking that historically legitimize dominant order. Modern terrorism, to be effective, must attack in order to *deconstruct dominant ideology*. For Vladimir, the attack must absolutely defy bourgeois logic, and in so doing, undermine the process of (re)producing hegemony:

The attack must have all the shocking senselessness of gratuitous blasphemy . . . it would be really telling if one could throw a bomb into pure mathematics. But that is impossible . . . What do you think of having a go at astronomy [the Royal Observatory]? . . . Such outrage combines the greatest possible regard for humanity with the most alarming display of ferocious hostility. I defy the ingenuity of journalists to persuade their public that any given member of the proletariat can have a personal grievance against astronomy.[100]

Historically, astronomy has been principally concerned with the cultural imagining of a relationship between time (an abstract measurement) and space (in the first instance, the positionality of celestial bodies, and later, in the form of mapping the globe to a high degree of mathematical accuracy). In its modern inflections, the study of astronomy has sought to describe—to objectify and quantify—this relationship in modern scientific terms, naturalizing the connection between time and space. More than this, astronomy is a science that attempts to establish an *order and a logic* to this relationship. Indeed, it is a science in which the conceptual ordering of space (through for example, cartography) is achieved through the ordering of time, and vice versa. Vladimir's choice of astronomy as a symbolically potent terrorist target can thus be read as an assault on the symbolic ordering of time and space in Western modernity, and by extension, the everyday—the spatial and temporal framework that structures modernity. This attack on astronomy, Vladimir claims, can send a message of "pure destruction." Similarly for Lefebvre, who claims that the true revolution will *annihilate* the everyday: "The revolution of the future will put an end to the quotidian . . . Not . . . restricted to the spheres of economy, politics and ideology; its specific objective will be to annihilate everyday life."[101] As we shall see, this impulse toward total destruction of the everyday has strong resonances with the ways the radical feminist project encoded its aims and objectives.

CHAPTER 5

Conjuring the Apocalypse: Radical Feminism, Apocalyptic Temporality, and the Society for Cutting Up Men

I'm not a lunatic, asshole, I'm a revolutionary.

Valerie Solanas[1]

Beginning in the 1970s, as second-wave North American feminism began to gain momentum and terrorism "at home" simultaneously became a prominent political and cultural concern for the United States, feminism and terrorism began to present in the cultural imaginary as isomorphic practices. I argued in Chapter Three that, in the first instance, feminism and terrorism were perceived as causally related. That is, feminism was constructed within dominant discourse as responsible for increased numbers of women participating in clandestine activities directed at overthrowing the state. However, perhaps more importantly, white urban terrorist groups were constructed as being dominated by women as both organizers and protagonists of the terrorist drama. In this context, feminism came to be thought as culpable for (white urban) terrorism per se in the United States.

What is often referred to as second-wave feminism comprised a spectrum of groups with widely divergent understandings of the problem of women's subordination and an equally divergent set of strategies for effecting cultural and political change. However, in the earlier phase of second-wave feminist activism, a small number of women's groups, those we have come to label "radical feminists,"[2] came to dominate the political scene of feminism. Ellen Willis writes that the radical feminist "movement took shape in 1968 and ended, for all practical purposes, five years later"[3]—a period coinciding with the peak of home-grown US "urban terrorism" carried out by various left-wing groups.[4]

I argued in Chapter Four that terrorism, as a tactical practice, signifies within the Western imagination as the apocalyptic end to modernity. This chapter argues that the crosswiring of radical feminism with terrorism that began in the late 1960s/early 1970s in the United States was made possible by terrorists' and feminists' shared articulation of an apocalyptic outlook culminating in a call to arms—itself an effect of envisioning the radical transformation of a society based on linear time. I exemplify this argument via an analysis of Valerie Solanas' *SCUM Manifesto*—a text that literalizes the idea of feminism as terrorism—in order to critique the gendering of Western modernity.

Valerie Solanas: Radical Feminist *Zeitgeist*

As the New Right has struggled to make sense, however inadequately, of the events of September 11, 2001 and their aftermath, these self-proclaimed moral watchdogs of US culture have breathed new life into the discourse that crosswires feminism with terrorism. As in the 1970s, for the New Right, feminism, once again, is responsible for the terrible affliction of terrorism. Feminism, as their language and imagery would suggest, is itself terrorist.

We will recall from Chapter Three that in a 1992 fundraising newsletter, Reverend Pat Robertson described feminism as "a socialist, anti-family political movement that encourages women to leave their husbands, kill their children, practice witchcraft, destroy capitalism, and become lesbians."[5] Phyllis Schlafly has warned that feminists not only "want to *kill* everything masculine" but also that "you can't negotiate with the feminists because you will lose. *They will slit your throat.*"[6]

It could be said that these constructions are at odds with the status accorded present day feminism in US dominant culture, where feminist principles now circulate widely in the popular domain, albeit in different forms, to varying degrees of acceptance, and often ambiguously or contradictorily. Feminist principles, that is, have a certain degree of cultural currency and legitimacy[7] and, as such, feminists and their demands are not ultimately all that unreasonable.

The paranoid fear of feminism, as a catalyst of terrorism, articulated by the New Right is however contextualized (though not excused) if we juxtapose Robertson's comments with the words for which Valerie Solanas, founder and sole member of the feminist terrorist organization known as SCUM—the Society for Cutting Up Men—is most notorious. Solanas is remembered for shooting Andy Warhol in 1968 and, in the shadow of her spectacular debut into infamy, what is often overlooked is that she authored one of the most angrily outspoken texts of US radical feminism. The *SCUM Manifesto*, self-published by Solanas in 1967, is one of the few concrete legacies of Solanas' existence. In the opening paragraph, she writes:

> No aspect of society being at all relevant to women, there remains to civic-minded, responsible, thrill-seeking females only to overthrow the government, eliminate the money system, institute complete automation, and destroy the male sex.[8]

Later in the manifesto, she describes SCUM's activities in this way:

> SCUM will always operate on a criminal as opposed to a civil-disobedience basis, that is, as opposed to openly violating the law and going to jail in order to draw attention to an injustice. Such tactics acknowledge the rightness of the overall system and are used only to modify it slightly, change specific laws . . . SCUM is out to destroy the system, not attain certain rights within it. Also, SCUM—always selfish, always cool—will always aim to avoid detection and punishment . . . SCUM will coolly, furtively, stalk its prey and quietly move in for the kill.[9]

Solanas' feminist vision operates at the discursive nexus of feminism and terrorism. An iconoclastic text, the *Manifesto* advocates a violent and clandestine politics that renders the extermination of the male species as the only plausible solution to the age-old problem of women's subordination. Solanas' manifesto is straightforward. She deploys the modern discourse of eugenics to argue that "the male is a biological accident"[10] whose continued existence is no longer justified. She writes: "The elimination of any male is, therefore, a righteous and good act, an act highly beneficial to women as well as an act of mercy."[11]

Opposed to the liberal feminist agenda of groups such as the National Organization of Women (NOW), which argued for women's equality *within* the system, Solanas' angry and incendiary stance was emblematic of the so-called radical edge of feminism that proposed the complete overthrow of the system itself. In 1977, interviewed for the *Village Voice*, Solanas described SCUM as: "hypothetical . . . There's no organization called SCUM . . . I thought of it as a state of mind. In other words, women who think a certain way are in SCUM."[12] If SCUM was a structure of thinking, a world view, then, in 1968, for a number of women at the forefront of the women's liberation movement, particularly the hard line "movement heavies,"[13] Solanas embodied the contemporary feminist *Zeitgeist*.[14]

When, on 13 June 1968, Solanas appeared in the State Supreme Court, she was represented by black radical feminist lawyer, Florynce "Flo" Kennedy,[15] who hailed Solanas as "one of the most important spokeswomen of the feminist movement."[16] Ti-Grace Atkinson, a New York NOW member being groomed for feminist leadership by Betty Friedan, heralded Solanas as "the first outstanding champion of women's rights";[17] her show of solidarity horrifying Friedan and other NOW members.[18] Atkinson later attributed her departure from NOW to form the radical women's liberation group, "The Feminists," to the influence of Solanas' manifesto. At an August 1968 meeting of representatives of women's organizations held at Sandy Springs, Roxanne Dunbar "read aloud excerpts from Valerie Solanas' *SCUM Manifesto* and proclaimed it the 'essence of feminism.'"[19] As Alice Echols writes, "Solanas' case became something of a *cause célèbre* among radical feminists . . . In the wake of the shooting, [the] *SCUM* [*Manifesto*] was finally published by Olympia Press and it became obligatory reading for *radical* feminists."[20]

While the term suggests a unitary movement defined by a coherent political agenda, "radical feminism" in fact developed in uneven and often haphazard ways,[21] encompassing the activities of numerous, often quite small, independent women's groups of the late 1960s and early 1970s, working to address the structural inequities that characterized the positioning of women both locally and nationally, and often globally and/or universally. There were several concerted efforts to establish a common agenda for women's liberation out of these disparate concerns and to mobilize women on a large scale. From 1968 to 1973, the issue of how to theorize and actively address the problems of women's subordination within dominant culture would be hotly contested, and eventually, "radical feminism" would give way to "cultural feminism."[22]

Nonetheless, in 1968, "radical feminism" within the broader women's liberation movement was a force to be reckoned with. It is clear that, for radical feminists, Solanas' outspoken misandry resonated with their own developing feminist beliefs. The formative work of feminists such as Dunbar, Atkinson, and Shulamith Firestone, for example, echoes Solanas' manifesto in both tone and content, arguing fiercely for the elimination of sexual difference and the annihilation of the structure of gender relations that underpins Western culture. In 1970, in a landmark text of second-wave feminism, *The Dialectic of Sex*, Firestone argued that "the end goal of feminist revolution, must be . . . not just the elimination of male *privilege* but of the sex *distinction* itself."[23] These women interpreted Solanas' call for "sexocide" as an attempt to shift the boundaries of, and reinvigorate, the debate that had been opened up by liberal feminists, and they boldly declared their solidarity with Solanas' understanding of the gendered biases of modernity.

It is this version of feminism—the radical feminist activist paradigm of which Solanas is perhaps the most extreme representative—that, since the late 1960s, has been discursively aligned with the phenomenon of (white urban) terrorism. And it is this version of feminism that was invoked and condemned by the New Right in the aftermath of September 11, 2001; imagined as, and standing in for, feminism more generically.

Radical Feminist Tactics

Throughout the late 1960s and early 1970s, radical feminists advocated a variety of activism that paralleled "revolutionary" terrorist tactics of the era. At the level of popular culture, this produced feminism as aligned with terrorism. Consequently, dominant culture tended to respond to both feminists and terrorists in remarkably similar ways, perhaps most notably by constructing them as mad. Like the "revolutionary terrorism" of the time, radical feminism's tactics of shock and disruption aimed to destabilize and eventually overthrow dominant order.

Radical feminism's transformative politics rested on a program, albeit largely uncoordinated, of *tactical* intervention. The radical feminist activist paradigm privileged the "action" as a key mechanism in the fight for gender equality. As Marianne DeKoven explains, within the New Left, "an 'action' could range from the familiar modes of march, rally, sit-in, leafleting, petition and protest, to various forms of street or guerrilla theatre, to a bombing or a bank robbery."[24] DeKoven notes that feminism adopted the New Left's commitment "to spontaneity, creativity and diversity in its expression."[25] Of the various forms of actions popularized by the New Left, radical feminism often opted for "guerrilla theater" to draw attention to their political message, or what the Yippies[26] called the "theatre of the apocalypse."[27] Like terrorism, feminism operated opportunistically. Radical feminism "extended the domain of the political . . . so that 'actions' could be almost anything and appear almost anywhere."[28] For example, at "the Miss America demonstration of August 1968 . . . young women crowned a live sheep to symbolize the beauty pageant's objectification of female bodies, and filled a 'freedom trashcan' with objects of female torture—girdles, bras, curlers, issues of *Ladies Home Journal*."[29] Like their terrorist counterparts, through their staging of spectacle, radical feminists seized public attention. As Echols notes, the Miss America Beauty Pageant protest "marked the end of the movement's obscurity because the protest . . . received extensive press coverage."[30]

Also in 1968, a group of New York based radical feminists including Robin Morgan formed a feminist activist group called WITCH. WITCH staged an impressive publicity campaign for the radical feminist cause in the late 1960s by performing—"dressed as witches and bearing broomsticks"[31]—a series of spectacular public "hexings," most notably on the stock exchange on Wall Street and on the annual Bride Fair at Madison Square Garden. WITCH's guerrilla theater was inspired by the Yippie-style activism popularized by Jerry Rubin and Abbie Hoffman.[32] The Yippies' political lineage itself can be traced back to the French radical avant-garde Situationist movement, which, like Michel de Certeau and Henri Lefebvre, conceptualized the everyday as a space for the expression of political dissent and the enactment of sociocultural transformation.[33] As with terrorism, shock and surprise were key elements of WITCH's political activism. Like terrorism, WITCH-style radical feminism sought to create a spectacle to expose the inadequacy of "the system" and force a space for radical critique. And like terrorism, WITCH had a publicity agenda. It sought to create "actions" that would capture the attention of the mainstream mass media in order to promote its political position.[34]

Crucially, WITCH articulated the importance of the everyday to its political program: "Our short-term purpose is to . . . attack where we are least expected . . . and to reveal that *the routine of daily life is the theatre of struggle.*"[35] Like terrorism, WITCH aimed to disrupt the routine of the everyday, and, in so doing, focus attention on the basic repression inhering in social order. Or in other words, radical feminists such as WITCH configured the everyday as a site of radical transformation. In deploying methods of tactical intervention, WITCH constructed itself in the mould of (metaphorical) terrorists. Indeed, the acronym WITCH stood for the "Women's International *Terrorist* Conspiracy from Hell." In this context, radical feminism looked like a form of terrorism.

Feminism, Modernity, and the Politics of Utopia

As Rita Felski points out in *The Gender of Modernity*, the relationship between "modernity" and feminism is by no means straightforward. If the term "modernity" signals both the variety of identifiable structural changes in the organization of everyday life that have taken place alongside the processes of modernization as well as the set of discursive practices that have legitimized those structural transformations, historically, in its challenge to the variety of forms of women's oppression, feminism has simultaneously shaped, and been shaped by, modernity itself.[36] Feminism's relationship with modernity is dialogical; it is produced by the subjects silenced by the grand narratives of modernity, empowered and in dialogue with those grand narratives themselves.[37] As a response to, or as an engagement with, the problems of women's subordinate status as it is prescribed by the conditions of modernity, feminism has both deployed modernity's dominant discourses and formulated its methodologies in relation to the idea of the modern.

Apocalypse and utopia, as important and complementary visionary motifs of secular modernity, have been deployed to drive the transformational project of a range of modern social movements. While the two discourses are intertwined,[38] they both perform distinct functions in the modern imaginary. Both discourses may be understood to have their roots in premodern religious rhetoric, but both have taken on specifically modern inflections in the modern episteme, which, among other things, replaces Divine Wisdom with individual Reason as the guiding principle of history, is structured around notions of progress that depend upon a linear conceptualization of history, and thinks representation through the structure of binary opposition. Both discourses have, to a great extent, been secularized, and it is their modern secular forms that I discuss here. Inasmuch as radical feminism's vision of social transformation is informed by these modern discourses of utopia and apocalypse, it articulates as a specifically modern movement for social change.

As Krishan Kumar notes, modern conceptualizations of utopia—beginning with the coining of the term by Thomas More in 1516—have differed in fundamental ways from its premodern (religious) antecedents. In modernity, utopia often gets reworked in terms of the dialectic, as the final and perfect resolution of the dialectical process, in the Hegelian sense of opposition between two contradictory but interacting forces (thesis and synthesis) and their continual reconciliation on a higher level (synthesis). In Hegel's formulation, this dialectical process always produces a residue that, in the next stage of the progress of history, gets cast as the new antithesis. Utopia occurs, then, when synthesis is reached without a residual.[39] Further, the modern concept of utopia is constructed as a goal that individuals in society can, and must, actively work toward.[40]

In modernity, the discourse of utopia has played an important role in imagining the ideal form of the modern nation-state,[41] which is envisaged as representing perfectly the society it governs by balancing uniformity, complete equality, and unlimited freedom for all its citizens through the perfection of its regulatory mechanisms. As Louis Marin has described More's utopia, it is

> [o]n the one hand, a free play of imagination in its indefinite expansion measured only by the desire, itself infinite, of happiness in a space where the moving frontiers of its philosophical and political fictions would be traced; on the other hand, the exact closed totality, rigorously coded by all the constraints of the law, binding and closing a place with insuperable frontiers that would guarantee its harmonious functioning.[42]

Given that the utopian vision of the perfect state is that which reflects perfectly the desire of all its citizens, representation is fundamental to the imagining of the utopian state in modernity. The utopian state—as the perfect expression of modern political formations—is that in which the spacing of representation, the space which produces difference in modernity, is overcome once and for all, revealing the fundamental sameness, indeed the synthesis, of the government and its people.

The imagining of a perfect society in which all conflict is resolved has provided much of the impetus for modern reform. As Kumar points out, "social movements need utopias."[43] He goes on to claim that second-wave feminism is a case in point,[44] and indeed, the liberatory promise of utopia has profoundly shaped the feminist call for equality between the sexes. The imagining of a society without discrimination based upon sex has inspired feminists to search for direct political activist strategies that enable them to challenge and transform what they envisage as the causes of women's subordination.[45]

Evolution versus Revolution: Feminist Discourses of Social Change

According to Felski, there are two main tropes through which feminism has envisaged the process by which modern society will attain perfection, namely through evolution and revolution. This troping influences the production of the two dominant paradigms of second-wave feminist activist strategy: ongoing reform as it is posited by liberal and institutional forms of feminism and the call for violent feminist revolution that characterizes radical feminism, respectively.

Discursively, the evolutionary paradigm configures the shift toward the feminist utopia as "an organic process of development"[46] whereby, through piecemeal reform, in the context of the inexorable flow of history, society gradually progresses toward a feminist vision of perfection. The evolutionary paradigm has profoundly shaped institutional feminism—such as that of NOW—in which the individual is understood as shaping history both from *within*, and in relation to, the state.

In feminist rhetoric, evolutionary progress toward utopia is juxtaposed with the revolutionary paradigm, which envisages "the violent overthrow of an existing régime, but . . . simultaneously encompasses a wider . . . process of radical and fundamental change."[47] The sense of the inevitability of the attainment of utopia is substituted here by an explicitly modern understanding of the centrality of the individual as dynamic agent of history. It encompasses a notion of individuals bringing on, forcing even, the advent of utopia.

Revolution is thus understood as a rupture of history "in that it affirms the schismatic nature of the transformative moment, as a qualitative leap towards an unimaginable future."[48] Revolution presents as the *Aufhebung*—the force gesture of the dialectic, the moment of fracture within the history of representation. Positioned as taking place, not from within the state, but from *outside* (and against) the state, it constitutes a challenge to the state's existence. And as a prerequisite for the achievement of utopia, it intersects with the eschatological discourse of apocalypse. In modernity, the apocalypse is secularized in terms of revolution.[49] Moshe Amon notes that "the twentieth century is rife with apocalyptic premonitions,"[50] which since the sixteenth century (and here we can understand Amon as referring to the rise of modernity) have characterized "the age of revolution." I suggest below that revolution in its apocalyptic formulation is necessarily based on a principle of *eradication* as opposed to one of synthesis.

The discourse of apocalypse has its origins in Judeo-Christian religious philosophy. In contrast to utopia, which works in terms of synthesis, the religious apocalypse turns upon a notion of eradication, that is, in terms of destruction, selection and elimination "of those who, depending upon the ideological context of the particular text, either have unwarrantedly harassed God's people and failed to acknowledge him, or failed to acknowledge the advent of his Son."[51] In the modern, secular reworking of the religious apocalypse, the focus has tended to be less on a revelatory promise and more on the advent of unmitigated destruction.[52]

The modern secular apocalypse is thought in terms that signal the ideal modern nation-state as embodying postapocalyptic harmony. In certain instances, the modern apocalypse is constructed, both by the state itself and by those who challenge the state from outside, as the event that will bring on utopia. In order to bridge the gap between the lived experience of society and the utopian vision, individuals must bring on the apocalyptic eradication of those who stand in the way of the dream.

For some theorists, the envisaging of utopias which, when put into concrete political practice, rely on an apocalyptic début, corrupts and contaminates the idea of utopia. Leszek Kolakowski, for example, states: "Utopias . . . have become ideologically poisonous . . . Their advocates managed to convince themselves that they had discovered a genuine technology of apocalypse to force the door of paradise."[53] In political practice, the version of utopia that relies on revolution as rupture or disjuncture is signaled by this notion of apocalypse as ushering in the new world. As Hans Magnus Enzensberger suggests, "the idea of apocalypse has accompanied utopian thought since its first beginnings, pursuing it like a shadow . . . [W]ithout catastrophe, no millennium, without apocalypse, no paradise."[54] In the modern vision of revolution, utopia and apocalypse are thus linked, manifesting themselves at distinct stages in the history of the end of the world. Apocalypse is that which comes directly *before*, and produces, utopia. Seen as a challenge to the state "from below," apocalypse can be equated with revolution.

Radical Feminism's Apocalyptic Vision of Revolution

In the radical feminist vision of the path to salvation, the apocalyptic presents in a particularly pronounced manner. It was not uncommon for radical feminists to preach violence as a way of forcing an apocalyptic end to social order in order to enable the rebuilding of society from scratch. As Echols notes, in the late 1960s, young radical feminists were strongly of the opinion that "nonviolent protest had long since outlived its usefulness."[55] Todd Gitlin writes that, in response to their perceived oppression both within and without the New Left, "the women's groups reacted . . . with their own version of revolutionary apocalypse."[56] At the level of popular culture, too, radical feminism was perceived in apocalyptic terms: "sisterhood is, indeed, powerful [and . . .] hastening the Last Days of Patriarchy."[57]

If terrorism's affect is generated by its rupture of the ordinary (linear and routine) time of modernity, so too, radical feminism relied upon the premise of linear and routinized time for its political effect. Radical feminist "actions" had rhetorical power because they unfolded against the backdrop of ordinary time. However, more fundamentally, radical feminism conceived of its transformative project in teleological terms. Radical feminism, like the New Left "Movement" out of which it grew, was built upon "the belief that the collapse of society was imminent."[58] Radical feminists perceived themselves as poised on the brink of total revolution. Morgan, a key figure in the early stages of radical feminism, described, in overtly apocalyptic tones, a world wreaked by the male-created havoc of "ecological disaster and nuclear threat."[59] And in 1971, journalist and feminist activist, Vivian Gornick, positioned the rise of radical feminism at the culmination of 25 years of postwar social protest in the United States, constructing it as the catalyst, indeed the *Aufhebung*, of total revolution:

> Beginning with a general loss of faith in the meaning and comfort of middle class capitalism, it has gathered momentum . . . sweeping through the country to include the hungers and protests and demands of a whole variety of "have-nots." Beginning, most notably, with blacks and then students, it has ended, most vociferously and *most dangerously and most radically*, with women . . . who are beginning to say "No, in thunder" . . . who are determined now . . . to make a lunge for that brass ring which threatens—more than any other element of social revolution abroad ever could—to bring Western society toppling.[60]

In the radical feminist imagination, women were bearing witness to the last days. In rising up against patriarchal oppression, women would destroy the system of gender relations that underpinned it. As DeKoven states, "this rising up was conceived teleologically, as a stage in the historical sequence of capitalism, imperialism and world socialist revolution."[61] In the aftermath of the revolution, configured in the radical feminist imagination as apocalypse, women would remake the world *anew*. But first, women would have to bring about the end—patriarchal society would be forced to confront its eschaton. In this sense, radical feminism constructed itself as positioned at the culmination of history, indeed, of modernity itself: the moment of the annihilation of the "old order."

Enzensberger has noted that "the apocalyptic fantasy [is] inescapably bound up with the terror, the demand for vengeance, for justice."[62] For those who witnessed radical feminism from the outside and those who practiced it alike, radical feminism presented as an "explosion" of "cumulative rage" bent on the destruction of social order.[63] For many radical feminists, this anger needed to be mobilized for the feminist revolution. As the anonymous authors of "What is Liberation?" stated, "women must learn the meaning of . . . the violence that liberates the human spirit."[64] It is often suggested that terrorism is born of the frustrated anger associated with perceived oppression.[65] In their harnessing of anger as a revolutionary tool then, the radical feminist vision resonated with contemporary terrorist visions. Indeed, for some sections of the early radical feminist movement, the parallels between feminism and terrorism would take a concrete form: women had to be prepared to use physical violence to force the revolution. For example, according to Echols, Atkinson excoriated "women's liberationists for failing to 'pick up the gun.'"[66] And Echols claims that, rather than drawing inspiration from the achievements and examples of earlier generations of US feminists, radical feminists looked to the tradition of armed revolution in the third world for inspiration.[67] This kind of radical feminist call to arms facilitates a discursive alignment of terrorism and feminism. However, radical feminism resonated with the practice of terrorism in ways beyond this, specifically in its conceptualization of the everyday as the site of both women's oppression and feminist transformation.

Radical Feminism and the Everyday

While Lefebvre is mostly silent on the role of gender in the reproduction of the everyday, he does note that "everyday life weighs heaviest on women,"[68] lamenting their humiliations, which include "child-bearing and child-rearing, basic preoccupations with bare necessities, money, tradesmen, provisions, . . . the survival of poverty and the endlessness of want."[69] While it goes unelaborated in his analysis, we can understand Lefebvre as articulating the idea that the routinization of the quotidian produces a fundamental power differential between beings gendered as "male" and those gendered "female"; that the everyday is a technology of the subordination of women to men. This is the nature of the "oppression" that radical feminism perceived so acutely, and it is this subordination against which radical feminism directed its energies.

Terrorism operates to render the power relations underpinning social order visible. So too, one of radical feminism's chief objectives was to expose the invisible structure of gendered power relations implicit in the everyday. Firestone powerfully claimed that "sex class is so deep as to be invisible,"[70] and that radical feminism's challenge lay in exposing the structures of women's oppression, "the organization of culture itself."[71] Her rallying call thus emphasized the need to address the conditions of lived experience, the organizational parameters of what I have described as "the everyday." As with terrorism then, the everyday became a key site for radical feminist tactical intervention.

As DeKoven states, in radical feminist politics, "resistance is as pervasive and diffuse as power itself, and . . . is seen to inhere in everyday cultural tactics, practices and modes of performance not themselves necessarily overtly political."[72] This idea took expression in the radical feminist catch-cry, "the personal is political," which shifted focus to "the realm of particular subversive or resistant or counter-hegemonic identifications, modes of subjectivity, *tactics of the everyday*, and cultural or subcultural practices."[73] To enact their agenda of the transformation of the everyday, radical feminists deployed "consciousness-raising" (known in radical feminist speak as "CR"). CR was conceived as a practice that could politicize women, educating them in the fundamental oppressions at the heart of "personal" and "ordinary" life. Its methodology consisted of women's discussion groups, designed to facilitate the recasting of women's experiences of "personal problems" as "social issues fought together rather than with personal solutions."[74] Radical feminists thus took the feminist struggle to the heart of everyday cultural practices, calling for women's negation of the everyday roles they inhabited, and in particular, the refusal of the gendering of the routines prescribed by the "domestic." In this sense, *radical feminism constituted the refusal of patriarchal routine*. It defied, outright, modern temporality.

The Terrorist Time of Radical Feminism

Julia Kristeva claims that the distinction between radical feminism and the forms of feminism that preceded it revolves around a difference in orientation toward time, around a temporal disjuncture. This claim can also be read as distinguishing between the "evolutionary" and "revolutionary" paradigms of feminist activism discussed earlier:

> In its beginnings, the women's movement, as the struggle of suffragists and of existential feminists, *aspired to gain a place in linear time as the time of project and history.* In this sense, the movement, while immediately universalist, is also deeply rooted in the socio-political life of nations . . . In a second phase, linked . . . to the younger women who came to feminism after May 1968 . . . *linear temporality has been almost totally refused . . .* This current seems to think of itself as belonging to another generation . . . in its conception of its own identity and, consequently, *of temporality as such.*[75]

Kriesteva suggests that feminism after May 1968, for which we can read "radical feminism," entails the conceptualization of a radically different temporality. If we accept that linear time is based on the routinization of the everyday, we can understand Kristeva as signaling radical feminism's refusal of the routine of (patriarchal) everyday life, conjuring the end of modern, linear and routinized time. Kristeva argues (and we should note her apocalyptic overtones here):

> The new generation of women is . . . *attempting a revolt which they see as a resurrection but which society as a whole understands as murder.* This attempt can lead us to a not less and sometimes more deadly violence. Or to a cultural innovation. Probably to both at once. *But that is precisely what the stakes are, and they are of epochal significance.*[76]

I have argued that terrorism politicizes the structural violence that makes modern social order possible. For Kristeva, feminism also operates in these terms: "Modern feminism has only been but a moment in the interminable process of coming to consciousness about the implacable violence (separation, castration, etc.) which constitutes any symbolic contract."[77] Radical feminism thus manifests as the reinvestment of the sociosymbolic violence experienced by women in relation to the foundational pact of modernity, namely the social contract. In making this claim, Kristeva understands the social contract as, in Carole Pateman's terms, a "sexual contract" that operates to the exclusion of women.

As Pateman states, the social contract is "structured through time by a permanent exchange between the two parties, the exchange of obedience for protection."[78] There are two points in traditional social contract theory accounts of the state that are of interest here. First, the state is understood to be constituted of rational individuals.[79] That is, the notion of the state operates according to a principle of exclusion that differentiates between rational individuals and their ("irrational") oppositional Other. Second, social contract theory posits the importance of the state in the protection of the individuals it governs from the threat posed by the Other. Together, these criteria define the boundaries of civil society. Importantly, a contract that only includes rational individuals characterizes those who are excluded as irrational and constructs them as a threat to the rational foundations of modern society—a threat from which the state must be protected.[80]

Pateman argues that the original social contract established not only political right but also *patriarchal* right. Citing a long history in which modern Western culture considers women to be fundamentally irrational, she argues that historically women have been excluded from membership of the state, which is founded, for social contract theory, in a contract between rational, consenting individuals.[81] Further, in drawing a distinction between the public and private spheres as a necessary prerequisite for the existence of civil society, patriarchal social order required the exclusion of women from the public realm. In other words, women are positioned as excessive to both the state and its operation in the public sphere.[82]

In a separate text, Pateman argues that there has been a broader cultural concern with what Rousseau termed "the disorder of women," dating back at least as far as the story of the Garden of Eden, but which becomes "a general social and political problem"[83] in modernity. Women come to represent the forces of chaos that threaten the ordered world of modernity "because their being, or their nature . . . necessarily leads them to exert a disruptive influence in social and political life. Women have a disorder at their very centers—in their morality—which can bring about the destruction of the state."[84] The belief in the disorder of women has functioned throughout modern Western history as a rationale for their subordination and containment, for example, within the family structure and the domestic realm. However, despite attempts to contain her, the threat of Woman never disappears. Indeed, such attempts arguably augment the threat of her (potential) subversion of order. If "women are seen as guardians of order and morality as well as inherently subversive,"[85] then, paradoxically, moral order depends upon the cooperation of women, that is, those who are positioned within the cultural economy as inherently subversive.[86] Positioned at the border between order and disorder, society and nature, Woman remains an unsettling reminder of the potential for the loss of order against which the project of modernity rails. In this way, women become representative of an enemy *within* the borders of "civilized" society. Or as Hegel expressed it, the community "creates its enemy for itself within its own gates," namely "womankind in general."[87]

Given that Woman is positioned as simultaneously necessary but subversively excessive to the gendered order of modernity, feminism mobilizes the terror of disorder that lurks beneath the ordered veneer of modernity.

Feminism—a movement that, within the Western cultural imagination, signifies the transgression and overturning of the gender laws that structure dominant order—signifies the unleashing of the terroristic threat of the disorderliness of women that lies at the heart of Western patriarchal culture. The threat is, as Eileen MacDonald puts it, that Valerie Solanas' "Society of Cutting Up Men . . . would triumph."[88]

Further, inasmuch as women are positioned as *integral* to the reproduction of society from one generation to the next, feminism represents for the modern imagination a movement against the naturalized order of the world that stems *from within*. Feminism desublimates the terror of the loss of (gendered) order that underpins and drives the organizational project of modernity—it mobilizes the destructive seed that lies within modernity itself. And it is radical feminism, speaking in terms of rage and violent retribution, that proclaims the revenge of "the disorder of women" most loudly.

For Kristeva, it is no coincidence that many women, post-1968, turned to terrorism as a solution to the problems of the world:

> When a subject is too brutally excluded from this socio-symbolic stratum . . . she may, by counter-investing the violence she has endured . . . combat what was experienced as frustration—with arms which may seem disproportional, but which are not so in comparison with the subjective or more precisely narcissistic suffering from which they originate.[89]

Kristeva reads women's participation in the political violence of terrorism as the reinvestment of women's rage at their exclusion from civil society. In this sense, radical feminism and terrorism are not, as dominant discourse seeks to convince us, causally related. Feminism does not lead to (female) terrorism. Rather, *feminism and terrorism are structural equivalents*. They respond to the sociosymbolic violence upon which modernity is predicated. And in doing so, they present in the cultural imagination as geminate practices.

Valerie Solanas' terrorist vision for the radical overthrow of patriarchal society constitutes a pronounced instance in which the radical feminist vision intersects overtly with the terrorist vision. Indeed, just as Joseph Conrad's *The Secret Agent* literalizes the idea of terrorism as the disruption of linear time, Solanas' *Manifesto* literalizes the terroristic threat of (radical) feminism.

Solanas and the Terrorist Spectacle

Genet just reports, despite what Sartre and de Beauvoir, two overrated windbags, say about the existential implications of his work. I, on the other hand, am a social propagandist.

Valerie Solanas from the locked ward at Bellevue Hospital in 1968[90]

In the early afternoon of 3 June 1968, the summer of the student uprisings across the United States, Valerie Solanas waited outside the new offices of Andy Warhol's retro-chic art gallery, the Factory, at 33 Union Square, New York. It was a warm day, but Solanas was heavily dressed and she had even applied a little makeup—from all accounts, something she reserved for special occasions. When Warhol arrived in a taxi with his assistant, Jed Johnson, Solanas rode with them in the elevator up to the gallery. Solanas and Warhol exchanged a few words, and then Warhol and his entourage went about their business, ignoring Solanas' presence. A few minutes later, Solanas pulled a .32 caliber automatic pistol from a paper bag and fired three times at Warhol. Only one bullet hit Warhol, but it seriously wounded him, "entering through the left lung and hitting the spleen, stomach, liver and oesophagus before penetrating the right lung and exiting from the side."[91] She then fired at a visiting art dealer, hitting him in the left buttock, before turning and catching the elevator down to the ground floor. Later that evening, having surrendered herself and the gun to a traffic policeman in Times Square, Solanas was taken to the 13th Precinct Booking Room where she openly confessed to the shooting of Warhol. It is this incident for which most people remember Solanas, if they remember her at all.

In characteristically egotistical fashion, Warhol attempted to subordinate Solanas' attack to his own agendas by framing it as a hostile attempt to mobilize his promise, made earlier that year, that "in the future everybody will be famous for 15 minutes." Undermining the political nature of her actions, he constructed Solanas' action as "a mere attempt to use him as a trampoline to fame."[92] However, Solanas' own conceptualization of the incident was radically different. Solanas clearly envisaged the shooting as a radical, tactical intervention that would seize public attention and focus it on her feminist politics. For Solanas, the attack constituted a propaganda stunt that would operate in the violent, spectacular, and publicity-centered terms of terrorism, to foreground a political agenda.

In the immediate aftermath of her arrest and questioning, confronted by "a mob of journalists and photographers shouting questions,"[93] Solanas referred them directly to her feminist manifesto: "I have a lot of reasons. Read my manifesto and it will tell you who I am."[94] In so doing, Solanas attempted to redirect popular attention to her political cause linking her "radical gesture" with the politics of feminist revolution outlined in her manifesto.

Solanas' attempt on Warhol operated according to the same propaganda principle that is central to terrorism. It must be recognized as "a carefully orchestrated and radically disturbing aesthetic performance"[95] that can be located within a twentieth-century paradigm of spectacular political intervention, which encompasses the rise of terrorism as an important weapon in the arsenal of resistance. However, in the media spectacle that followed the shooting, her manifesto received very little attention, and the seriousness of her revolutionary aims was lost; her guerrilla action was always already mediated by her victim's celebrity status. As Germaine Greer, one of the few people to consider Solanas with any seriousness, wrote, Solanas "was too easily characterised as a neurotic, perverted exhibitionist, and the incident was too much a part of Warhol's three-ring circus of nuts for her message to come across unperverted."[96] Splashed across the front page of *The New York Times*, Solanas' story was relayed as a vicious personal vendetta, emptied of its feminist politics.[97] Overshadowed by Warhol's seductive public persona, Solanas was labeled as the crazy woman who shot Warhol. Cast as a man-hating lesbian, Solanas enjoyed no more than a fleeting flirtation with infamy that almost completely obscured the political views she stood for. The unanimous conclusion of the media was that Solanas was mad.[98]

It is not merely Solanas' choice of target that enabled her attack to be written off as an act of insanity. Her casting as "crazy" expresses much about the way she is positioned in relation to dominant culture and the nature of the fear she inspires. Madness, as many theorists from Thomas Szasz to Michel Foucault have argued, is one of the tools by which dominant culture contains the threat posed by those who challenge its modes of operation, its legitimacy, or both.[99] Madness is one strategy by which the political valence of the terrorist is nullified. We can thus read Solanas' "madness" as a mark of her positioning within dominant discourse as a (female) terrorist.

Solanas' actions can be understood as a subversion of the practice of terrorism as one which is only "permissible" or "tolerated" if it is employed under the auspice of male defined aims and objectives. Solanas appropriates a masculine method of revolution for the purposes of feminist objectives, challenging the gendered nature and, by implication, the very form of the modern state. As such, she inhabits the space of the (male) terrorist. She thus manifests as the "inversion of the inversion,"[100] and by way of containing the threat she represents, dominant culture responds by classifying her as mad.

Solanas represents the most extreme manifestation of the feminist political struggle; the willingness to take the fight for women's liberation to its most terrifying and confronting limit. Her ideas and her program for action constitute for the state the most disastrous and threatening possibility of women's participation in terrorism. It was her politics—namely, the vision of violent feminist revolution that she outlines in the *SCUM Manifesto*—that constituted her as "terrorist."

Solanas' manifesto resonates as a form of terrorism in several key ways. First, and perhaps most obviously, like terrorism, Solanas' revolutionary project is configured as a clandestine movement that deploys violence to political ends. The genocidal vision of Solanas' one-woman organization is based on terrorist tactics:

> SCUM will not picket, demonstrate, march, or strike to attempt to achieve its ends. Such tactics are for nice, genteel ladies who scrupulously take only such action as is guaranteed to be ineffective . . . If SCUM ever strikes, it will be in the dark with a six-inch blade.[101]

However, beyond this, the *Manifesto* can be read as a radical critique of the (gendered) organization of power within the state. Like terrorism, then, Solanas' program for action is perceived within dominant discourse as an attack on the state. The manifesto can be understood as an apocalyptic text that conjures the implosion of the gendered order that underpins modernity. Her program for clandestine and violent revolution proposes a *tactical* intervention that politicizes the terror of the loss of order that lies at the heart of modernity. In these ways, the blueprint for feminist revolution that Solanas lays out operates according to the same principles as the revolutionary terrorism of the era. It signifies the apocalyptic end to the ordered world of (patriarchal) modernity.

Reading the *SCUM Manifesto* as an Attack on the State

Solanas' manifesto is an apocalyptic text, and in this sense, it resonates with contemporary forms of terrorism. Lois Parkinson Zamora argues that the difference between apocalyptic and utopian literature is a matter of focus. She writes:

> Effective apocalyptic literature has always focused its descriptive powers on the imperfect old world rather than the perfect new world . . . Its focus is on the "before" rather than the "after."[102]

Further, while "the apocalyptic narrator's psychological investment is in the 'happily ever after,' his [sic] narrative emphasis is on the 'lived,' that is, on time rather than eternity."[103] Solanas' ideal society is shaped by a utopian vision. She envisages a world in which competition, which she constructs as the primary cause of unhappiness, is eliminated, and peace, love, and happiness reign. She writes, "the female function is to explore, discover, invent, solve problems, crack jokes, make music—all with love. In other words, create a magic world."[104]

However, the *SCUM Manifesto*'s emphasis lies on the shortcomings of the lived experience of modern Western patriarchal society. In the introductory pages, Solanas writes, "the male . . . has made the world a shitpile."[105] She goes on to paint her apocalyptic vision in no uncertain terms. Her tone is millennarian; her call to action couched in the language of urgency, situating SCUM's arrival on the political scene at the moment of the apocalypse. She dedicates approximately two thirds of the manifesto to an annotated list of the myriad atrocities that shape modern American life and for which men can be held accountable, among them war, mental illness, the suppression of individuality, racial, ethnic and religious prejudice, ignorance, boredom, hate, violence, disease, and death. As Gornick notes, Solanas "describes everything as dead or dying."[106] Solanas envisions, that is, a world on the brink of apocalypse—indeed, in the grip of suicidal autoimmunity.

In Gornick's estimation, Solanas' enraged treatise against men crystallized radical feminist wrath:

> [Hers] is the voice of one *who can no longer be satisfied with anything less than blood*. Set in such a mental framework, Solanas speaks the true feelings of the quintessential feminist heart, and those feelings are feelings of black rage. Rage of an ungiving, unstinting, unmediating nature. Rage to the death. Rage out of the racial unconscious which accumulates the experience of centuries and drops onto each woman as she is born.[107]

The kind of "black rage" that Gornick claims motivates the violent activist strategy of *The SCUM Manifesto* is characteristic, as I have noted, of what Enzensberger has labeled "the apocalyptic fantasy."[108] That is, the unbounded rage that frames the pages of the manifesto positions it within the apocalyptic genre. Further, though, underneath the blatant fury and the allocation of the blame for women's subordination to men, Solanas' manifesto may be understood as a critique of the exercise of male power and its relation to women's subaltern position in the modern democratic nation-state.

One of the characteristics of the text, which has rendered it an unpalatable read for many, and which has been used to justify its dismissal, is its appropriation of prominent male-generated cultural and scientific theories to justify Solanas' call for the termination of men's existence. In modern Western culture, these theories have achieved cultural dominance by appearing to have universal significance, and likewise, appearing to be scientifically objective. However, as Genevieve Lloyd discusses, this theoretical tradition has played a crucial role in the legitimation of male domination of the female.[109] Thus, for Solanas to assume these theories in support of the notion of female superiority marks a confronting inversion of Western thought and a source of discomfort for the modern reader.

Solanas bases her powerful call for feminist revolution on arguments borrowed from the science of eugenics.[110] Her theory revolves on a notion of men's genetic, and consequently emotional, inferiority, delivered in the language of biological determinism.[111] Claiming that women are the superior beings of the human race, Solanas argues that it is thus necessary—indeed urgent—that women embark on a process of what we might call "gender cleansing." In this sense, Solanas' critique parallels the eugenics argument that shaped Hitler's apocalyptic project of cleansing the German nation.

In claiming that men are imperfect versions of women, Solanas inverts the notion popularized in Western thought since Greek times that women are imperfect incarnations of the male, and consequently dangerous.[112] She reverses the idea that women's imperfect biology demands their subordination and asserts that the "natural" order of things is one encompassing the subordination of men to female control. In Solanas' theory:

> The male is completely egocentric, trapped inside himself, incapable of empathizing or identifying with others, of love, friendship, affection or tenderness . . . His responses are entirely visceral, not cerebral; his intelligence is a mere tool in the service of his drives and needs; . . . He is a half dead, unresponsive lump, incapable of giving or receiving pleasure or happiness.[113]

Solanas confronts head on the gender binary on which the modern state turns, challenging the modern cultural construction of men as rational and women as irrational by inverting the body of modern theory that has established women's fundamental irrationality as scientific fact.[114] Thus, one of the origins of the threat Solanas poses to the state is her complete inversion of the dichotomy of gender difference that forms the basis for the logic of the state as it is elaborated in social contract theory.

More explicitly, if we understand the state in Anthony Giddens' terms, as the institutional apparatus that governs social life,[115] then Solanas argues passionately that men's institutional command constitutes an important mechanism by which men achieve and retain power over "the superior sex"[116] in the modern world. Paralleling Pateman's critique of the state as a gendered entity, Solanas argues that modern social organization is based upon the systematic exclusion of women from civil society. She alludes to women's exclusion when she addresses the methods by which women must make amends. She writes:

> Dropping out is not the answer; fucking up is. Most women are already dropped out; they were never in. Dropping out . . . strengthens the system instead of undermining it, since it is based entirely on the non-participation, passivity, apathy, and non-involvement of the mass of women.[117]

In her suggestion that women "are already dropped out," Solanas echoes Pateman's suggestion that the state, and by extension the social order it implies, is patriarchal and exclusive of women.[118] In this sense, *The SCUM Manifesto* resonates within the cultural imagination as an attack on the modern state, and therefore as terrorist.

The *SCUM Manifesto* as an Attack on Modernity

Like terrorism, the call for sexocide expressed in Solanas' manifesto is a possibility produced by the conditions of modernity. For example, technology—which, in the dominant cultural imagination, represents the essence of modernity—is central to the realization of the goals of the manifesto. Solanas claims that, with modern reproductive technologies, "it is now technically possible to reproduce without the aid of males . . . and to produce only females. We must begin immediately to do so."[119] Solanas privileges technology as central to the emancipation of women from "male control"; it is the tool that provides the feminist revolution with its *Aufhebung*. She writes, "the male changes only when forced to do so by technology . . . when 'society' reaches the stage where he must change or die. We're at that stage now, if women don't get their asses into gear fast, we may very well all die."[120]

Women are constructed here, in a particularly modern sense, as the rational agents of history's transformation, indeed its termination. And technology, so central to both the imagining and the implementation of modernity, provides them with the means to achieve their ends. In this sense, SCUM's use of technology marks a moment of reversal, the turning of modernity against itself.

I have suggested that terrorism configures the everyday of modernity as the site of the apocalyptic implosion of the order of modernity. Terrorism attacks the regulation and systematization of everyday life on the terrain of the everyday. It marks, in Derrida's terms, the (terror of the) moment of "suicidal autoimmunity." I have also discussed how radical feminism constructs the everyday as the site of women's oppression and the site of radical transformation of gendered order. If we think back to the quotation from Solanas' *SCUM Manifesto* that I cited at the beginning of this chapter, the routine time of the everyday features as the site of SCUM's "radical gesture." Solanas claims that "SCUM will coolly, furtively, *stalk its prey* and quietly move in for the kill."[121] Stalking exploits the predictability of a victim's behavior, a predictability that is produced by the routinization of quotidian life. Solanas' program for political action, like terrorism, thus registers as tactical. It relies upon the routine of the everyday in order to intervene and turn the order of the everyday of modernity against itself. Like terrorism then, Solanas' feminist vision draws attention to and exploits the seeds of destruction—in this instance, the linear and routine time of the everyday—implicit in the structural configuration of (patriarchal) modernity. In so doing, the manifesto calls up the apocalyptic implosion of modernity and as such resonates as similar in form to terrorism.

Solanas advocates that women seize control of the institutions that shape the production of everyday life, not in order to exercise bureaucratic power, but in order to systematically destroy it. Not content to wage a war for women's equality within the framework of conventional feminism, Solanas demands the destruction of "the system." She writes, "SCUM is out to destroy the system, not attain certain rights within it."[122] In this way, Solanas differentiates SCUM from more liberal and/or institutional forms of feminism in that her terrorist statement aims directly at dismantling the entire fabric of society; a complete overturning of the status quo and its replacement with something entirely novel. Like forms of revolutionary terrorism carried out in the United States in the late 1960s and early 1970s, Solanas demands the radical revision of society.

Importantly then, Solanas is not interested in merely attacking the state. *She wants, wholeheartedly, to dismantle it.* She writes, "SCUM is against the entire system, the very idea of law and government."[123] It is in this claim that the apocalyptic temporality—the very same conceptualization of time that underpins the practice of terrorism—that shapes Solanas' version of feminist revolution is most apparent. In her anarchist call to abolish law and government, we can understand Solanas as conjuring not just the end of the state but, perhaps more importantly, apocalyptic end-time. If the modern state is both embedded in, and imagined as the supreme expression of the order implied by the linear and routine time of modernity, then Solanas' attack, in summoning the end of the state, also musters the apocalyptic end of modernity itself. While it is dependent on linear time for its actualization, Solanas' call for the complete destruction of the state expresses the apocalyptic temporality that I have argued characterizes both terrorism and radical feminism.

The manifesto, noting that women make up the majority of the population, goes on to say:

> If a large majority of women were SCUM, they could acquire complete control of this country within a few weeks . . . The police force, National Guard, Army, Navy and Marines couldn't squelch a rebellion of over half the population, particularly when it's made up of people they are utterly helpless without.[124]

It is perhaps this image, an image of masses of newly empowered women wrenching control from the patriarchal state in the most violent way, that is the most powerful threat to modern social order that Solanas envisages. With this image, Solanas invokes the reinvestment of that "implacable violence"[125] to which Kristeva refers—namely women's anger at their exclusion from the social contract—that lies at the heart of the foundational sociopolitical contract of modernity. Gornick, deploying apocalyptic signifiers, similarly reads the manifesto in terms of the reinvestment of the violence of women's exclusion:

> Solanas' fury had been prophetic . . . Solanas had understood, from the very beginning in the savage, guttersnipe terms of her generation's mad, stripped-down expressiveness—the rage beyond reason—that the dispossessed of the world are beginning to spill onto civilization's ground. She had understood *that having been pent up so long, having swallowed their humiliation time and time again . . . women, like blacks, were about to go genuinely mad with the anger that comes to the dispossessed like a flash flood*, upon the heels of the first dawning realization of what has actually been taken from them.[126]

Solanas thus takes the threat to male society implicit in feminism to its absolute limit, an action that can only inspire the most paranoid and repressive reaction from the state that operates upon women's exclusion, since it is a threat that stems from the excluded themselves—a threat that, according to the tenets of social contract theory, must be contained for the protection of society. In the passage quoted above, Solanas makes reference to women's uprising as a "rebellion of over half the population . . . made up of people [men] are utterly helpless without."[127] Here Solanas can be read as highlighting the ambiguous positioning of women within modern social order. That is, while women are constructed as excluded from civil society, they are nonetheless necessary to the smooth functioning of modern social order. In this sense, women's disenfranchisement notwithstanding, the threat of female insurrection Solanas beseeches signifies, like terrorism, as a threat *from within*. In this context, like terrorism, Solanas' vision—a vision that entails the empowerment of the dispossessed—represents the threat of the rise of the subaltern classes to power. But more crucially, it unleashes the terror held in check by the gendered order of modernity, the terror upon which the "sexual contract" is founded. It summons the violent and terrorizing revenge of the "disorder of women." This revenge implies the end of the linear and routine time of (patriarchal) modernity, and by extension, the apocalyptic finale of (patriarchal) modernity itself.

The Death of Modern Representation

In *Je, Tu, Nous: Toward a Culture of Difference*, Luce Irigaray writes that:

> Certain modern tendencies, certain feminists of our time, make strident demands for sex to be neutralized. This neutralization, if it were possible,

> would mean the end of the human species . . . To wish to get rid of sexual difference is to call for a genocide more radical than any form of destruction there has ever been in History.[128]

Solanas' project of annihilating the entire male population constitutes one method by which this neutralization of sex might take place. This would indeed constitute a genocide of unprecedented proportions. However, what makes Solanas' proposition a radical one is not only the literal destruction of material bodies; it is also the obliteration of the binary structure that underlies the symbolic order of gender relations in Western culture. In this context, the *Manifesto*'s method for ushering in a feminist utopia represents not only the end of the male sex but also the end of the representational order of gender relations underpinning modern order—an eradication that summons the apocalyptic end of (gendered) modernity.

Greer writes of Solanas that "more than any of the female students she had seized upon the problem of the *polarity* which [places] men and women . . . in a limbo of *opposite sides*."[129] Here Greer signals Solanas' engagement with modern forms of representation as a technology of (patriarchal) power.[130] Indeed, the problematic of modern forms of representation constitutes a central concern of Solanas' manifesto. As DeKoven notes, the call for

> [n]ot just insight and change from men, [but also] retribution, possibly to the extent of total annihilation . . . is elaborated . . . fully and unambivalently by Valerie Solanas in the *SCUM Manifesto* . . . This is very different from eliminating oppression or even from anarchist acts of targeted assassination. The target here is an entire identity category.[131]

As I have argued, the othering of Woman enables modernity to be constituted as a gendered project of imposing order. Solanas' call to exterminate men is a form of genocide that transfers the category distinction from race to sex; what I have been calling sexocide: it bears certain similarities with Hitler's genocide of the Jews and raises similar issues concerning representation in modernity.[132]

The utopian vision of the state is often conceptualized in terms of absolute homogeneity. That is, the modern nation-state is integrally concerned with the problem of perfect representation. As Jon Stratton argues:

> The nation is thought of as the *undifferentiated entity* made up of individuals who represent themselves to themselves as an imagined community having the identity of a particular nation. The state represents the nation, something expressed through the importance of voting to the modern state.[133]

For the modern state, the apocalypse, as a method by which utopia can be ushered in, gets constructed in terms of the eradication of those who impede the homogeneity of the nation-state. That is, apocalypse engages with the problem of representation.

In modern historical terms, the solution to this problem of perfect representation by the state has, under certain conditions, been thought to lie in the practice of genocide. It is in this context that "the discourse of race [has been] appropriated by the state as the most important way of limiting membership of the nation."[134] As Zygmunt Bauman identifies, genocide only becomes thinkable in modernity:[135] when technology is privileged as the major vehicle of progress and bureaucracy becomes central to the functioning of the modern state, mass extermination becomes a realizable goal. While this is true, there is a further feature of modernity that facilitates the possibility of thinking genocide, namely the modern representational order based on binarisms—Othering—that enables the "classifying out" of certain groups of people from society.

Historically speaking, perhaps the most powerful example of genocide, in terms not only of scale but also of impact on the modern imaginary, is Hitler's extermination of the Jews and other groups seen to pollute the homogeneity of the state such as gays, gypsies, and the intellectually disabled, during the Second World War. This "event" is commonly described in terms of the apocalypse: For example, the usual claim made about the term "Holocaust" is that it means "burnt offering" and is used to describe the Nazi genocide because of its connotations of widespread or total destruction. Similarly, the Hebrew term commonly used in Israel is *Shoah,* meaning destruction. Jonathan Boyarin argues that we live "in the shadow of the apocalypse . . . The specific event I am thinking of as casting that shadow is indeed the Nazi genocide."[136] It is possible to think of the Holocaust as apocalypse not only because it involves widespread destruction and decimation reminiscent of the Last Days, but also because it is organized around a principle of eradication, a central feature of apocalypse thinking. This idea of eradication is only possible because of the process of Othering that characterizes modern representation.

Raphael Lemkin, who coined the term, defines genocide in the following way: "Genocide is directed against the national group as an entity, and the actions involved are directed against individuals, not in their individual capacity, but as members of the national group." He constructs genocide as depending upon "a conceptualisation of a group of people, and all the social and cultural things associated with that group, as a totality."[137] That is, it is dependent upon the identification of certain individuals as Other ("them") to the imagined community (the "we") that forms the basis of the nation-state.

Stratton states, "it was the modern, discursive production of Otherness that made genocide a meaningful possibility."[138] It is in this context that genocide registers as a specifically modern possibility and that Boyarin can claim that the Holocaust represents "the funeral pyre of the Enlightenment and of a certain culminating vision of Europe as the problem of difference resolved."[139]

Just as modernity renders genocide a thinkable practice, the modern structure of gender representation—dependent as it is upon the binary opposition of Man and Woman, operating in a society that privileges technology as progress and administered by the bureaucratic state—gives rise to the possibility of sexocide. It is this possibility that Solanas articulates. The invocation of a revolution based on a notion of eradication is foregrounded by Solanas' allusions to the gas chambers of the Nazi Holocaust. In the final section of the *Manifesto*, she draws on Holocaust narratives that describe how Jews were led to the shower rooms of concentration camps and gassed to death. She beckons the day when, "the few remaining men can . . . go off to the nearest friendly suicide centre where they will be quietly, quickly and painlessly gassed to death."[140] In Solanas' view, the path to feminist utopia is not based on a notion of synthesis, on the resolution of the dialectic configured in evolutionary terms. Rather, it is based on revolution and is intricately bound up with the issue of representation in modernity.

Solanas' manifesto, while it inevitably draws upon the binary structure of representation characteristic of modernity in order to make its case, when imagined in practice, powerfully undermines that very system of representation. In this sense, in a manner that parallels the practice of terrorism, SCUM represents a manifestation of the "suicidal autoimmunity" of patriarchal modernity. That is, like terrorism, the manifesto exploits the terrain of (patriarchal) modernity in order to mobilize the de(con)structive potential of (patriarchal) modernity in the service of obliterating (patriarchal) modernity itself. Solanas' apocalypse marks not only the end of this world as we know it, but also the end of gender representation. As Gornick notes, "of course, to contemplate such a world is also to contemplate the eventual end of the family as we know it, competitive society as we know it, sexuality as we know it."[141] In other words, Solanas puts into play a vision of apocalypse beyond which modernity is no longer thinkable or representable, let alone operational. Like terrorism, she conjures (gendered) modernity's *dénouement*.

Postscript: The Erasure of Solanas From Feminist Histories

While Solanas was hailed as an inspirational figure by radical feminists in the late 1960s, feminists have, on the whole, shown a marked reluctance both to engage critically with Solanas' work and to allocate a place to her in the history of the US feminist movement. In the extensive body of theoretically diverse feminist academic research that exists today, Solanas is barely mentioned, let alone acknowledged as worthy of in-depth critical analysis. If she is remembered, it is in passing: she is alternately paid homage for expanding the boundaries of the feminist debate and making "normal female anger seem reasonable in comparison"[142] and dismissed as the woman who went "too far" and gave feminism a "bad name."

And yet, constructed within dominant readings as the lunatic fringe of feminism, Solanas' specter looms. She is the repressed that, in Freud's terms, always threatens to return and unravel the "good" work of "legitimate" feminism. She manifests as the stereotypical figure of the man-hating, crazed lesbian—a figure all too easily deployed by feminism's adversaries to discredit the feminist movement as nothing but the ravings of irrational women.

The dominant culture ascription of Solanas as mad is perhaps one justification for feminists to distance themselves from either Solanas herself or her plot to exterminate men. Historically, feminists have had a difficult task establishing the legitimacy of their claims in a cultural context that has often conflated feminist demands with the culturally prescribed markers of insanity. Perhaps then, Solanas may be understood to blur the boundaries that feminists have sought to assert between feminism and madness, constituting a reason for feminists to dissociate themselves from her. However, given the feminist tradition of questioning the processes by which madness is ascribed to women in Western culture,[143] this explanation is unfitting as it fails to scrutinize why feminists have been so eager to uncritically categorize, and dismiss, Solanas as mad.

As I have begun to suggest, by the mid-1970s, radical feminism was commonly thought to have been superseded by "cultural feminism," and "feminism" or "women's studies" began to be constituted as a legitimate intellectual discipline.[144] Concurrent with feminism's mainstreaming and institutionalization, its relationship to "violence" began to transform. Whereas radical feminists had celebrated Solanas, the female terrorist, as inspirational, by the mid-1970s, the female terrorist had become a much more problematic figure for feminism. Rather than seeking to annihilate sexual difference, cultural feminists—some who had originally identified as radical feminists—attempted to revalue those qualities traditionally associated with femininity. For example, motherhood began to be (re)valorized by feminists in the United States as an exclusively feminine experience that offered up a vision of an alternative world based on women's values.[145] At this point in the history of second-wave feminism, the alignment of women with "peace" and men with "violence" gained rhetorical significance within US feminist thought. Against this backdrop, cultural feminists constructed the female terrorist, not

as a celebrated icon of revolution but, rather, a victim of "male violence"—
explained away as the "demon lover."[146]

It was not until the mid-1970s that histories of second-wave feminism
began to be written, by which stage, the last vestiges of radical feminism had
either disappeared or been reworked and subsumed by the cultural feminist
project.[147] Bearing in mind the problematic positioning of the female terrorist at this time, it is not surprising that Solanas only appears momentarily.
However, it is not just that the female terrorist resonates uneasily with the
cultural feminist project. Imagining the feminist revolution in the apocalyptic
terms of eradication outlined by Solanas has important implications for
feminism. Given that feminism as both a social and philosophical practice
draws upon the binary distinction between men and women as its fundamental organizing category, Solanas' proposed annihilation of the male sex poses
a profound threat to the production of identity that is so crucial to the feminist project, and in this sense threatens the existence of feminism itself.
Proposing an *apocalyptic* methodology for attaining the feminist promise of
equality, which is formulated not in terms of synthesis, but in terms of *eradication*, threatens the structure of representation that enables feminism to constitute itself as a forceful and legitimate social movement of modernity.
Solanas' manifesto thus describes a limit case for modern feminism, a historical end point beyond which feminism becomes both unimaginable and
impracticable. Positioned at the beginning of second-wave feminism in
North America, Solanas' manifesto gets ignored by feminists because it
implies the destabilization of the defining category, the differentiation
between men and women, that forms the basis of feminism's ability to represent itself—at a point in time when feminists were struggling to construct
women as a category in order to effect (institutional) social and political
change.

CHAPTER 6

Abjecting Whiteness: "The Movement," Radical Feminism, and Genocide

> From the embers of the old movement, a new one rose scorching—sisterly, factional, wild, egomaniacal, furious with insight and excess, the voice of millions of women, living survivors of the death and transfiguration of the New Left.
>
> Todd Gitlin[1]

In 1970, in the introduction to her anthology of writings from the women's liberation movement, radical feminist, Robin Morgan, mused:

> I can no more countenance the co-optive lip service of the male dominated Left which still stinks of male supremacy than I can countenance the class bias and racism of that male "Movement." I haven't the faintest notion what possible revolutionary role white heterosexual men could fulfill, since they are the very embodiment of reactionary-vested-interest-power. But then, I have great difficulty examining what men in general could possibly do about all this. In addition to doing the shitwork that women have been doing for generations, possibly not exist? No, I really don't mean that. Yes, I really do. Never mind, that's another whole book.[2]

By the turn of the decade, then, Morgan was beginning to wonder, like many radical women and some white men themselves, what purpose white heterosexual men served in the revolutionary struggle. She also expresses—vacillating, somewhat hesitant and perhaps tongue-in-cheek—the desire to see men "disappear" once and for all, but promptly dismisses the thought with: "Never mind, that's another whole book." Of course, that "another whole book" had already been penned by Valerie Solanas a number of years earlier. What is interesting about Morgan's inner dialogue is that, as with Solanas' manifesto, her target is not an abstracted "women's oppression" but men themselves. As Marianne DeKoven states: "The target here is an entire identity category rather than a position of power, or its symbolic representative, within an oppressive system."[3] Morgan's idea is that of a metaphorical genocide that targets the system of representation producing and enforcing women's material oppression: the same idea that forms the basis of Solanas' *SCUM Manifesto*.

While radical feminists celebrated Solanas, the female terrorist, as a key inspirational figure, they were simultaneously concerned to reinterpret her manifesto for those who rejected it on the basis of a literal interpretation. Solanas' proposed sexocide, they argued, should be read as a metaphor for the obliteration of the system of culturally ascribed "sex roles."[4] The *Manifesto*, radical feminists insisted, deployed the trope of genocide to convey both the fury and the sense of urgency felt by women with an awakened feminist consciousness, but ultimately, its call was for the destruction of the cultural system that prescribed the valuation of gender roles—what we might call "gen(der)ocide," as opposed to a literal sexocide.

So why does genocide emerge as a meaningful trope in the conceptualization of the radical feminist political project? And how does the radical feminist idea of gen(der)ocide play into the discursive alignment of (radical) feminism and terrorism? To unpack these questions, I analyze the (radical) feminist deployment of genocidal narratives and situate them in the context of the apocalyptic temporality articulated by the broader social protest "Movement."[5]

Sketching the Movement: Eschatological Temporality and Despair

Reflecting on the culminating years of the 1960s, Morgan mobilizes the vision of impending apocalypse—of widespread and inevitable death and destruction—circulating with prominence within both dominant culture and the social protest movement:

> Decades of non-violent civil rights activity were exploding into black rage, black manhood, Black Panthers. Television screens bled full-color Vietnam carnage each evening onto the dinnertime news . . . College students back home set fire to the US flag in protest against the war . . . Rap Brown was declaring that violence is as American as cherry pie, and the nation was still reeling in the aftermath of the assassination of John F. Kennedy. The ghettos were afire with poverty and powerlessness, the campuses afire with guilt and idealism. Even the staid *New York Review of Books* ran a recipe for making Molotov cocktails, and Leonard Bernstein hosted a fund-raiser for the Black Panthers.[6]

Writing in 1968, Judith Brown observed, "the media warn us daily of a national or even international Apocalypse,"[7] suggesting a US cultural imaginary overdetermined by a distinctly eschatological temporality.[8] Further, Jonah Raskin writes that, in the 1960s, "it seemed to many citizens that America was headed toward Armageddon . . . an immense conflagration that would bring . . . armies . . . into final battle with one another and that would result in the ultimate breakdown of society."[9] This sense of living at the end of time, "in the last days," was particularly acute among the myriad groups calling for social change that comprised the Movement.

When I refer to "the Movement" here, I use the term loosely. There was never a single unified Movement. Rather, in the late 1960s, what was known as the Movement had metamorphosed into a collection of left-wing issue and/or identity-based groups calling for radical change. As Sara Evans states, "above all the term 'movement' was self-descriptive. There was no way to join; you simply announced or felt yourself to be part of the movement—usually through some act like joining a protest march."[10] I focus here on the Movement in the later stages of its development—the late 1960s—in its various manifestations in the northern cities of the United States. There was no single central organization that coordinated the activities of these disparate groups. However, it must be said that groups such as Students for a Democratic Society [11] often saw themselves as actively working to construct alliances between the various groups coalescing as the Movement and consequently perceived themselves as providing an overarching leadership. And there were several concerted attempts to establish greater unity and solidarity: for example, the National Conference for New Politics (NCNP) held in August 1967 in Chicago was an attempt to "pull together a 'movement' out of the new left's increasingly diversified strands—black and white, adult and student, anti-war and anti-poverty."[12] However, by and large, these attempts never translated into lasting cohesion.

While there was no single, all-encompassing agenda, these groups did understand themselves as sharing common ground. As Evans suggests, "almost a mystical term, 'the movement' implied an experience, a sense of community and common purpose."[13] Many involved were "graduates" of the civil rights movement in the south in the early 1960s and based their organizational methods and tactics of resistance on those that had been successful there. Further, perpetuating the idea of the "beloved community"[14] that had been central to the civil rights vision of interracial harmony in the early 1960s, the issue of race continued to be a preoccupation for many of these groups,[15] and the Movement aspired to the production of a racially inclusive utopia.

Broadly speaking, these groups embraced a Marxist critique of society, defining their interests in terms of "class oppression" and outspokenly condemning a nefarious "system" that thrived at the expense of subaltern groups. For these groups, the US state was a mechanism of morally bankrupt institutions responsible for "genocidal" practices such as widespread racism within the United States and the devastation of the Vietnam War. Among the New Left, these acts were thought to signify the *apocalyptic* end of a fundamentally corrupt and rotten society: this society was not just headed for Armageddon, it *was* Armageddon. Judith Brown, a white female activist declared, "we who have experienced the movement . . . know so well that for many people the Day of Doom has been the measure of their years and the only Revelation of their lives."[16]

Within this apocalyptic outlook, there was also an optimism that, if the New Left could hold out through the last days, and even escalate its counter-hegemonic activities, it could deliver the "inevitable" utopian society.[17] And despite the Movement comprising a conglomerate of diverse groups with varying agendas, there was often a sense, however illusory or transient, of the unity of the Movement. As J. Muncie states, in the "spate of university sit-ins, marches and demonstrations of 1968 . . . the strange agglomeration of black militants, students, drop-outs, draft dodgers, mystical hippies and women's liberationists seemed to be momentarily united."[18] This fueled a palpable feeling of hope among young radicals that the apocalypse was about to end and utopia would emerge. This optimism was not entirely misplaced. Riding the momentum of achievements such as the civil rights, anti–Vietnam War, and free speech protests, the Movement, in large part because it succeeded in sustaining the attention of the news media, made significant inroads. As Sheldon Wolin writes:

> The varied forms of action developed to oppose the war and to extend civil rights were destructive of a certain simplistic understanding of national unity, of some racist folkways, and of a mindless patriotism, and they also exposed the shallowness of consensus politics and its ideal of a depoliticized citizenry. Both the civil rights movement and the antiwar protests politicized hundreds of thousands of Americans and simultaneously contested the boundaries of the political domain, its forms, and the monopoly on action enjoyed by the elites.[19]

In 1968, then, it appeared that incredible gains were being made toward the attainment of a new society. Indeed, Theodore Roszak crowed that "the alienated young are giving shape to something that looks like the saving vision our endangered civilisation requires."[20] Political and cultural transformation seemed imminent.

However, as Todd Gitlin suggests, "although partisans and antagonists alike saw a single 'spirit of the sixties,' there were . . . crosscurrents and zones of confluence, [as well as] tensions and interference patterns."[21] By the end of the 1960s then, the "zones of confluence" were markedly less visible, and the contradictory forces that had given the Movement vibrancy and legitimized its claims had, in effect, radically undermined any sense of its cohesion.

The fact that "by 1969 it was becoming clear that revolution was not a natural process which must occur because people willed it to"[22] further accentuated the perception of the Movement's disunity. Disagreements erupted about how the revolution should proceed, producing a perceived crisis in a leadership that had in fact always been fraught by the difficulties of difference.[23] In particular, some factions now claimed that it would be necessary to force the door of utopia: in this context, terrorism became a meaningful form of political resistance. The Movement's spirit of unity, hope and faith began, among certain segments, to dissipate, and despair began to set in.

It is commonly claimed that the Movement "disappeared," "self-destructed," or was "killed off" at the end of the 1960s.[24] This was certainly the case for some incarnations of the Movement, and in particular the Movement as it is remembered by "white" activists. I use the word white here advisedly, as a highly contingent category.[25] For the purposes of this chapter, I refer to white radicals as those who were positioned as such in the context of the shift within the civil rights movement toward "black power," and on that basis, as we shall see, were excluded from leadership and participation in the Movement.

The "Disappearance" of the Movement

While the black/white dichotomy operated with discursive power, it simplified a very complex "racial" politics.[26] Many of the white activists to whom I am referring were, in fact, Jewish, and therefore only problematically white.[27] As Karen Brodkin illustrates in her sophisticated analysis of the history of Jewish "whiteness" in the United States, it was not until the postwar period, when Jewish organizations supported, broadly speaking, a policy of Jewish assimilation, that Jews came to be considered white.[28] The Movement's Jewish radicals were thus among the first generation of North American Jews to enjoy the everyday benefits of "invisibility" that whiteness proffered. However, while Jewish radicals were regarded as white by dominant culture, for many, this was experienced ambivalently, particularly in relation to their activities within a highly racialized Movement. It was these activists who experienced most acutely a sense of the "implosion"[29] and "disappearance" of the Movement at the end of the 1960s.

Rather than disappear, however, it is more accurate to suggest that the Movement transformed. In the late 1960s, the civil rights movement had metamorphosed into the black power movement—a movement that, often with the support of white radicals, claimed that black people, whose history of oppression gave them unique insight into the "human condition," would lead the way forward. As Evans observes, "black power was at its zenith . . . Whites . . . could admire and emulate from a distance the black movement which remained the touchstone of 'true radicalism.'"[30] White activists, many of whom had previously considered themselves, alongside their black counterparts, the vanguard of the revolution, found themselves not just alienated but often excluded from that same revolution.[31] This was compounded by black leaders' often open antagonism toward white radicals. Evans notes that "the centre of the black struggle in the north had imbibed the bitterness and hostility of the urban ghetto . . . Blacks were ready to lash out at whites wherever they could be found."[32] Rap Brown, for example, alongside claiming that the leadership of the Movement belonged to blacks, "refused to talk to white radicals"[33] (otherwise known as "honkies") at the NCNP in Chicago in 1967. In the face of black militants' claims "that blacks, by virtue of their most-oppressed status, possessed the moral authority to direct the Movement,"[34] the place of white people, not only in the Movement but also in the dominant vision of the new society, now seemed radically uncertain.

Since at least as early as 1967, there had been a sense among the white constituents of the Movement that their whiteness was proving to be increasingly problematic. The usefulness of white revolutionaries, it seemed, had expired. As radical journalist, Andrew Kopkind, writing of the summer of 1967, expressed it:

> To be white and radical in America this summer is . . . to watch the war grow and know no way to stop it, to understand the black rebellion and find no way to join it, to realize that the politics of a generation has failed and the institutions of reform are bankrupt, and yet to have neither ideology, programs, nor the power to reconstruct them.[35]

This mood was compounded by the relative lack of success of white radicals in organizing "the ghettos of the (white) poor" in the northern United States, compared with that of "black" radicals mobilizing their black constituents around the issue of race. A highly racialized division of labor emerged; as calls for black self-determination gained increased momentum, "blacks" assumed the exclusive right to organizing around the issue of race, and "whites were pushed out of the black movement."[36] Previously, whiteness, as a marker of privilege, had been almost entirely invisible. However, the emphasis on black self-determination crystallized the demarcation of racial identities, and increasingly, whiteness, within the Movement, became a much more visible category with highly pejorative connotations. Whiteness, that is, was beginning to be a problematic signifier, marking out "the othered enemy."

In a desperate attempt to remain valuable collaborators in the revolution, whites turned their attention to mobilizing "the poor," articulating this shift as a desire to work in "their own communities." However, the majority of the Movement's whites, being from middle- or professional-class backgrounds, were not, in terms of class at least, "members" of these poor communities. In the claim to be working among "their own" then, they, like their black counterparts, were articulating a sense of racial community. However, due to the othering of whiteness within the broader Movement, this sense of community could not be deployed to politicize and mobilize an alliance of the poor, resulting in the difficult and contradictory situation of white radicals' constituency being defined in racial terms. White radicals were constructed at least tentatively (remembering their Jewishness), as insiders, but with their project being defined in terms of class, most were cast as outsiders to the very communities they sought to organize.

Constructing a sense of community around the common denominator of poverty proved impossible in two further senses. While blacks could usefully deploy the codings of race to unite their constituency, for whites, there was no visible distinguishing (embodied) feature that readily identified "the poor" as members of an oppressed class. In addition, a deeply entrenched sense of poverty as the result of personal failure, rather than a failure of society to provide for its members, prevailed among poor, white communities.[37] These factors greatly hampered white radicals' efforts to politicize large numbers of people in support of the revolution. Meanwhile, the Movement increasingly drew both its energy and its credibility from the achievements of black organizers. Thus, white radicals suffered increasingly as a result of their higher visibility within the Movement. As Gitlin remembers, "we could not imagine any life without the movement, but the movement no longer held any life for us. The demonstration rituals felt stale and—for militants—increasingly dangerous."[38] For white participants then, the Movement appeared to be committing a metaphorical *genocide*— an erasure of whiteness—that marked "the end of the interracial 'beloved community.'"[39]

At times, this "genocidal" impulse of the Movement was articulated highly explicitly. For example, at the NCNP in 1967, a conference whose overarching agenda "was to develop a unified left program and to nominate for the

1968 elections a presidential ticket headed by Martin Luther King and Benjamin Spock,"[40] emotions ran high. I quote Evans here at length:

> When whites met with blacks . . . they seemed desperate to receive validation from them. Black delegates in turn needed to unleash their fury at American racism on the whites at the conference. For both, these pressing emotional needs proved far stronger than the desire for a strategic alliance . . . [T]he moralism of middle-class guilt clashed head on with the morality of righteous anger. Black delegates shouted: "Kill Whitey!" as they repeatedly insisted that they should cast 50 percent of the conference vote and occupy half of the committee slots though they constituted about one-sixth of the convention . . . Each time the conference capitulated to black demands, the majority of whites applauded enthusiastically in apparent approval of their own denunciation.[41]

In the call to "Kill Whitey!," we see the discourse of genocide—extermination on the basis of race—being used to police the Movement's racial hierarchies, pointing to the ambiguities that structured the categorization of whites within the Movement. As Evans notes, the black militants' challenge to whiteness—expressed as a call for genocide—was posed to an "audience full of Jewish radicals"[42] and cannot have failed to conjure the specter of Hitler's genocide for the "white" audience.[43] This was further accentuated by black militants' demand for conference delegates to denounce Zionism in the Middle East, right at the moment when Israel was going to war against its neighbors to defend its "homeland" in the Six-Day War. In calling for the denunciation of "Zionist imperialism," black militants were aligning themselves with Jordanian, Syrian, and Egyptian Israeli border inhabitants, an alignment based on the conceptualization here of Israel's adversaries as (black) colonized peoples. This, in opposition to the "white" and Jewish Israeli "aggressors."

However, the postwar transition to being considered as members of the white race still firmly within living memory—in some senses still "incomplete"—Jews were far from considering themselves categorically white. And an often first-hand knowledge of recent Jewish history, however sublimated by the assimilationist demands of dominant culture, provided these white radicals with grounds for sympathy with other (black) subaltern groups. Given this, we can understand the ambiguous response of "white" radicals (their "enthusiastic applause") to black militants' advocacy for a white genocide and the denunciation of Israel's Zionist claims in the Middle East. While Evans collapses whiteness and Jewishness in the quote above, expressing surprise at the response of white radicals to "their own denunciation," it is the Jewishness of these white radicals—in a sense, their simultaneous "whiteness" and "not-whiteness"—that provides the key to understanding their ambiguous support of black militants' demands. Rather than an expression of "timidity" or the "moralism of middle class guilt,"[44] we have here the evidencing of problematic whiteness, articulated by white, predominantly Jewish, radicals.

The response of white radicals to their increasingly ambiguous position within the Movement was varied. A significant number of young, white men and women embraced increased militancy as a way of continuing to render their radicalism relevant. These partisans formed militant organizations such as The Weathermen; some decided that revolutionary violence—what the establishment labeled "terrorist violence"—was the only way forward and promptly went underground to carry out their version of the revolution. The alternative to this revolutionary nihilism was to "drop out" and join the counter-culture, and they did so in droves. Gitlin comments:

> Some veterans, burned out by the infighting, brooding with visions of impending apocalypse (concentration-camp roundups, urban riots), found this a propitious moment to slip off into communes . . . relinquishing any illusion that they could shape history.[45]

In opting to leave the Movement, whether to go underground or to join the counter-culture, these white radicals were in a sense complicit with the genocidal drive of the Movement, their departure enabling a further erasure of whiteness. Importantly for our purposes, their sense of despair was also gendered, in that it was particularly acute for white men. As Alice Echols notes, "white men . . . wondered what role, if any, they could comfortably play in the struggle."[46] But for white women, while some joined revolutionary terrorist groups, and many moved into the communes of the counter-culture, there was also a third option. While "most of the old New Left men—those who weren't on trial or immersed in defense committees—felt paralyzed,"[47] Gitlin suggests, white women, the "survivors" of the New Left's collapse,[48] "could take refuge, find community and political purpose in the women's movement."[49] The women's liberation movement became a kind of political hospice to which white women could turn when the Movement, always tenuous but seemingly unified, imploded.

A White Women's Movement

It was thus amid an atmosphere of white chromatic anxiety and despair that the women's liberation movement began to assert its position as a legitimate political force on the spectrum of left-wing dissidence. Echols suggests that feminism erupted just as "the [New Left] Movement was . . . becoming a less congenial place for white women."[50] And Jeremy Rabkin points out that, "the remarkable thing about the women's liberation movement was that it took off at the very moment when the original [white] student movement was collapsing into confusion and despair."[51] Women's involvement in the feminist movement grew at a quick pace. Evans notes that, "the proliferation of women's groups that had begun in the fall of 1967 continued . . . into 1968 at an astounding rate."[52]

It has often been noted that early second-wave feminism in its originary form was an overwhelmingly white women's movement.[53] A handful of black women such as Florynce Kennedy, Cellestine Ware, and Frances Beale became prominent in the movement for their attempts to draw out the connections between masculinist culture and racist culture. However, women's liberation, until the mid-1970s, remained predominantly white in terms of both its active constituency and its conceptual blindness to the differences, most prominently perhaps of race, but also of class, that structured women's experience.[54] Further, women's liberation was understood by black women as "white women's business." This was because women's liberation was based upon an understanding of liberation that turned on assumptions of white privilege—often misplaced assumptions, that is, about women's homogeneity as a group. As Echols states, "middle-class, white women were struggling for those things—independence and self-sufficiency—which racial and class oppression had thrust upon black women."[55] However, the (ir)relevance of white women's feminism for black women was also very much circumscribed by the idea of genocide.

Radical feminism, from the outset, was a white movement framed by racial anxiety, but not the kind of white anxiety that has characterized white colonial history.[56] This was not, that is, the kind of anxiety that derives from a desire to reproduce a position of *dominance*. Rather, white feminists were anxious about *their own exclusion* from a burgeoning Movement poised for the overthrow of society. Their anxiety revolved around their (in)ability to secure their own inclusion in the process of shaping the new utopia, a kind of internalized *terror* of white impotence. This anxiety, I argue, was a key motivating factor in the formulation of feminist aims and objectives and formed the backdrop against which feminists positioned themselves politically. This is not to deny that feminism was responding to the injustices inherent in the material conditions of (white) women's everyday existence. Many early second-wave feminists explicitly positioned their feminism as a direct response to their lived experiences of sexism, particularly living and working with the male left.[57] And of course, then, just as now, feminism played a crucial role in critiquing and rectifying the failings of a culture that positioned women as inferior and/or subordinate. However, the discursive practices of women's liberation—the putting into language of the feminist movement's struggle and the conceptualization of their tactics of resistance and overthrow—were framed, sometimes paranoiacally, by the politics of race.[58]

In this context, it is not surprising that early radical feminism was notoriously an angry movement. As Evans points out, "although women's liberation was shocking and alienating to many, especially as seen through the magnifying lens of a hostile media, the reactions to the outcry on behalf of women's equality indicated that feminism had tapped a vein of enormous frustration and anger."[59] The white women who comprised the majority of the participants in early radical feminism were doubly angry; they were not only legitimately angry about their experiences of sexism, both within and outside the Movement, they were also angry about a Movement that denied them a place in the revolution on the basis of their skin color. With this history in mind, we can see why, for young white women of the feminist movement, genocide was a meaningful description of women's historical subordination.

Radical Feminism and Genocide

In the 1960s, both liberal and radical feminists alike frequently constructed the history of women's experience as one of deep and enduring suffering. In this context, feminists began to draw analogies between women's everyday lives and that of the quintessential (post)modern figure of human suffering, the Nazi concentration camp inmate. As early as 1963, North American Jewish liberal feminist, Betty Friedan claimed that the conditions framing the quotidian experience of the average suburban housewife were comparable to those under which Hitler's prisoners existed. Friedan outlined what she called "the problem with no name"—the systematic destruction of women's sense of identity, purpose, and individual fulfillment in "the comfortable concentration camp that American women have walked into, or been talked into by others."[60] She wrote, "the conditions which destroyed the human identity of so many [Nazi concentration camp] prisoners were not the torture and the brutality, but conditions similar to those which destroy the identity of the American housewife."[61] As Rabkin notes, Friedan seemed to "suggest that 'genocide' might, after all, be appropriated to answer the 'name' problem."[62]

A number of *radical* feminists picked up on Friedan's comparison, weaving it into their analysis of patriarchy. From the outset, their critiques were characterized by a much greater sense of urgency than those of liberal feminism. Like Friedan, they invoked the image of *genocide*, painted in the *apocalyptic* language of decimation, destruction, and annihilation. Shulamith Firestone spoke of the "massacre" of women,[63] and Solanas constructed man as a being who lived at woman's expense[64] and whose "proving [of] his manhood is worth [to him] an endless amount of mutilation and suffering, and an endless number of lives."[65] And Roxanne Dunbar advocated the "total annihilation of a system which *systematically destroys half of its people*."[66] In 1969, Atkinson claimed that:

> *Men neatly decimated mankind by one half* when they took advantage of the *social* disability of those men who bore the burden of the reproductive process; men invaded the being of those individuals now defined as functions, or 'females' . . . The original 'rape' was political, *the robbing of one half of Mankind of its Humanity.*[67]

For radical feminism then, claims of the genocide of women under patriarchy became an important ground for their rallying cry. As the movement grew, radical feminists "regularly compared the plight of women with that of blacks in the segregated South, oppressed colonial peoples, and starving masses in the Third World,"[68] aligning women with other subaltern groups that had been subjected to the genocidal practices of the dominant class/"oppressor."

This was an important discursive strategy for a fundamentally white women's liberation movement. The feminist portrayal of a "genocide against women" paralleled the tactics of other groups within the Movement who were simultaneously emphasizing the genocidal tendencies of dominant US thought and practice in relation to the populations of the "third world" and thus translated the struggle of women into terms with cultural currency. For example, the civil rights movement had begun to insist on the need for violent militancy in order to counteract the "genocide" against black people in the United States, while the antiwar movement mobilized against the "colonial genocide" being enacted on behalf of US citizens in Vietnam and elsewhere. In this sense, feminism's establishment of a critique of the genocide of women helped legitimize the cause.[69]

However, there is a further dimension to radical feminism's positioning of women as victims of genocide. In this redrawing of borders, we can detect a displacement of white women's experience of exclusion from the Movement. If, in the experience of white (female) radicals, the Movement itself had committed a metaphorical genocide—an erasure of whiteness—then, for radical women, this became displaced onto a concept of a genocide against women. This displacement, by radical white feminists, of the white experience of Otherness within the Movement, constitutes a disavowal of the racial parameters that construct the Movement's exclusivity/inclusivity. In this sense, the radical feminist construction of a genocide against women not only legitimized the feminist cause by encoding it in the language of the larger Movement, but also relegitimized, and thereby recuperated, *white* female activism. However, this recuperation of white female activism depended upon a repudiation of whiteness. Indeed, this denial of racial difference was to become a trademark of radical feminism.

In this context, then, white radical women came to experience their whiteness as abject. This abjection of whiteness had far-reaching consequences for radical feminism's conceptualization of the project of women's liberation, culminating in the call for a male genocide, of which Solanas' manifesto is perhaps the most extreme example.

Abjecting Impossible Whiteness: Feminism and the Call for Gen(der)ocide

In the late 1960s, to be both white and radical was an extremely uncomfortable experience, and one that often provoked a very *visceral* response. Morgan writes:

> My white skin disgusts me. My passport disgusts me. They are the marks of an insufferable privilege bought at the price of others' agony. If I could peel myself inside out I would be glad. If I could become part of the oppressed I would be free. I must do something, something far more confrontative of the system than I've done so far. Besides, I believe the oppressed are going to win—and I want to be on the winning side.[70]

In Morgan's description of the "disgust" she feels at being white, we witness the kind of response that characterizes a subject's reaction to the abject. Elizabeth Grosz writes, "the subject's reaction to [the abject] is visceral; it is usually expressed in retching, vomiting, spasms, choking—in brief, in *disgust*."[71] Morgan experiences the physical manifestation of her whiteness—her white corporeality—as impossible: impossible in that whiteness, a subjectivity that is usually invisible in Western cultures because it enjoys the privilege of being the marker of dominance, is, within the Movement at this point in time, suddenly highly visible. Morgan's whiteness is thrust upon her, it confronts her. She is painfully aware of it (as never before), helpless to remedy it, and its denial is problematic. How to claim that one is not "white" when it is "obvious," "verifiable," that one is? How to deny "whiteness" when the label is not yours to apply, when your whiteness is inscribed on your body by others? How does one claim, or more importantly prove, that one is *not* "*white*" (and) *on the inside*? "Impossible."

Morgan's whiteness is also the thing that defines her as an outsider to the Movement: the barrier to her inclusion, preventing her from being "on the winning side."[72] It is that which she *must* transcend, but which is also *impossible* to transcend. And so Morgan abjects her whiteness: for Morgan, the experience of her whiteness as *Otherness* produces the sense of "a burden both repellent and repelled."[73] This abjection is illustrative of a current of feeling prevalent among white radicals in the late 1960s. Their whiteness, deeply stigmatized by the larger Movement, was simultaneously irrefutable and abhorrent.

For Julia Kristeva, who reworks the concept from Freud, the abject is "something rejected from which one does not part."[74] The abject is not an entirely differentiated Other: rather, the abject is simultaneously Same *and* Other, both "within," or a part of the subject, and "outside," rejected by the subject. As Grosz says, "the abject is that *part of the subject* (which cannot be categorized as an object) *which it attempts to expel*."[75] Two things are key here in relation to the formation of the (white) feminist speaking position.

First, the abject is an Otherness *within* the Self that produces a sense of terror: a terror of inescapability, the terror of trapped-ness. For Kristeva, the horror of abjection is strongest when the subject discovers that the abject, abominable, and othered, resides *within*, "when it finds that the impossible constitutes its very *being*, that it *is* none other than abject."[76] In relation to the Movement, it becomes clear why whiteness should provoke such intense revulsion—even terror. It is the white radicals' discovery, rather late in the piece, that the enemy—previously coded as the "oppressor" or "capitalism" or "the bourgeoisie," but now coded as "whiteness" or "honkiness"—lies within; that white people *themselves* constitute the enemy. Hence, Morgan's claim that "if I could peel myself inside out I would be glad."

The anger of radical feminism, then, was not only an anger at the injustices suffered by women, nor a straightforward anger at the erasure of whiteness. This was an anger *fueled by the energy of abjection*, tapping an anger "from deep down and way back."[77] This leads us to the second characteristic of the process of abjection—that the "discovery of the impossible within" leads to the expulsion, the rejection, the jettisoning, of the abject.

As Grosz points out, the response to the terror inspired in the subject by their discovery of the abject residing within is to attempt to annihilate the abject. While the abject can never in fact be obliterated, nonetheless, the desire for its obliteration perseveres. Importantly, for both Kristeva and Grosz, it is the disavowal and/or the annihilation of the abject that brings the subject into being. As Grosz suggests, "The subject must disavow part of itself in order to gain a stable self."[78] The recognition of the abject and the production of the self, that is, are simultaneous processes. Both Kristeva and Grosz are speaking of individual identity formation. However, as Freud himself argued, the production of collective, or social, subjectivities, in the psychoanalytic understanding, can be understood to mirror the production of individual subjectivity.[79] Through the abjection of whiteness, then, radical feminism, as the voice of a collective of white women, emerges as a (temporarily) "stable" speaking position.

If we accept that for white radicals, whiteness constitutes the abject, then we can understand the emergence of radical feminism as a sublimation by radical white feminists of the process of abjecting whiteness. As the abject, whiteness threatened the very possibility of claiming a place, an identity, within the Movement. It had to be transferred, named as something else, that is, *objectified*, for it is through a process of sublimation/objectification that the terror of the abject can be managed. As Kristeva notes: "In the symptom, the abject permeates me, I become abject. Through sublimation, I keep it under control."[80]

Thus, the abjectness of whiteness translates into a radical feminist conceptualization of (white) men as the enemy. Objectified, (white) men stand in for the unnameable abject whiteness that must be obliterated. For this reason, a genocide against men, as called for by Solanas, or a metaphorical gen(der)ocide that will destroy the system of binary oppositions that establishes women's subordination, as proposed by radical feminism's reinterpretation of Solanas' call, begins to resonate with the white women of the Movement. A gen(der)ocide becomes a legitimate response to the "age-old" genocide against women. In this move, radical feminism itself, angry and vengeful, is called into being.

This abjection of whiteness proceeds, however, in a bipartite manner. On the one hand, (white) men are now defined in opposition to (white) women, converting the abject into an object against which a defense can be mounted, holding it, temporarily, at bay. As Kristeva notes, "the unconscious contents remain here *excluded* . . . clearly enough for a defensive *position* to be established."[81] In a limited way, this enables the abject to be mastered, producing subjectivity. Grosz suggests that "by naming it or speaking it [the subject] can maintain an imperilled hold on the symbolic and a stable speaking position."[82] On the other hand, however, the distance produced in this attempt to objectify the abject is always about to close. The abject is distanced but still threateningly close, "within" the space of the subject, and exposing it to "perpetual danger."[83] The abject threatens, it terrorizes, the subject. It is "immoral, sinister, scheming, and shady: a terror that dissembles."[84] And "from its place of banishment, the abject does not cease challenging its master."[85]

Radical feminism responds to this terror with its own form of terror—a call for genocide. But this terroristic response is only possible if whiteness is continually, obsessively, disavowed. Thus, radical feminism continues to emphasize the "meaninglessness" of race, to insist on a sisterhood based on women's fundamental sameness regardless of other acknowledged but downplayed differences of race, class, sexuality, and so on. Abject whiteness, then, is held at arm's length, and radical feminist subjectivity is established by projecting abject whiteness onto (white) men, and disavowing difference. As Kristeva suggests, "the *deject* never stops demarcating his universe whose fluid confines . . . constantly question his solidity and impel him *to start afresh*."[86]

Here, the deject, the subject of abjection, is a radical feminism that sublimates the abject, whiteness, onto an external object, (white) men. The provisionality of the deject's subjectivity motivates the deject to continually "start afresh," producing the apocalyptic temporality that, as I suggested in Chapter Five, characterizes the radical feminist vision.

Feminists frequently configured the women's liberation movement as the necessary culminating gesture of an apocalyptic era. For example, Judith Brown wrote, in 1968, that, "we must be liberated so that we can turn from our separate domestic desperation—our own Apocalypse of the Damned— toward an exercise of social rage against each dying of the light."[87] In the late 1960s, radical feminists argued, the productive forces of revolution were converging, and women's moment to rise up and radically *remake* the system had arrived. There was an expressed will among radical feminists, guided by a utopian vision of society, to "go back to the beginning." In May 1969, Ti-Grace Atkinson wrote:

> Those individuals who are today defined as women must eradicate their own definition. Women must, in a sense, commit suicide, and the journey from womanhood to a society of individuals is hazardous . . . We must create, as no other group in history has been forced to do, *from the very beginning*.[88]

We have here, on the one hand, a dramatic ending, the finishing of time, and on the other, the urge to start afresh that Kristeva describes as accompanying the process of abjection. This sense of time current within the radical feminist movement, and in slightly different ways within the Movement more generally, then, is not only the *temporality of apocalypse* but also the *temporality of abjection*. It is thus a worldview marked by the *apocalyptic temporality of abjection* that Solanas claimed SCUM represented when she stated that SCUM "is a state of mind."

Destabilizing the Boundaries between Legitimate and Illegitimate Violence

As part of their feminist agenda, radical feminists argued vehemently for women's right to control their own bodies.[89] The issues of women's access to abortion, contraception, and childcare were key aspects of the radical feminist vision, and practice, of women's liberation. In Firestone's view, women needed to liberate themselves from "the tyranny of their reproductive biology."[90] This framing of the radical feminist agenda in terms of reproductive independence marked radical feminism as a *white* women's movement. As Jane Gerhard recounts, "black women had long felt suspicious about the women's liberation movement."[91] For black feminist, Cynthia Washington, the emphasis on sexual liberation and reproductive control alienated women of color. She explains that black women

> [h]ave been raised to function independently . . . White women were demanding a chance to be independent while we needed help and assistance . . . Abortion, which white women were fighting for, did not seem an important issue for black women . . . they needed a means to support children other than welfare, a system of childcare, decent homes and medical attention.[92]

Thus, for Washington, radical feminism was written through with the privilege of whiteness.[93]

Barbara Solomon, of the feminist separatist group, The Furies, argued vehemently that white women needed to address this privilege. She argued, in particular, that white women's call for reproductive freedom had the potential to be used against "third world women," including black women in North America, and pronounced loudly that black women think "women's liberation . . . [is] a pile of shit. They think that women's liberation means that women should be able to have babies and that whites would tell them that they shouldn't."[94] This claim betrays the extent to which radical feminism's call for reproductive rights was over-determined by narratives of genocide. Not only did radical feminists explicitly call for gen(der)ocide, they inadvertently played into—with detrimental effects—black women's fears of a (black) genocide.

For some time, certain leaders of the black power movement had promoted black women's return to the hearth as a necessary component of the revolution, "producing children for the black nation."[95] More paranoid segments of the black power movement suggested that the increasing availability of contraception was part of a carefully orchestrated government strategy, veiled by the language of sexual freedom, to commit a genocide of blacks. As such, they advocated "'black matriarchy' and the duty of black women not to use birth control."[96] In this climate of racial anxiety, the fight for women's rights to contraception and abortion, when combined with the often-explicit call by radical feminists for a (metaphorical) genocide, had, for many black women, very ambiguous, if not sinister, connotations. Thus, in many senses, radical feminism's call for genocide undermined white women's claims to be organizing on behalf of *all* women and helped to consolidate the impression that radical feminism was an exclusively white women's movement. In this way, radical feminism—a movement forged by, and embedded within, the racial politics of the Movement more broadly—ultimately reproduced those same politics. Further, radical feminists' call for guaranteed access to contraception and abortion, in combination with their couching of the idea of feminist revolution in the language of genocide, conjured, for certain black women, the specter of *state terrorism*. I return to this idea in a moment.

If radical feminists intended to frighten those with a vested interest in maintaining patriarchal social order, then frighten they did. Preaching violent retribution, often inscribed in the language of genocide, some, such as Solanas, also pointed out that women made up more than half the population, gesturing a sizeable threat to dominant gender relations, especially in light of feminism's growing impact on US women. From the late 1960s and well into the 1970s, large numbers of women "joined" the women's liberation movement and feminist ideals began to infiltrate the cultural realm with unprecedented effect. Feminism it seemed, to those it threatened most, was increasingly something to worry about.

In particular, feminism directly threatened women's role as lynchpin of one of the foundational institutions of modern social order, the nuclear family. In the radical feminist call for reproductive self-determination, feminism's adversaries perceived a genocidal threat to the future of the (white) dominant class, popularly interpreted through the lens of women's positioning as mothers within dominant culture. Directed at men and/or the system of identity production that underpins gendered modernity, feminist calls for abortion and birth control resonated as tools of genocide and conjured the "myth of the murderous, devouring mother."[97] We can hear this fear in Beverly LaHaye's proclamation that feminism is "a philosophy of death."[98] This same anxiety gets mapped onto the female terrorist, seen as the limit case manifestation of feminism within the popular Western imagination:

> [T]here is great pressure for the female terrorist to keep proving herself . . . If she is the leader and feels she is losing control of the male terrorists in her command, outrage overtakes discipline . . . [T]o preserve her status as an operative, she is more *likely to kill children*.[99]

Feminism thus represented a wholesale threat to the possibility of women bearing and rearing children in the regulated manner that forms the basis of social order, and as such, constituted, like terrorism, a threat *to the future* itself. These anxieties around feminism's destabilization of the nuclear family were—and continue to be—most explicitly articulated by the then-emerging

New Right. In the rhetoric of the New Right, feminism's attack on the family signifies the end of modern social, economic, and sexual order. Indeed, the New Right's fight against feminism has frequently played out across the temporal space of the apocalypse. For example, Jerry Falwell has exhorted good Americans to "preserve family values" by invoking the apocalyptic scenario: "We cannot wait. *The twilight of our nation could well be at hand.*"[100] In these ways then, radical feminism's reproductive agenda signified, from the outset, the threat of revolutionary terrorism.

However, as I have suggested, in the explicit call for gen(der)ocide, along with the genocidal implications of their reproductive agenda, radical feminism invoked the specter of state terrorism. The idea of state terrorism, as distinguished from state-sponsored terrorism,[101] encompasses violence or repressive action carried out by governments against either their own populations (or segments thereof) or the populations of other states. Historically, the idea of state terrorism has been associated with the practice of genocide—Hitler's Nazi Germany providing the archetype for both state terrorism and genocide. Thus, in their call for a gen(der)ocide, radical feminists none-too-subtly aligned themselves with the practice of state terrorism. However, radical feminists' articulations of genocide were ambiguous: not only did they advocate gen(der)ocide, they simultaneously claimed that women were themselves the victims of gen(der)ocide—they had a foot in both camps.

Radical feminists' relationship to terrorism was also ambiguous. On the one hand, radical feminism resembled revolutionary terrorism, deploying spectacular tactics and speaking in the language of apocalypse. On the other hand, it resembled a form of state terrorism. From this perspective, feminism looked slippery and elusive, just like the figure of Woman in whose name it acted. This was perhaps the most terrifying and destabilizing feature of feminism. For, in simultaneously invoking revolutionary *and* state terror, radical feminism problematized the distinction between legitimate and illegitimate violence upon which the state is premised in Western modernity. It politicized the continuum of terror that both underlies order in Western modernity and that must be disavowed in order for Western liberal democracy—Lefebvre's "terrorist society"—to endure. That is, in highlighting the arbitrariness of the distinction between legitimate and illegitimate violence, radical feminists drew attention to the way that the organization of the everyday that is facilitated by this distinction is in fact premised on the circulation of terror. From this perspective, LaHaye's description of feminism as "a philosophy of death" looks like a projection of the fear associated with the "suicidal autoimmunity" of Western modernity.

CHAPTER 7

Nuclear Terrorists: Patricia Hearst and the (Feminist) Terrorist Family

This is the Age of the Terrorist. There is, and will continue to be, more than one Tania. The intensity with which the world was gripped by the Patty Hearst story is not hard to understand. Almost every family today has its Patty, girl or boy, lost, stolen, or strayed, dropped out, kicked out, left out, or flipped out.

David Boulton[1]

So far in this book, I have described the ways that radical feminism—which, within the late 1960s and early 1970s North American cultural milieu, stands in for feminism more generally—resonated as a terrorist threat to dominant order. This chapter examines how this threat was mapped onto the figure of the female terrorist by analyzing the high-profile kidnapping and "conversion" of Patricia Campbell Hearst by the Symbionese Liberation Army (SLA) in 1974. In what follows, I suggest that the threat of both feminism and (feminist) terrorism are perceived to problematize—indeed, terrorize—the institution of the family, and that the family thus becomes an important site for the recuperation of the (feminist) terrorist threat and the reassertion of dominant order.

As I suggested in Chapter Five, the inscription of madness is a key strategy by which dominant order seeks to contain any threat to itself. In this context, the construction of the female terrorist as "mad" operates to annul the political valency of the threat she poses. We have seen how this occurred in the case of Valerie Solanas. By contrast, however, the case of Patricia Hearst was not so clear-cut. The unfolding of the Patty Hearst event in the mainstream media saw Hearst apparently reject the comforts of her upper-class lifestyle in favor of a terrorist career.[2] When Hearst radically declared her solidarity with the SLA in a taped communiqué to the media, it was met with speculation that she had been brainwashed, drugged, or tortured or had fallen in love with a male SLA member. That is, Hearst's behavior was rendered comprehensible by framing it within the range of acceptable feminine behaviors—as the passive victim of the terrorists or a victim of the feminine propensity for madness and/or malleability. When Hearst was tried in 1976 for crimes committed while she was ostensibly a member of the SLA, her defense team explained the radical transformation of the young heiress into a "ruthless" female terrorist via a claim of "coercive persuasion." While the idea of psychological duress has been used by other female terrorists to explain away their behavior upon their reintegration into mainstream society,[3] in the Patty Hearst event, this strategy failed and Hearst was sentenced to seven years in prison. I argue that her defense was rejected because, as a member of one of the United States' most wealthy and prominent families, Hearst's decision to engage in terrorist warfare resonated as an event that threw the perceived failure of the institution of the family into sharp relief—it very publicly revealed the family in crisis.

There has been much popular debate around Hearst's role in, and the extent of her agency in relation to, the activities of the SLA, and the speculation continues. I am not concerned here with the question of whether or not Patricia Hearst can be considered a terrorist, but rather with the ways our culture's description of her as a terrorist articulate with broader cultural narratives about terrorism itself, the position of women in Western cultures, and, in particular, how the category of gender works to structure and order Western cultural and political responses to terrorism.

Terrorist Fiction before Terrorist Fact

> Someone had kidnapped her and kidnapping always had a reason, however twisted it might be. Ransom, maybe . . . the senator was a wealthy man and could be counted on to raise an immense sum to get his only daughter back . . . or maybe . . . She whimpered again, and her belly knotted and churned . . . Maybe . . . oh, God, not that . . . maybe it was one of those ritual things, with the "love children" planning to do their hideous thing against her as they had . . . against the Tate party.[4]

In 1972, an obscure and short-lived San Diego publisher, Regency Press, released a paperback novel written under the pseudonym of Harrison James and entitled *Black Abductor*. Set in the immediate aftermath of the student uprisings of the late 1960s, when portions of the Movement became more militant and went underground, the novel traces the kidnapping of Patricia Prescott, daughter of a wealthy, popular but conservative law-and-order politician by a campus-based terrorist group, loosely affiliated with the black liberation movement. Led by an embittered black man, the revolutionaries kidnap the drunk and disheveled Patricia from her boyfriend's car late at night, leaving him badly beaten. On taking Patricia hostage, the terrorists demand the release of Bolivar Gunter, a comrade awaiting trial in prison for the murder of a National Guardsman at a student riot.[5] The terrorists' intention is to wait for the government to capitulate to their demands and then murder Patricia so she would not be able to identify her captors. However, in the time between the abduction and the authorities' receipt of the first communiqué from the terrorists, the gang realizes that "there was going to be time to kill while the establishment was running in circles . . . Maybe it would be amusing to give this dumb broad an education."[6] And so the revolutionaries—the well-hung black leader of the gang, his two white male sidekicks, and a black lesbian—subject their captive Patricia, "the political ingénue with fairly conventional sexual experiences,"[7] to a "reeducation" that consists of her forced participation in a variety of sexual escapades "worthy of finely conditioned acrobats."[8]

At first, Patricia resists the sexual advances of her abductors until, realizing she is helpless, she resolves to cooperate in order to survive. However, the moment of her initial rape in the novel is not one of victimhood for Patricia, but of sexual and political awakening. As the novel progresses, Patricia comes to see the world through the eyes of her captors. As Angie, the only other female of the terrorist organization remarks, "Shit, you act like you're a house guest instead of a hostage . . . Christ Trish! You're sure as hell one of us!"[9] As Al Ellenberg argues, "Patricia's sexual and ideological education is so successful, she literally becomes a member of the tiny guerrilla family."[10] In Ellenberg's analysis, Patricia's membership of the terrorist *family* is bound up with her sexual and ideological education, or to be more precise, her *reeducation*.

Sold primarily through a handful of independent retail outlets dealing in adult literature, *Black Abductor* never achieved mainstream circulation. However, it is noteworthy in that it anticipates, in remarkable detail, an event that, just two years later, rocked the United States and much of the Western world.

In 1972, *Black Abductor* described Patricia Prescott's kidnapping as the United States' "first political kidnapping."[11] On 21 August 1973, Richard H. Ichord, the chairman of the US House Committee on Internal Security, released a report in which he could still claim that "the United States has been fortunate to escape the rash of political kidnappings that have shaken the world in the past few years."[12] Six months later, on the evening of 4 February 1974, the United States experienced its first real "political kidnapping' when the left-wing SLA kidnapped Patricia Campbell Hearst in a violent attack on her home near the University of California's Berkeley campus. This kidnapping, foretold with eerie prescience in *Black Abductor*, began an ordeal that would see the US public spellbound by an intense media spectacle that lasted for over two years. In the aftermath of her abduction, so the dominant narrative goes, Hearst was held captive in a closet for a couple of months, subjected to a rigorous process of "brainwashing"[13] and, like the fictional Patricia, subsequently declared that she had decided to join the terrorist group in their fight against "the corporate enem[ies] of the people."[14] Authorities treated this declaration with some degree of disbelief until Hearst was caught on security camera wielding a rifle in a bank robbery executed by SLA members in San Francisco. The event caused sensation, not only because the kidnapping was perceived to attack the heart of the US establishment, but also because, in announcing her new loyalty to the "revolution," Hearst had vehemently denounced her family. Strong public speculation about the nature of Hearst's involvement with the SLA continued until well after she was arrested and tried for bank robbery in early 1976.

As Ellenberg notes, the similarities between the novel and the kidnapping of Hearst "challenged probability sufficiently to have prodded the FBI into obtaining a copy of the novel after the parallels were listed in a *New York Post* story on 15 February 1974."[15] However, when the FBI investigated, they were reportedly unable to track down the author, the publisher, or the distributor.[16] Conspiracy theories abound as to how a porn novel published in California in 1972 could predict with such alarming accuracy a course of events that was to unfold in the 1974 Patricia Hearst kidnapping, what I refer to here as the "Patty Hearst event."[17] Indeed, the existence of this novel has formed the basis of enduring speculations that Hearst masterminded her own abduction or that Regency Press was owned by the Hearst Corporation and that Randy Hearst, Patricia's father, orchestrated his daughter's kidnapping to instigate a law-and-order crackdown that would serve his political and economic interests.

The SLA formed out of a black inmate visitation scheme known as "Venceremos" run by left wing radical activists at California's Vacaville Prison in the late 1960s and early 1970s. However, the group did not officially cohere until after the 5 March 1973 when Donald DeFreeze (Cinque) escaped from Soledad State Prison. The only black member of the SLA, DeFreeze became its titular leader. Then, on 6 November 1973, the SLA murdered Marcus Foster, the first black Californian Superintendent of Schools, in a daylight shooting—an incident that is echoed in *Black Abductor* by Bolivar Gunter's shooting of the National Guardsman. It is possible that the SLA had read *Black Abductor* and, from it, gained a blueprint for radical action. Indeed, it is possible that the author of the novel knew of or had a connection with the SLA and modeled the fictional terrorist gang of *Black Abductor* on its members. However, it is not important to establish a direct causal link between the two texts. Further, it is not surprising that *Black Abductor*, coming out of a genre of "transgressive" literature, appears before the Patty Hearst event takes place. Rather, both *Black Abductor* and the Patty Hearst event articulate anxieties, or tensions, that lie at the core of Western modernity, and *Black Abductor*, as "adult" literature, gives expression to narratives that underpin, yet are disavowed by, dominant constructions of the Patty Hearst event. Both texts, I argue, articulate modern anxieties around the stability of the institution of the nuclear family and terrorism as a threat to the structure of sexual relations that orders modern society.

To illustrate the ways both *Black Abductor* and the Patty Hearst event articulate cultural anxieties about the nuclear family, it is useful to turn to one of the more inventive twists in the plot of *Black Abductor*: Patricia's incestuous relationship with her brother, Will. In the first chapter of the novel, as Patricia awakens from the chloroform-induced slumber that enabled her abduction, we learn that some time earlier, "the numbing realization had come over her that Will was unique—that she would never find his match in another man."[18] Later, with her reeducation well underway, Patricia concludes that her enjoyment of sex with Dory, the black terrorist gang leader, is a sublimated form of her desire for her brother:

> Because she could never have [Will] as long as she should live, her subconscious must have wanted her to belong to him in every way that a woman could give herself to the man she loved. Now, hostage in a terrorist plot, forced to indulge in unspeakably vile acts, she was sublimating them! She was throwing herself into them with wild pleasure, her subconscious pretending that Dory was Will. And every new degradation that Dory subjected her to would strengthen that subconscious merging of identities.[19]

At the end of the novel, it comes to light that, unbeknownst to Patricia, Will has been an active member of the underground arm of the radical student movement. Using his contacts in the movement, Will arranges for Patricia's newly found comrades to go underground. The novel closes with the siblings sharing a passionate kiss and Will's hand on Patricia's crotch. And, one presumes, the revolution goes on.

Ellenberg argues that, while *Black Abductor* parallels the Patty Hearst event in many ways, the incest theme marks one of the most significant divergences between the two texts.[20] To the contrary, both texts articulate a Western cultural preoccupation with incest or, rather the taboo against incest, and the incest theme is fundamental to understanding why the Patty Hearst event resonated so strongly with Western audiences. While the preoccupation with incest is not explicit in the event's narrativization, as it is in the plot of *Black Abductor*, it nonetheless structures dominant understandings of the kidnapping. As such, we can use the text of *Black Abductor* to deconstruct the narratives that make sense of the Patty Hearst event for mainstream audiences.

"It's a Family Affair": Reading Patty Hearst through the Nuclear Family

Patricia Hearst was a member of one of the most influential families in San Francisco's Bay Area. Her father, Randolph (Randy) Hearst, was chief executive of the media empire inherited from Patricia's millionaire grandfather, William Randolph Hearst, whose life inspired the film, *Citizen Kane*.[21] Patricia's mother, Catherine Hearst, was the daughter of a wealthy family from Atlanta. At the time of Patricia's kidnapping, Catherine was a member of the University of California's Board of Regents—a conservative body that implemented several restrictive policies to curb the revolutionary activities of the student movement in the late 1960s and early 1970s. As a result of her position on this committee, Catherine had been the victim of a failed assassination attempt in 1972.

From the moment when Randy and Catherine Hearst presented themselves to the media on the steps of their Hillsborough mansion in San Francisco the morning after Patricia's kidnapping, the Patty Hearst event was constructed by the establishment as a breach against the nuclear family. Even before the SLA's first taped communiqué was broadcast, the mainstream media, along with state representatives and the Hearsts themselves, unanimously began describing the 20-year-old Patricia in ways that positioned her as a member of a family, sometimes as a child but primarily as a daughter. Catherine appeared dressed in black, assuming the role of a mother grieving for her disappeared daughter, and newspaper reports were filled with stories detailing the "kidnapping of Randolph Hearst's daughter" accompanied by sympathetic images of Randy, head bowed with fatherly concern. The Hearsts' performance in the initial days of the Patty Hearst event thus constructed the abduction in terms of an attack on the Hearst family, and in so doing, their plea for the safety of their daughter tapped public sympathy by appealing to fears and concerns about the vulnerability of families more generally.[22]

As Hearst pointed out in a subsequent communiqué addressed to her parents, *everyone* was implicated in this attack: "This is a warning to *everybody* . . . This is a political issue and this is a political action [the SLA] have taken."[23] And it seems this breach hit a raw nerve with the wider US public. For example, Jerry Belcher, a journalist for the *San Francisco Examiner*, with a daughter of similar age to Patricia, recalls going home the evening after the kidnapping and removing the nameplate from his family's mailbox: "Silly, probably. But Randy Hearst never thought his daughter would be kidnapped either."[24] David Boulton, too, notes that the event tapped the latent fears of every family[25] but had an immediate impact in particular on upper-class North American families.[26] As the case developed, Hearst came to signify, as Shana Alexander so aptly expresses it in the title of her account of the trial, "anyone's daughter."[27] That is, the event was experienced by the general public as an attack against *all* families. At the level of discourse, the abduction of Patricia Hearst posed a more generalized threat to dominant order and those everyday families who, in the Marxist terms of the SLA, were complicit in perpetuating that order. Why was, and is, Western-dominant culture so anxious to construct the Patty Hearst event as an attack against the institution of the family? The extent to which the myriad representations of the Patty Hearst event are couched in terms of the nuclear family smacks of a recuperation.

By the mid-1970s, the nuclear family was commonly perceived to be in crisis. The reasons for this included the counter-culture's challenge to the nuclear family through the establishment of communes in the late 1960s, and the cultural and institutional repercussions of second-wave feminism, including the changing of divorce laws in many US states, legalization of abortion, women's entry into higher education and the workplace, and increased numbers of women exercising their rights to contraception. Indeed, of the Patty Hearst event, Alexander writes, "it was a family event occurring at a time when the family as an institution was in disunion and disrepair, when real families withered and shattered, and pseudofamilies thrived. The SLA itself was a pseudofamily."[28] The Patty Hearst event, then, provided a timely opportunity to reassert the importance of the middle-class institution of the family.

Beyond this, however, the event tapped latent fears about the stability, or lack thereof, of the nuclear family, which are always already present in, and fundamental to, modernity. The perception that the family is under threat of disappearing has been a characteristic of modern social engineering discourse since at least as far back as the nineteenth century.[29] In Western culture, we experience the threat of the practice of terrorism through this anxiety about the instability of the nuclear family. That is, it is not just the terrorism of the SLA that was perceived as a threat to the nuclear family, but terrorism as a practice more generally. Further, experienced as a threat to the nuclear family, terrorism is also perceived to threaten the libidinal economy that structures capitalist exchange in modernity and the structure of gender relations on which that economy turns. It is for this reason that we see the kinds of preoccupations with terrorism and the family that are present in *Black Abductor* and in representations of the Patty Hearst event.[30]

The Terror of Incest: The Primal Horde and the Terrorist Family

In his study of indigenous social systems, *Totem and Taboo*, first published in 1913, and later in *Moses and Monotheism*, Sigmund Freud formulates a theory of the origins of human social organization by applying his developing theory of individual psychosexual development to the broader subject of society—to the collective. Freud traces the origins of "civilized" society, and by this we can take him to mean "modern" society, back through the kinship structures of indigenous societies to the mythic story of the primal horde. A distinctly modern myth,[31] the value of this story lies in its provision of a rationale, from a modern Western perspective, for the libidinal economy that structures modern society. Its universalizing and essentializing tendencies notwithstanding, I use the story here, not as a scientific description, but as a cultural product, to illustrate how the discursive reproduction of the logic of modern fraternal society takes place.[32] I suggest that Freud's story, as a product of fraternal culture, is structured by the very same modern concerns that shape the narrativization of the Patty Hearst event, and, for that matter, the plot of *Black Abductor*. As such, Freud's story can be used to help explain why the Patty Hearst event is constructed in particular ways, and why this renders the event intelligible for Western audiences.

Freud explains the myth of the primal horde:

> The story is told . . . as though it happened on one single occasion, while in fact it covered thousands of years and was repeated countless times . . . The strong male was lord and father of the entire horde and unrestricted in his power, which he exercised with violence. All the females were his property— wives and daughters of his own horde and some, perhaps robbed from other hordes. The lot of his sons was a hard one: if they roused their father's jealousy they were killed or castrated or driven out. Their only resource was to collect together in small communities, to get themselves wives by robbery, and when [possible] . . . to raise themselves into a position similar to their father's in the primal horde.[33]

At the center of this tribal "pseudo-society" (for Freud is very careful to point out that the primal horde is presocial[34]) is a jealous patriarch with a *monopoly* on sexual access to the women of the tribe. Sexual relations within the primal horde take place within a closed circuit that revolves around the father's desire and his unlimited access to the women. Indeed, the father's monopolization of the women is the only law that governs sexual relations in the primal horde. Second, the patriarch defends his right to the women, and rules over his sons, with violence. His is a reign of terror—a regime maintained by the brothers' terror of being murdered, castrated, or driven out of the horde. Importantly, the sons/brothers excluded from this violently guarded closed circuit of sexual relations simultaneously despise their father for his position of privilege and desire to emulate him—to attain his position of power and sexual supremacy. Freud writes, "we suppose . . . that they not only hated and feared their father but also honoured him as a model, and that each of them wished to take his place in reality."[35] Freud's story assumes from the outset the contemporaneous existence of more than one horde. In Freud's telling, the only way for a son to achieve the patriarch's position of privilege is to *steal* women from others—either from the father of his own horde or from the fathers of other hordes—in order to have the women necessary for him to establish a horde of his own. We have here then a "pseudo-society" based not only upon a patriarchal monopoly of sexual access to women maintained by violence and terror, but also upon theft. Indeed, the requirement of a monopoly on sex that operates within each primal horde produces the imperative to thieve.

Miraculously, so the story goes, one day, the rules change: "The expelled brothers, living in a community, united to overpower their father and, as was the custom in those days, devoured him raw."[36] Having thus murdered and consumed the father, the brothers, reflecting the ambivalence with which they regarded their father when he was alive, are at once glad to be rid of him and the structure of sexual monopoly he enforced, and experience remorse for his murder. To expiate the crime that binds them together in guilt, the sons agree that, in the absence of the father, no one will seek to raise himself to the position formerly held by the patriarch. Each of the brothers abrogates his desire for his mothers and sisters, entering a kind of contractual agreement to exogamy that respects the wishes of the dead father. In this respect, the patriarchy lives on, regulated by a fraternal pact. Or in the words of Herbert Marcuse, in modern society, we see "the replacement of the patriarchal despotism of the primal horde by the internalised despotism of the brother clan."[37] For Freud, it is this agreement that marks the rise of the incest taboo.[38]

In making this argument, Freud implies that the taboo on incest, whose corollary is the "injunction to exogamy,"[39] brings the nuclear family into existence, and in so doing, constructs the social order. He writes, "the first form of [modern] social organisation came about with a *renunciation of instinct*, the introduction of definite *institutions* [such as, we can assume, the nuclear family], pronounced inviolable—that is to say, the beginnings of morality and justice."[40] For Freud then, society is based on the psychosexual structure of the nuclear family and regulated by the incest taboo.

Under this new regime, we witness the beginnings of modern social organization in which, as Juliet Flower MacCannell argues, patriarchal power is supplanted by fraternal power.[41] The new society, based on fraternity, is defined by way of men's access to women and, as such, preserves the basic principle that defines the pseudo-society of the primal horde. While in the pseudo-society of the primal horde, the patriarch has access not only to the women of his horde but potentially to the women of other hordes via theft, modern society is based upon a scarcity of women that circulate between men in organized ways, within a rigid structure of exchange. As Marcuse writes, "the development of the paternal domination into an increasingly powerful state system administered by man is thus a continuance of the primal repression, which has as its purpose the ever wider exclusion of women."[42]

The incest taboo is thus both a prohibition and a repression that marks the origins of modern society. In psychoanalytic theory, as Freud writes, "repression . . . involves a loss of memory—an amnesia."[43] What is it that the incest taboo represses? And, by extension, what is "forgotten" with the implementation of modern social order?

We can argue that the memory that must be repressed is the guilt trauma the brothers suffer in the aftermath of the father's murder. However, in addition to the traumatic memory of the patricide itself, we might also add the traumatic memory of what the patriarch represented for the brothers: namely a regime of terror and violence under which their sexual desires were systematically denied. In this sense, if the incest taboo expresses a repression, and this repression marks the rise of modern social order, then modern society is based not only upon the repression of patricide, but also upon the repression of the primal horde. Or to put it differently, the institution of the nuclear family, produced by the incest taboo as the basis of modern social order, enables the sublimation not only of the brothers' instinctual desire for their mothers and sisters but also the sublimation of violence and terror. As with the narratives, discussed in Chapter Four, of social contract theory, and those that locate the rise of democracy in Robespierre's reign of terror, the story of the primal horde tells of modern social order supervening terror.

As Freud outlines, the prohibition of an instinct does not abolish it: "Both the prohibition and the instinct persist: the instinct because it has only been repressed and not abolished, and the prohibition because, if it ceased, the instinct would force its way through into actual operation."[44] In other words, that which is repressed always threatens to return. In this logic, then, behind the smooth veneer of exchange held in place by the incest taboo, in the social unconscious, lurks the repressed memory of the primal horde, which threatens to return and "restore the prehistoric and subhistoric destructive force of the pleasure principle"[45] that characterized "pre-social" life. Thus, the memory must continue to be repressed if society is to continue to exist. It is through this threat of the return of the primal horde that the practice of terrorism gets narrativized in Western culture and is rendered comprehensible for Western audiences. This "return" structures the ways terrorism is *represented*, and thus understood in fraternal culture.

Exchanging Women: Legitimate and Illegitimate Forms of Capitalism

In "Women on the Market," drawing on the story of the primal horde from the psychoanalytic tradition and reading it through a Marxist analytical framework, Luce Irigaray argues that society is based upon relations between men. She writes, "the law that orders our society is the exclusive valorization of men's needs/desires, of exchanges among men."[46] For Irigaray, "women's bodies—through their use, consumption and circulation—provide for the condition making social life possible."[47] The exchange of a woman between two men is marked, argues Irigaray, by branding women with the "name-of-the-father," and this "determines their value in sexual commerce."[48] Women are thus circulated as commodities, in the Marxian sense, as items of exchange between men in patriarchal society. Like all commodities, women's value takes two forms: a use value, which for Irigaray is a reproductive value produced in relation to individual men's desire in *private*, and an exchange value whose production is fundamentally *social/public*, carried out by, and between, men.[49] The exchange of women forms the legitimate basis for relations among men, and as such, constitutes the "symbolic system"[50] that structures both the collective process of imagining "society" and the relations between men, which, under patriarchy, comprise the social.

Applying Irigaray's argument to the kidnapping of Patricia Hearst, it was the "legitimate" exchange of women, and the social order it reproduces, that the SLA threatened to undermine. In her account of Hearst's trial, Alexander describes the SLA's tactic of kidnapping as "this new form of *illegitimate* capitalism,"[51] positioning Hearst as a commodity in a relationship of exchange between men. In the first instance, the SLA's intention was to secure the release of their imprisoned colleagues, Joseph Remiro and Russell Little, in exchange for the safe return of Hearst.[52] However, when it became clear that the state would not capitulate to these demands, the SLA resorted to a different strategy. Unbeknownst to the "outside" world, they held Hearst hostage in a closet for almost two months, subjecting her to a rigorous process of thought reform, or "brainwashing," as it became known in popular cultural representations. Eventually, in a communiqué on 3 April 1974, Hearst declared her decision to join the terrorist gang and fight for the "revolution."[53]

This moment in the Patty Hearst event marked, for Hearst's parents, representatives of the state and the Western audiences who were watching, the SLA's possession of Patricia Hearst. They marked their new possession as their own by renaming her "Tania," after Che Guevara's mistress. The Hearsts and the mainstream media responded with claims that Patricia had been coerced—drugged, hypnotized, tortured, or, as Randolph Hearst stridently and publicly asserted, brainwashed. The sexual overtones of these assertions were barely submerged. For example, the spokesperson of the antipsychiatry movement, Thomas Szasz, described her as the apparent "victim of mind-rape."[54] It was automatically assumed that Hearst's decision to join the SLA was the mark of her sexual domination, and from that point on, Hearst became, for those involved, the illegally acquired "property" of the SLA and her exchange value in "legitimate" relations between men was undermined. She was now, in Irigaray's terms, "off the market."

Thus, in kidnapping Hearst, the SLA violated the rules of exchange that underpin modern society, breaking the taboo upon which social order is based. As Don West and Jerry Belcher point out, to Patricia's fiancé "Steven Weed and the Hearst family . . . Patricia Campbell Hearst was a woman stolen by force—all that followed and will follow stems from that central violence."[55] The SLA stole Hearst from the men to whom she "rightfully" belonged—her father, her fiancée—in an attempt to force a relationship of exchange with the state. That is, they used Hearst as an item of exchange in order to construct themselves as legitimate political actors, legitimate parties to the process of exchange between men.

In Freud's reading of the story about the behavior of the primal horde, prior to the killing of the father and the implementation of the incest taboo, we will remember that the brothers, if driven from the primal horde either by jealousy of the patriarch or because of his wrath, would establish hordes of their own by stealing women from other clans. If, as Freud suggests, the primal horde story describes, not a single episode, but a pseudo-social structure that predominated over a long period of time, we can assume that the primal horde operated to a large degree via the theft of women. The SLA's kidnapping of Patricia Hearst, an act of theft that defies the incest taboo, might be thought of as an act that is characteristic, not of society, but of the pseudo-social primal horde. In this sense, the SLA comes to represent the primal horde, the repressed memory upon which modern social organization is based. As such, the event represents, in dominant discourse, a fundamental threat to both the institution of the family and society itself.

It is not just the act of stealing Hearst from her "rightful" owners that positions the SLA as the primal horde within the representational structures of the event. The SLA, like many other radical groups of the era, operated on principles of "free love" and open sexual relations as a deliberate strategy of destabilizing the structure of the bourgeois family. In theory, this meant that both the men and the women of such groups were free to interact sexually with any other member of the group, but in practice, this often meant that the men of these organizations simply gained increased access to the women. In this sense, the SLA mimicked the *disorder* of sexual relations extant in the primal horde.

If, as I have argued, the incest taboo represses the incestuous instinct and, by extension, society represses the primal horde, then the SLA's terrorism operates not only in terms of the threat of random violence in a society that disavows violence, but also as the desublimation of incestuous desire and the threat of the return to the primal horde. The SLA threatens, that is, the libidinal economy that produces the nuclear family, and thus society, as meaningful constructs, and it is for this reason that dominant Western culture responds by narrativizing the kidnapping through the discourse of the family. Thus, constructions of the Patty Hearst event betray an anxiety about the possibility of the disintegration of the nuclear family into the mythical primal horde, and by extension, an anxiety about the possibility of the demise of society. It is this possibility—a possibility disavowed by dominant readings of the Patty Hearst event—to which *Black Abductor*, as a morally transgressive text, gives expression. Indeed, for Steven Marcus, if an idea, a work, or an act emerges as a strong preoccupation in adult sex fiction, it is "the most reliable indicator of how much a society is frightened of that thing, how deeply it fears its powers, how subversive to its settled order it conceives [it] to be."[56] In order for modern society to continue to exist, the repression of the primal horde must be consistently reproduced. But, as Freud suggests, the prohibition of a forbidden instinct is "noisily conscious."[57] In the context of the Patty Hearst event, the prohibition that facilitates the repression of the primal horde is indeed "noisily" rehearsed.

"Your Sons and Daughters Are Beyond Your Command": The Crisis in Socialization

Approximately one month after Hearst was photographed by security cameras wielding a gun in an SLA bank robbery, the FBI executed a stakeout of an SLA safe house in Oakland, Los Angeles, in which six members of the terrorist group burned to death in a drama of violent state retaliation that was broadcast live on national television. Later that day, the only two other remaining members of the SLA, Emily and Bill Harris, became embroiled in a shoplifting incident at a sporting goods store. Hearst reportedly fired shots into the store from a parked car in order to secure her comrades' escape. Amid speculation that she had died in the "holocaust" in Oakland,[58] Hearst released another communiqué in which she "eulogized the bravery and 'badness' of her dead comrades, while declaring her feelings for slain SLA member William Wolfe . . . whom she described as 'the gentlest, most beautiful man I've ever known.'"[59] Hearst remained underground until she was captured, along with the Harrises, and charged with bank robbery on 17 September 1975. After weeks of psychological testing to determine whether she was mentally fit to stand trial, the spectacle of Hearst's trial finally began on 4 February 1976—two years to the day after she was snatched from her home.

Hearst testified that the violence committed against her was of both a psychological and a physical nature. After her abduction, she had been confined in a closet for approximately two months, blindfolded and with her hands tied. She was not allowed out of the closet except to visit the bathroom, accompanied by one of the terrorists. Although the SLA fed Hearst regularly, she had been unable to eat and consequently lost a large amount of weight. She lived in an extreme state of anxiety induced by the ongoing threat of being murdered at the terrorists' whim. To exacerbate her suffering even further, she was raped by the leader of the terrorist organization. At her trial, Hearst recounted how, during her time in the closet, the members of the SLA frequently lectured her about left wing politics, giving the impression that they were just one cell of a nationwide underground army preparing for imminent revolution. The remainder of the time, she would attempt to sleep or, terrified, would listen to the clicks of shotguns being loaded and unloaded as the terrorists went about their target practice. She claimed she had been forced to join the SLA as a matter of ensuring her own survival. In her autobiography, *Every Secret Thing*, she writes, "the truth was, of course, that I *did* want to join them! But not for the reasons they supposed . . . I wanted to join them so that I would survive."[60] Expert psychiatric evidence was given at Hearst's trial attesting that she had in fact suffered extreme sensory deprivation and been subject to a rigorous process of "thought reform." However, despite this evidence, the court rejected her defense and sentenced her to seven years in prison. In his closing summary, the judge noted, in highly paternalistic terms, that "*her* conduct could not be condoned, that a lesson must be made of *her* to serve as a deterrent to others."[61]

By all accounts, Hearst enjoyed all the comforts of an upper-middle-class upbringing and was considered by those around her as an exemplary young woman. However, while still in high school, Hearst fell in love with her young mathematics teacher, Steven Weed. When he accepted a teaching fellowship at the University of California's Berkeley campus, she moved in with him, despite not being married, and studied art history at the radicalized campus—decisions that her parents were less than enthusiastic about. On the request of her parents, shortly before Hearst was kidnapped, Patricia and Steven announced their engagement. In the aftermath of her very public denunciation of her family, and again when Hearst was finally arrested in 1976, Hearst's history of minor revolt was disinterred by journalists seeking to locate her conversion within a familiar narrative about rebellious teenagers and deviant sexual experiences. That is, narratives emerged within the popular domain to explain the hypersexualized terrorist "Tania" who had proclaimed her love for her male revolutionary comrade and her despise of bourgeois values and institutions, problematizing the image of Hearst as an exchangeable woman, "a young woman who was living the American dream—born to a happy family, well-educated, financially secure, and soon to be married."[62]

The Hearst family responded to this public scrutiny of Patricia's upbringing by releasing images from their family photo album for publication, attempting, as Nancy Isenberg notes:

> to reclaim Patty's image through photographs that normalized her upbringing, publicly displaying snapshots from her seemingly unexceptional life . . . Photographs of this kind capture images of happy families, but most importantly, the dignity of the family is reinforced by Patty's carefully coded sexuality, which is contained through safe and normal images.[63]

The publication of the Hearsts' family photos—images that ranged from her First Communion to cheerleading shots—operated to locate Hearst within the normative framework of feminine sexuality, reinforcing the image of the integrity of the family,[64] and, as such, modern social order. The photographs were used, literally, to construct the normalcy of Hearst's female psychosexual development in black-and-white "truth"-speaking terms. The photographs also worked to assert Hearst's pedigree in proper *socialization* within the closely guarded structure of the nuclear family, a point that Randolph Hearst was keen to affirm when the shadowy gun-toting figure of "Tania" made her high-profile début: "We've had her for twenty years. They've had her 60 days, and I don't believe that she is going to change her philosophy so quickly and permanently."[65] Here, Hearst attempts to contain the subversive threat of "Tania" by asserting "his prior claim as the progenitor of her true identity."[66] The strength and durability of the family is produced discursively through the idea of socialization, which grounds the family within the structure of linear and routine time, granting it a sense of permanence. Nonetheless, as

Isenberg suggests, "as a sign and commodity, *'Tania' threatened the most basic beliefs of socialization*."[67]

This perceived threat to the process of socialization was by no means particular to the Patty Hearst event. For example, many considered Bob Dylan the inadvertent spokesperson of the 1960s and 1970s North American counter-culture, giving voice to the complexity of experiences of a generation of youths swept up by, and instrumental in, a process of rapid societal change. In his archetypal protest song, "The Times They Are A-Changin'," Dylan says:

> Come mothers and fathers across the land
> And don't criticize what you can't understand
> Your sons and your daughters are beyond your command.[68]

Here, Dylan signals what the Birmingham Centre describes as "the nightmare of a society which, in some fundamental way, had lost its sway and authority over its young, which had failed to win their hearts, minds and consent, a society teetering towards 'anarchy.'"[69]

Indeed, the late 1960s and early 1970s witnessed major transformations in civil society and a fundamental crisis in the power and legitimacy of the state. This overtly political and ideological challenge to liberal hegemony was unleashed by the younger generation, who were determined not just to refashion society, but to dismantle the institutional and ideological matrix that sustained it and to construct an alternative, utopian society in its place. The various factions within the Movement mounted this challenge to dominant order in different ways. However, despite the divergence in the conceptualization and practice of "revolution," the composite Movement was interpreted within the popular realm as both a failure of the socialization of the younger generation, and an attack on the processes of socialization that ensured ongoing social order. The Movement represented a threat to the bourgeois nuclear family that stemmed from within the entity of the family itself.

For example, the emergence of the counter-culture differed qualitatively from many other youth movements of the era in that it represented a fundamental challenge to the liberal hegemonic order from *within* that order. Antonio Gramsci defines hegemony as the winning and shaping of consent to grant legitimacy to the dominant class through an ascendancy of social authority, not only within the state but within civil society itself; that is, the ruling class demonstrates leadership at the level of ideology and culture. The power structure of cultural hegemony is stable, but always contested, and thus, the rule of one group over the rest of society in modernity depends not only on material power, but also on the establishment of "its own moral, political and cultural values as conventional norms of practical behaviour."[70]

The majority of participants in the counter-culture comprised white, educated, middle-class youths who explicitly rejected everything dominant culture stood for. In this sense, the counter-culture constituted a crisis in the ideological interpellation of the youth of the dominant class that resonated as a crisis from within the confines of the nuclear family.

Riding on the crest of the civil rights movement, the peace movement and the free speech movement, all of which gained considerable momentum on the radicalized university campuses, most notably at the University of California's Berkeley campus,[71] droves of young people "dropped out." Their method involved a kind of voluntary "ghettoization"—a policy of nonpartici-pation in mainstream society and the creation of an alternative society based on new patterns of living, family, and (non)work (the counter-economy).[72] The counter-culture directly opposed mainstream society and signaled a severe weakening of the institutions that facilitated the maturation of middle-class youths into responsible bourgeois citizens. Implicit in the counter-culture's rejection of bourgeois values and social formations was an interrogation of the nuclear family as an instrument of socialization that interpellated individuals as "good citizens." The counter-culture sought to destabilize the hegemonic nuclear family by rejecting monogamy and pro-moting communal living arrangements.[73] For dominant culture, this attack on the nuclear family and the process of socialization it implies signaled the unraveling of the power of the state itself.

As the movement grew and the violence and militancy of its opposition to the state increased, there was a visible shift in the methods of control exer-cised by the state. Deploying the rhetoric of the need for "law and order" and a "crackdown" on the permissive society, the state mobilized a range of coer-cive mechanisms in order to enforce its hegemony, resulting not only in a strong police and military presence at public demonstrations,[74] but also in a stream of arrests, charges of conspiracy and drug use, court trials, and the incarceration of dissident youths. This response further reinforced the sense of a crisis in the hegemony of the ruling class that was being played out within, and in relation to, the nuclear family. And this sense of crisis was further fueled by the rising momentum of the women's liberation movement.

Monstrous Mothers and Feminist Automatons: The Feminist Threat to the Family

As early as 1970, Robin Morgan claimed to be able to sense feminist victory in the wings, citing the report of a "blue-ribboned Presidential panel on the status of women," which urged the establishment to respond swiftly to sexual discrimination, lest "a new feminist movement that preached revolution" present "a danger to the established order."[75] Her account suggests that, at the turn of the decade, the US government perceived feminism as a serious, if not terroristic, threat to dominant order.

Henri Lefebvre's *terrorist society* is one in which "opposition is silenced either through being condemned as a perversion and thus invalidated, or by integration."[76] By the mid-1970s, while more militant forms of feminism were still dismissed within dominant culture as the manifestations of female madness, the debate over women's liberation had shifted significantly enough for dominant culture to begin to *integrate*—albeit hesitantly and partially—the threat of feminism. (Radical) feminist ideas, that is, had begun to infiltrate the US popular imagination, and increasingly informed the practice of gender within the realm of the everyday.[77] Sara Evans provides a snapshot of feminism's incursions into the sphere of everyday cultural politics:

> Although women's liberation was shocking and alienating to many, especially as seen through the lens of a hostile media . . . feminism had tapped a vein of enormous frustration and anger. Previously, ambivalence and fear of change had made women even less likely than men to advocate greater sexual equality. By 1975 a new sense of rights and possibilities had led women to assert their belief in equal rights and opportunities for females in greater numbers and with greater intensity than men. Within the context of such massive shifts of opinion, as millions of women readjusted their view of themselves and of the world, many thousands also moved to activism and into the burgeoning women's movement . . . The issue of sexual equality had become a subject of dinner conversation in households across the nation.[78]

Indeed, (radical) feminism had begun to assert itself as a formidable force for social and cultural change, reflected in, and bolstered by, significant legislative gains masterminded by "institutional" feminists of organizations such as the National Organization of Women—including the Equal Rights Amendment in 1972, followed quickly by the US Supreme Court's 1973 legalization of abortion.[79] US attitudes toward the "fairer sex" began to undergo a paradigm shift, manifesting in, for example, new modes of speech— such as "Ms," "chairperson," and "congressperson"—and novel conceptions of advertising's female target audience. (Radical) feminism had thus begun to stake a sizeable claim on the "mind share" of popular audiences.[80]

Radical feminists had, by the mid-1970s, paved the way for the mainstreaming of feminism. Jane Gerhard notes that, "core values forged in 1969 had, by 1976, been edited, expanded, and transformed as feminism itself became useful to more and more women."[81] As the brainchild of young, white, middle-class women, (radical) feminism originally resonated, like the counter-culture, as a threat from within the dominant class that evidenced the failure of the socialization of the younger generation. By 1975, however, (radical) feminism had found a much more mainstream constituency.[82]

In particular, the radical feminist practice of consciousness-raising (CR) had captured the imagination of large numbers of women from all walks of life. As Evans notes, through CR, "hundreds of thousands of women transformed their perceptions of personal inadequacy into a political analysis of women's oppression."[83] CR was to be perhaps radical feminism's most significant contribution to the radicalization of large numbers of women. Indeed, as the decade wore on, CR was advocated and adopted not just by radical feminists but also by more liberal feminists, evidencing the ways that "radical ideas and co-operative forms of the women's movement were re-shaping the more conservative, tightly structured 'women's rights' branches."[84]

CR was key in rendering the (radical) feminist slogan "the personal is political" meaningful to women. In providing a space for women to analyze the events and assumptions that shaped their everyday lives, CR facilitated the recognition of a shared experience of oppression. Drawing attention to the belief system underpinning women's subordination and locating women's subordination in the very practices of everyday life, it politicized women's internalization of dominant cultural norms and practices. Further, CR provided a social and communication network that could support women as they actively renegotiated their interpellation as subordinate citizens, and implemented feminist practices, within the structures of the everyday. In the context of CR, the family, and the domestic realm more broadly, were configured as key sites of women's everyday oppression and came under intense scrutiny. CR thus often translated into micro-changes in the structuring of family life and domestic labor—a reworking of the routine of the everyday. The overwhelming success of CR contributed to a widespread sense that "all the bulwarks seemed to be crumbling . . . For a time it seemed that the power of an aroused, united mass movement of women was irresistible."[85]

In the context of these gains, along with the growing membership of the women's liberation movement, (radical) feminism began to be described in terms of contagion[86]—as an evil and deadly plague that threatened daily existence. In particular, this took shape in the inflated claims of the emergent New Right.[87] That the New Right constructed (radical) feminism in these terms is testament to the perceived threat of feminism in the mid-1970s. For the New Right, (radical) feminism manifested as an attack on the institution of the nuclear family; indeed, within the New Right's apocalyptic vision, feminism was seen as *antifamily*—it *terrorized* the nuclear family. At least as far back as the publication of Betty Friedan's *The Feminine Mystique*, feminists of different persuasions had critiqued women's subordination via their confinement within the domestic realm and the nuclear family. However, this was expressed most vociferously by radical feminists. As Valerie Solanas put it:

> The reduction to animals of the women of the most backward segment of society—the "privileged, educated," middle-class, the backwash of humanity—where Daddy reigns supreme, has been so thorough that they try to groove on labor pains and lie around in the most advanced nation in the world . . . with babies chomping away on their tits. It's not for the kids' sake, though, that the "experts" tell women that Mama should stay at home and grovel in animalism, but for Daddy's . . . He strives to be constantly around females, which is the closest he can get to becoming one, so he created a "society" based on the family—a male-female couple and their kids . . . who live virtually on top of one another, unscrupulously violating the female's rights, privacy, and sanity.[88]

Solanas constructs the nuclear family as the fulcrum of a fundamentally corrupt society that is (falsely) premised on the violation of women. In Solanas' reading, the family operates as a disguise for male inferiority. Shulamith Firestone provides a comparatively tame analysis of the nuclear family. Deploying Freud to dismantle patriarchy, she argues the need to undo "the link between families and reproduction, a link that depended on women."[89]

Radical feminism registered as a fundamental threat to the libidinal economy of modernity, and it was this threat that the New Right latched onto in the early 1970s in order to mobilize against feminism. In 1973, Paul Weyrich established a conservative think tank, the Heritage Foundation.[90] Weyrich was fiercely antifeminist and practiced the New Right's signature form of scaremongering. Describing feminists, tellingly, as "people who want a radically different political order who are not necessarily Marxists," he excoriated the women's liberation movement for its "*restructuring of the traditional family*, and particularly . . . the downgrading of the male or father role in the traditional family."[91] In effect, rather than confront feminism head-on in a time of rising popularity of feminist principles, this New Right policy institute launched a crusade that configured its assault on feminism by systematically coding itself as a *defense* of the traditional family.[92]

The New Right's framing of its antifeminist political agenda in terms of the defense of the family gestures the dimensions of the feminist challenge to dominant order. While the New Right protested most loudly, it by no means had a monopoly on anxieties about feminism. As Susan Faludi suggests, "the mainstream would reject [the New Right's] fevered rhetoric and hellfire imagery, but the heart of their political message survived"[93] in the popular imagination.[94]

According to Johanna Brenner, the second-wave feminist movement reached its pinnacle from the late 1960s to the mid-1970s.[95] Patricia Hearst was charged with bank robbery in September 1975. These events were deeply interconnected in the backlash imagination. Backlash has a double-edged operation: it is at once a recuperative gesture that attempts to contain a perceived threat and, paradoxically, reproduces the sense of the very same threat it seeks to contain. The backlash against second-wave feminism marked not only a "counter-assault" designed to thwart it, but also the recognition that women's liberation posed a formidable threat. In this context, the dismissal of the brainwashing defense and the sentencing of Hearst to seven years of incarceration can be read as an opportunistic attempt to rehearse the importance of the nuclear family, strike a blow at the forces of feminism, and reassert dominant order and the structure of gender relations it implies.

Indeed, the SLA was commonly perceived as a feminist revolutionary terrorist organization. Although ostensibly led by a black man, at the time of Hearst's kidnapping, the SLA comprised predominantly female cadres.[96] Media coverage frequently asserted that, "women are the dominant force, the leadership of the Symbionese Liberation Army."[97] And terrorism studies proponents such as H. H. A. Cooper claimed that the SLA's "theoretical underpinnings . . . were the creation of women, and its operations were executed by a majority of female participants."[98]

While the implementation of feminism within the everyday life of this terrorist "family" appears to have been, at best, limited,[99] the women of the SLA—among them two self-identified lesbians—publicly constructed their commitment to revolutionary terrorism as a form of feminist revolution, and their actions were heavily informed by radical feminist theorizations and tactical warfare.[100] Thus, the SLA's "appropriation" of Hearst both resonated with fears about the stability of the nuclear family that are a permanent feature of modernity and foregrounded the threat to the family implicit in (radical) feminism.

If Hearst's abduction was interpreted as a feminist attack, then, even more so, was the heiress' transformation into "Tania." Just two days after "Tania's" debut performance in the Hibernia National Bank robbery, in the same stunning communiqué that denounced her family and declared her allegiance to the SLA, "Tania" also announced, in coded terms, her feminist awakening. Insisting that speculation that she had been brainwashed was "ridiculous to the point of being beyond belief," she lashed out at the men associated with her former identity, in particular, her ex-fiancée, Steven Weed, saying "I don't care if I never see him again. During the last few months, Steven has shown himself to be a sexist [tape garbled] pig."[101]

"Tania" publicly proclaimed (radical) feminist solidarity until she underwent pretrial psychological testing.[102] As such, to the outside world, "Tania" sounded more and more like the product of an intensive experience of feminist CR.[103] In light of her repeated claims to have become a "revolutionary feminist," speculation about Hearst's brainwashing was revived and assumed new dimensions. Hearst's problem, it seemed, was that she had succumbed to a process of *feminist* brainwashing. Hearst's was thus a dual betrayal—she had defected to a terrorist group but, worse, to a *feminist* terrorist group. Similarly, not only did the SLA represent the terrorist family—the return of the repressed primal horde—but perhaps more potently, *a terrorist family in the control of feminist women.*

With this understanding, we can see why the state was so keen to exact retribution and to "make an example" of "Tania" for the rest of civil society. If the SLA had used "Patty" as "an example and a symbolic warning . . . to everyone"[104] about the vulnerability of social order in the face of the (feminist) terrorist challenge, then the legal apparatus of the state used "Tania" as a counter-assault. She was an admonition to the masses of "unruly," antiestablishment, young, feminist women that feminist "brainwashings" would not be tolerated and that feminists would be held accountable for their actions. In this sense, Hearst's imprisonment can be understood as a recuperation of the feminist threat to dominant order.

However, there is a further dimension to the state's decision to reject Hearst's brainwashing defense. It can also be seen as a response to the feminist politicization of the idea of brainwashing in the 1970s.

Tabula Rasa: The Discursive Uses of Brainwashing

The term "brainwashing" did not gain popular currency until after the Korean War. However, the *idea* of brainwashing existed, in an embryonic form, well before 1950 when the first official reports of the Chinese communists' brainwashing of US prisoners of war (POWs) in Korea began to filter back to the US public through the mass media. Historically, the origins of the discourse of brainwashing in the English-speaking world may be traced to the late 1930s and the US preoccupation with totalitarianism. The Western world first began to contemplate the methods used by totalitarian states to cultivate mass support for their ideological agendas in reaction to Stalin's Great Purges of the 1930s, which were renowned for the spectacular nature of the confessions they elicited, suggesting that the Soviets had invented powerful psychological techniques of persuasion.[105] While the terroristic methods employed on behalf of the Soviet state against these so-called dissidents played a large part in achieving their confessions, the Great Purges represented a far more threatening prospect for the West; namely, the totalitarian state's drive to gain complete *psychological* control of its citizens through the institutionalization of terror. As Hannah Arendt wrote in 1951, "totalitarianism is never content to rule by external means . . . totalitarianism has discovered a means of dominating and *terrorizing human beings from within*."[106] Although technically, within Lefebvre's schema, totalitarian states are "over-repressive" societies, this idea of brainwashing resonates with the ways Lefebvre's "terrorist society"—a society in which "compulsion and the illusion of freedom converge"[107]—achieves hegemony via individuals' internalization of terror. Indeed, the *institutionalization of terror* to achieve the psychological obedience of the masses was understood to be one of the most terrifying aspects of totalitarianism.

Fueled by the sense of an increasingly divided world that characterized the early postwar period and the onset of the Cold War, this Western concern about totalitarianism quickly escalated into widespread fear about the potential for totalitarian states to use psychological coercion to achieve world domination. In the late 1940s and early 1950s, this new emphasis on psychological control, or "totalism,"[108] derived increasingly from the West's understanding of the processes of political indoctrination that established support for the communist revolution in China in the 1940s. In the Chinese doctrine, political dissent was constructed not as a crime that required punishing, but as a psychological malady that must be dealt with therapeutically. In its emphasis on the therapeutic responsibilities of the state, this marked Chinese totalitarianism as uniquely modern. In an oft-quoted speech, Mao Tse Tung declared:

> If a man has appendicitis, the doctor performs an operation and the man is saved. If a person who commits an error, no matter how great . . . is genuinely and honestly willing to be cured . . . we will welcome him so that his disease may be cured and he can become a good comrade.[109]

Control of the citizenry thus depended upon "curing" dissenting individuals to accept their place in the communist society and then reintegrating them in productive roles.

By the late 1940s, then, Western understandings of the nature of the totalitarian threat had shifted from emphasizing the centrality of repressive institutional apparatuses characteristic of Soviet totalitarianism, to emphasizing the kind of therapeutic approach employed by Mao Tse Tung. Within North American popular culture, fear of totalitarianism's potential to achieve total control of the human individual entered a range of popular fictional texts, permeating, for example, the dystopian vision of George Orwell's 1949 novel, *Nineteen Eighty-Four*.[110] It is in this context that North America entered the Korean War and that the discourse of brainwashing emerged.

The coining of the term brainwashing is most commonly attributed to Edward Hunter in 1951[111] and was used to describe the practices used by the Chinese to convert US military personnel to the communist cause during the Korean War. The experience of the Korean War shaped the discourse of brainwashing in two ways, which would impact profoundly on the reception of Hearst's brainwashing defense.

First, in the 1970s, most US citizens gleaned their understandings of brainwashing through "watching television, the average American's principal source of news and drama,"[112] but also through the print media, radio, and film. As Robert Jay Lifton states, "the Western world . . . heard mostly about 'thought reform' [as brainwashing is otherwise known] as applied in a military setting."[113] Approximately 10,000 Americans were taken prisoner by the Chinese in Korea, and as all were male this produced brainwashing as a highly masculinized discursive construct within the popular imagination. Upon repatriation, 192 American men were charged with "serious offences against comrades of the United States," but only 11 were convicted "due to a wave of public sympathy" for, in Congressman William Wampler's words, "mere country boys victimized by a shrewd propaganda technique."[114]

Hearst's defense team adopted an approach that appealed to this public understanding of "brainwashing."[115] Given that the image of brainwashing that circulated in the mainstream media was so thoroughly masculinized, the young, wealthy, *female* heiress' claim to be the victim of an extensive "thought reform" campaign failed to tap into the same public sympathy that had been afforded male POWs captured in Korea.[116] The jury, it seems, were unable to place such a claim within a familiar framework of meaning. Indeed, the prosecution successfully exploited the gendering of the discourse of brainwashing to gain a conviction. For example, "in his closing argument, [the prosecutor] Browning emphasized gender differences by reminding the jury that the SLA was 'overwhelmingly female.' With derision, he added, '*This* was the army.'"[117] Thus, brainwashing was seen as a military, and therefore masculinized, discourse, which "ruled out"[118] Hearst's claim to have been brainwashed by the SLA.

Second, the initial cases of brainwashing in Korea marked the West's first direct contact with totalitarian methods of coercive persuasion, exacerbating the United States' growing fear of totalitarianism as it became obvious that Chinese domestic practice was just as effectively applied to (male) US subjects. Liberal democracy, it was held, was under serious threat *from outside*. In response to this deep sense of vulnerability, the US government deployed the discourse of brainwashing to demonize their communist enemies, emphasizing the violence and the deprivation of individual freedom that brainwashing techniques depended upon to gain their ends. Further, upon the repatriation of these American POWs, the discourse of brainwashing was mobilized to nullify the threat these men posed to dominant order, both explaining how "good American boys" could return home to the United States espousing communist views and operating discursively to reintegrate "stray" and ostensibly male members of the fold back into mainstream society.

Brainwashing, dominant discourse suggested, was the work of the communist enemy. Fundamentally "un-American," it could not take place on US soil. In the rejection of Hearst's brainwashing defense then, we can read the state as seeking to dictate the terms by which the discourse of brainwashing could legitimately operate; parenthesizing counter-discursive uses of the idea of brainwashing and, thus, asserting authorial control of its cultural meanings.

Washing Women's Brains: Feminism and Brainwashing

In an article written at the height of Hearst's trial in 1976, Szasz wrote:

> A person can no more wash another's brain than he can make him bleed with a cutting remark . . . [Brainwashing] stands for one of the most universal human experiences and events, namely for one person influencing another. However, we do not call all types of personal or psychological influences "brainwashing." *We reserve this term for influences of which we disapprove.*[119]

In this article, Szasz argues that "brainwashing" is a concept that operates in the service of establishment order—that, like "terrorism," it is a tool in the contest for power. Szasz, who, in this piece, critiques institutional psychiatry's use of brainwashing, takes issue with the *dominant discourse* of brainwashing. As Richard Terdiman contends, whenever a discourse becomes "dominant," it simultaneously becomes available for redeployment in ways that challenge naturalized modes of thought and practice.[120] By the late 1960s, while "brainwashing" was used within dominant discourse to describe the activities of totalitarian states, it simultaneously began to assume counter-discursive meanings within US popular culture.[121]

While popular myth posited brainwashing as a threat from outside the United States, with the publication of critiques of US consensus culture such as Theodore Roszak's *The Making of a Counter Culture* and Marcuse's *One Dimensional Man*,[122] the idea of brainwashing began to resonate uneasily with the modes of producing consensus *within* dominant culture. Brainwashing, it was seen, shared features with other forms of persuasion characteristic of late capitalist Western culture, such as advertising, education, and psychiatry.[123] The implication was that US liberal democratic consensus culture resembled those totalitarian cultures from which it sought to differentiate and distance itself, employing methods of "mind control" that paralleled the production of consensus, via individuals' internalization of terror, within the "terrorist society."[124]

In the late 1960s and into the 1970s, the idea of brainwashing was picked up by (radical) feminists in the United States and used to describe the conditions that established women's subservience to men. In the *SCUM Manifesto*, Valerie Solanas painted a picture of US culture that chillingly suggested that women's subordination was the result of a culture-wide brainwashing and declared that she was "too impatient to hope and wait for the de-brainwashing of millions of assholes"[125] to accept women as equals. Similarly, when radical feminists protested against the Miss America beauty pageant in August 1968—an event that received extensive mainstream media coverage—they attacked the brainwashing of women, chanting, "We won't let 'em bend our minds no more."[126] (Radical) feminists politicized the discourse of brainwashing, appropriating the terms of dominant discourse to enact a critique of dominant order. They turned a discourse that usually operated to reinscribe the (gendered) power relations underpinning US consensus culture against those very same power relations.

In their linkage of brainwashing with women's oppression, feminists drew comparisons between the techniques of brainwashing and key elements in the production of women as subordinate citizens. According to Lifton, to achieve "thought reform" first requires the isolation of the subject from others in order to facilitate the stripping of the subject's identity. The subject is rendered dependent upon their captors for their every need, reducing them to a state of "infantile dependency." Second, in a period of intense interrogation, the subject is accused of crimes that may or may not be specified and encouraged to make a confession.[127] Once the confession is obtained, the subject is submitted to a rigorous routine of reeducation in which he—remembering that the subject of brainwashing is ostensibly male—must learn to regurgitate the views of his captors.[128] The result of this process is a "symbolic 'death and re-birth.'"[129]

In accordance with this schema, many feminists named isolation within the domestic realm, dependency, and the destruction of women's identities as key features of women's subordination. For example, Solanas wrote:

> Our society is not a community, but merely a collection of isolated family units . . . [T]he male seeks to isolate [his woman] from other men and from what little civilization there is, so he moves her out to the suburbs, a collection of self-absorbed couples and their kids.[130]

Similarly, in 1970, Alice Embree famously argued that "Corporate America" isolated women in the suburbs and bound them in the menial routines of the nuclear family. In an image that conjured the antifeminist nightmare of robot women haunting the supermarket aisles in the 1975 film, *Stepford Wives*,[131] Embree described the destruction of women's identities—their production as objects, not subjects: "Her life must be routinized, her thoughts must be in terms of commodity. She must be the object, not the subject, of her world."[132] And Pat Mainardi drew a comparison between the "reeducation" phase of brainwashing and television commercials targeted at women in domestic roles when she wrote:

> We women have been brainwashed more than even we can imagine. Probably too many years of seeing television women in ecstasy over their shiny waxed floors . . . Men have no such conditioning.[133]

The radical feminist claim about women's brainwashing centered on a concern with "conditioning" or "programming" as the mechanisms by which gender difference, and therefore a system of gender exploitation, is reproduced through time. Women's socialization as gendered subjects, we should note, was also a key concern for the (radical) feminist CR project, which aimed to undo women's conditioning in order to liberate them from the conditions of subordination that were seen to inhere in women's everyday lives. In this sense, (radical) feminist claims about women's brainwashing intersected with other forms of feminist praxis.

Importantly, the (radical) feminist critique of socialization as a form of brainwashing politicized *the family* as a site of (gendered) power. Given that the family is configured as an important, if not the most important, medium of socialization within Western culture, (radical) feminists implicitly attacked the family as the place where nongendered individuals *learn* to be gendered subjects. Thus, feminism's linkage of brainwashing with the process of gendered socialization intersected powerfully with terrorism's challenge to the nuclear family. If terrorism signified as the threat of the return of the primal horde, then (radical) feminism, too, destabilized the nuclear family, problematizing the family as the "natural" site of socialization and, thus, of order in modernity. It attacked at the heart of the institution upon which the exchange of women is premised.

With this understanding of the ways that feminism colonized and politicized the discourse of brainwashing, we can understand not only why the Patty Hearst event was framed so extensively—even paranoiacally—by recourse to the discourse of the family, but also why Hearst's brainwashing defense was destined to fail. If Hearst's defense team ran a case that attempted to draw upon popular understandings of brainwashing, then, for both the jury in the courtroom and the public "jury" that sat in judgment on the case via the mass media, Hearst's defense strategy was crosscut with ambiguities. While brainwashing provided a "logical" explanation for Hearst's behavior while a member of the SLA, the discursive codings of brainwashing prohibited it from operating as a reasonable defense of a young woman from a well-to-do family whose "coercive persuasion" was carried out on US soil. Hearst's public declarations of feminist solidarity gave the appearance that, if she had been brainwashed, she had become the puppet of radical feminists—an impression that, given dominant cultural hostility toward feminism in the climate of 1970s antifeminist backlash, did little to win Hearst public sympathy or support.

Beyond this, however, (radical) feminist counter-discursive reworkings of the idea of brainwashing must certainly have provided a reference point for interpretations of the Patty Hearst event. As I have suggested, (radical) feminists problematized the distinction between brainwashing—a process carried out by US enemies—and the socialization of women as gendered subjects within, and in relation to, the nuclear family. This is precisely the same challenge that the discursive operation of the "Patty"/"Tania" double personality posed for her audiences. Morgan argues that Hearst had survived many "brainwashings," describing her as "a human being who has been shaped and reshaped—by the Hearsts, the SLA, the FBI, lawyers, psychiatrists, chaplains, media interviewers, and the US prison system itself," adding that "after that many 'brainwashings,' one's brain might well feel a bit faded or shrunk."[134] This point was not lost on Hearst. In late 1978, in an interview with Morgan at the Federal Correctional Institute at Pleasanton, California, where she was serving her sentence, Hearst said:

> What happened to me happens to women all the time. I've been kidnapped, held prisoner, threatened, beaten, humiliated, raped, battered. I've been lied to and lied about and disbelieved. The only difference between what happened to me and what happens to other women is that mine was an extreme case.[135]

In this statement, Hearst established her solidarity with other women via the assertion of a commonality of experience within the gendered everyday.

Throughout the duration of the case—from abduction to incarceration—Hearst had two primary, and competing, exchange values that were played off against one another and, remarkably, continue to structure the ways the Patty Hearst event is mythologized today. On the one hand, "Patty" was the soon-to-be-married daughter of one of the wealthiest families in the United States, who studied art history and enjoyed going on shopping sprees. "Patty" was shadowed, on the other hand, by the malign rifle-wielding guerrilla, "Tania," who denounced her family, declared her dedication to the (feminist) revolution and went on a shooting spree. What all contemporary readings of the event ultimately failed to acknowledge was that "Patty" and "Tania" were *strategic* performances of gender, roles demanded of her by a culture that thinks in binary terms. As Isenberg notes, the two images, "bride-to-be" and "guerrilla," "were dangerously similar because *both required socialization, indoctrination and brainwashing.*"[136]

Given this, we can read the state's handing down of a prison sentence in order to "make an example" of Hearst as an attempt to reassert the boundaries between brainwashing and socialization as a legitimate function of Western liberal democratic culture. That is, the state's response to Hearst's brainwashing defense represents an effort to "rule out" feminist readings of socialization as the goal-oriented manipulation of individual subjects and to reclaim and renaturalize the family as the site of social order. Remembering that the SLA was positioned within the representational order of North American dominant culture as a *feminist* terrorist organization, the state's punishment of Hearst was as much about containing the threat posed by (radical) feminism in the context of the mid-1970s antifeminist backlash as it was about containing the threat of terrorism. This act of recuperation addressed the feminist (terrorist) threat posed to the family by the SLA's abduction and conversion of Hearst.

Postscript

The era encompassing both the rise of radical feminism and the recognition of home-grown "urban terrorism" as potent political threats in the United States is bookended by the "terrorist careers" of the two women discussed in this book: Valerie Solanas and Patricia ("Patty"/"Tania") Hearst.

The Patty Hearst event—in which a daughter of the dominant class became a daughter of the revolution—was framed within dominant discourse as an assault on US social and cultural order emanating from, and resonating with, the crisis *within* the nuclear family itself. It constituted a site where competing definitions of the family and anxieties about the failure of the socialization of the younger generation played out. As I have argued, both terrorism and (radical) feminism can be understood as political practices grounded in an apocalyptic temporality—challenging dominant order on the terrain of linear and routine time and subverting the order of the everyday. In this context, dominant culture's obsessive need to construct the Patty Hearst event as an attack on the family, along with the state's rejection of Hearst's brainwashing defense, can be read as attempts to reassert the order of modern time and negate the apocalyptic challenge of both terrorism and (radical) feminism. At a time when "pseudo-families" seemed as if they were growing in number and might eventually outweigh the morally sanctioned bourgeois institution of the nuclear family—when (radical) feminists, alongside organizations like the Symbionese Liberation Army (SLA), the Manson gang,[1] and Jim Jones' family of the People's Temple were actively challenging the validity of the nuclear family—the Patty Hearst event was deployed to do the "cultural work" of reproducing dominant social formations.

The brainwashing defense turns on a claim to insanity as a way of annulling individuals' responsibility for their actions. Under different circumstances, madness has been an important discourse for the state in delegitimizing the actions of terrorist women—nullifying their political valence by drawing on the historical association of women with madness, such as occurred in the dominant cultural construction of Solanas as "the crazy woman who shot Warhol." On one level, then, Hearst's claim to have been brainwashed reinforced dominant order in that her purported madness fell into the category of typical female behavior.

However, when their terrorist engagements are over and the time comes for terrorist women to reinvent themselves as "ordinary" members of mainstream society, the discourse of madness is sometimes deployed as a method of reintegration.[2] In this sense, Hearst's resort to a claim of brainwashing may be understood as a practice of subaltern power: just as she apparently went along with her terrorist comrades as a way of negotiating her survival, Hearst chose the brainwashing defense as a tactic to guarantee her reintegration into mainstream society. However, the second-wave feminist movement's linkage of the discourse of brainwashing with a critique of male power rendered Hearst's defense problematic for the state. At a time when women were actively and aggressively challenging the gendering of dominant order, the state could not afford to legitimize the practices of subaltern power; nor could it allow the delegitimization of the routine interpellation of women as subordinate citizens. For these reasons, the state was compelled to defend its right to rule; it had to draw the line, and make an example of Hearst by punishing her harshly.

The Patty Hearst event unfolded as radical feminism's influence on the second-wave feminist agenda began to decline. Both Alice Echols and Ellen Willis argue that, by the mid-1970s, radical feminism had been superseded by "cultural feminism."[3] While *radical* feminists had celebrated Solanas, the female terrorist, as an inspirational figure that catalyzed women's transformative rage, under the rubric of cultural feminism, she became a problematic figure for "women's liberationists."

Indeed, the rise of cultural feminism is deeply imbricated with the figure of the female terrorist. Although she identified as a radical feminist, Jane Alpert is frequently credited with having written the founding text of cultural feminism, "Mother Right: A New Feminist Theory."[4] In 1969, Alpert had been arrested on charges of "conspiring to bomb federal property" for activities carried out while she was a member of the Jackson–Melville Unit[5]—a small underground terrorist organization responsible for a spate of bombings against "military and war related corporate buildings"[6] in Manhattan, which had informal ties to the Weather Underground. Alpert wrote "Mother Right" after jumping bail in 1970 and going underground, publishing it with the help of her close friend, prominent radical feminist, Robin Morgan.

"Mother Right" begins with an open letter to Alpert's "Sisters in the Weather Underground," situating her conversion to the radical feminist cause and her development of a "new feminist theory" as responses to both her encounter with "the sexual oppression of the left"[7] before and after she went underground and her process of coming to terms with her role in the "political violence" of the late 1960s. While falling short of a full renunciation, Alpert explains her participation in a "group of radical bombers" as the effect of "pressure . . . of the kind peculiar and common to male-female relationships," namely the threat that her lover Sam Melville would leave her if she "backed out."[8] In doing so, Alpert constructs her engagement with terrorism as the result of the seductions of what Morgan would later label the "Demon Lover."[9] This same logic dominated feminist sense making of Patricia Hearst's conversion to SLA terrorist. Rather, then, than an icon of feminist agency— such as Solanas had represented for hard-line radical feminists in 1968—the female terrorist, by the mid-1970s, signified in the North American feminist imagination as a victim of "male violence."[10] This shift in the feminist construction of the female terrorist can be read as symptomatic of the problematic positioning of the female terrorist in relation to second-wave feminism in the mid-1970s.

In one sense, Alpert's vehement denunciation of the male left and its violent (patriarchal) politics can be read as an attempt to recuperate her "terrorist" actions by embracing feminism. However, beyond any potential personal motivations pertaining to her "reintegration," Alpert's text speaks to the perceived need on the part of feminists to distance "feminism" from the figure of the female terrorist, at the levels both of practice and of symbolic imaginings. In the final part of the essay, Alpert outlines her feminist "political/religious vision" for a matriarchal social order that will "affirm . . . the power of female consciousness, of the Mother."[11] This matriarchy, which, for Alpert, "means nothing less than the end of oppression," will foreground the "maternal" qualities of "empathy, intuitiveness, adaptability, awareness of growth as a process rather than goal-ended, inventiveness, protective feelings towards others, and a capacity to respond emotionally as well as rationally."[12] The antithesis of the apocalyptic calls for violent retribution demanded by radical feminists in the late 1960s, cultural feminism's emphasis on peaceful transformation, based on the revaluation of "feminine" qualities, can be read as a response to feminism's perceived need to undo the cultural cross-wiring of (radical) feminism with (female) terrorism, at the historical moment in which the New Right launched its vitriolic campaign against second-wave feminism's accumulating institutional and cultural achievements. While Alpert's text outlines a blueprint for the new feminist society, it simultaneously banishes the late 1960s radical feminist (metaphorical) call to arms from the horizon. In the same way that the modern state supervenes terror in social contract theory, the cultural feminist matriarchy supervenes the apocalyptic politics of radical feminism—whose most extreme expression is the female terrorist—prioritizing an evolutionary model of social change and binding the future of feminism in the ontology of the modern state.

Despite the changing face of feminism in the mid-1970s, it was radical feminism, in particular, that the New Right seized upon in its inflated characterizations of the key threat to dominant culture arising from women's liberation. I have argued that radical feminism, as both an activist methodology and a revolutionary theory, operated in the same terms as the contemporary urban terrorism. Like terrorism, radical feminists' "guerrilla theater" deployed spectacle to politicize the terror that underpins the everyday in modernity. Importantly, radical feminism resonated as a form of terrorism because it operated according to an apocalyptic temporality that refuses the (patriarchal) routine of the everyday, and in so doing, conjures the end of (gendered) modernity—the implosion of modern (gendered) order. Emerging in the late 1960s as the movement imploded and the (white) women's liberation movement gained momentum, Solanas' *SCUM Manifesto*, in particular, epitomized the radical feminist *Zeitgeist*. Solanas took the (white) radical feminist threat to its logical extreme. For feminism's adversaries, SCUM marked the reversal of (patriarchal) order, which in practice is based on the containment of women within the linear and routine time of the quotidian. Further, in her call for sexocide, Solanas pushed the representational logic of (gendered) modernity to its limits. Solanas' combination of radical feminism and a radicalized terrorism had a catalyzing effect on the (white) radical feminist movement. Tellingly, however, Solanas' feminist politics and her violent praxis were never understood, within dominant culture, as anything but "madness."

Radical feminism's advocation of violent modes of political praxis has been an uncomfortable topic for historians of second-wave feminism. Indeed, feminism's historical relationship to violence is often overlooked—disavowed, even—by Western world feminists. And yet, popular culture's trope of the violent, man-hating, "crazy" feminist—the image that is conjured in relation to Solanas' memory—is all too often deployed by feminism's adversaries to discredit the very legitimate claims of all manner of feminisms, locking us into the binary opposition between the "Good" and the "Evil" Woman.

The female terrorist—the dissembling figure of hyperfemininity and hyperterrorism—reminds us that such binaries constitute the space of necessary contestation, that Western modernity's structures of thinking are everywhere permeated by symbolic violences, and that these must be a key focus for feminist interventions. To be clear: this is not to advocate material violence. Rather, it is to advocate that feminisms everywhere adopt a "terrorist mentality" directed at continually undoing the easy assumptions that underpin Western modernity's constructions of gender. In this light, it is imperative that feminisms of all kinds confront their relationships to, and implication in, forms of violence both material and symbolic. But to pursue this idea in detail requires, as Robin Morgan might say, "another whole book."[13]

Notes

Introduction

1. Cooper (1979, 152–53).
2. In the vast literature that emerged in response to September 11, 2001, the gendering of both terrorist practice and terrorist subjectivity has gone largely ignored, reflecting a more generalized neglect of the study of the gendering of terrorism. The small number of feminist and queer analyses of terrorism include, for example, Hawthorne and Winter, eds. (2002); Morgan (2001); and Puar (2007).
3. Cooper (1979, 152–53).
4. *I Shot Andy Warhol*, directed by Mary Harron (Los Angeles: Orion Pictures/Samuel Goldwyn Company, 1996), 35mm film.
5. Soliah's sentence was passed down amid the human rights scandal concerning the extraterritorial detention center at Guantanamo Bay.
6. *Guerrilla: The Taking of Patty Hearst*, directed by Robert Stone (New York: Magnolia Pictures/New Video Group, 2003) 35mm film; *The Weather Underground*, directed by Sam Green and Bill Siegel (Sausalito, CA: Roco Films, 2002), 35mm film. *Guerrilla* represents Patricia Hearst's terrorist metamorphosis, which is discussed in detail later in this book.
7. Berendse and Cornils (2008, 7).
8. Berendse and Cornils (2008, 14).
9. I have placed "radically unfamiliar" in quotation marks here because, although the events of September 11 were most often encoded in dominant cultural representations as "extra-ordinary" and "unfamiliar," part of terrorism's ability to generate affect lies in its invocation of the "familiar" Western imagining of the end of society (see Chapter Four).
10. For example, Cronin and Ludes, eds. (2004) collate the views of "some of the world's finest experts, people who have made the study of this rising menace their life's work" ("Attacking Terrorism," *Georgetown University Press* online, accessed 28 March 2014, http://press.georgetown.edu/book/georgetown/attacking-terrorism); and Rapoport, ed. (2005), is a four-volume set that reprints historical literature on terrorism. For further examples, see also: Jenkins (2003); Hoffman (2006); Laqueur (2001, 2004a, and 2004b); Cooper and Redlinger (2006); Rapoport, ed. (2001); Rapoport and Weinberg, eds. (2001); Wilkinson (2006); and Nye et al. (2003).
11. Zwerman (1992, 140).

12. Herman and O'Sullivan (1989).
13. In many places in his work, Bauman theorizes modernity as a project of constructing order. See, for example, Bauman (2001c).

1 Conceptualizing Terrorism

1. Johnson (1978, 268).
2. Horowitz (1983, 38–39). Horowitz here refers to "external guerrilla power": acts of terrorism "from below" that are "external" and therefore threatening to the institutions of the state.
3. Quainton (1983, 53).
4. Laqueur (1977); Freedman and Alexander, eds. (1983); Crenshaw, ed. (1983b).
5. See, for example, Barnhurst (1991); Jenkins (2003); and Crenshaw (1983a, 1–37).
6. Jenkins (2003, 18).
7. Jenkins (2003, 18).
8. Jenkins (2003, 18).
9. Jenkins (2003, 18).
10. Jenkins (2003, 17).
11. Laqueur (1978, 262).
12. Laqueur (1978, 262).
13. Hage (2003, 126).
14. Jenkins (2003, 18).
15. Jenkins (2003, 18).
16. Borradori (2003c, xiii).
17. This approach is informed by Jacques Derrida's observation that "the most powerful and destructive appropriation of terrorism is precisely its use as a self-evident concept by all the parties involved" (Borradori, 2003b, 152). As Borradori suggests, "the deconstruction of the notion of terrorism is the only politically responsible course of action because the public use of it, as if it were a self-evident notion, perversely helps the terrorist cause" (Borradori, 2003c, xiii).
18. Freedman (1983, 3) (my emphasis). See also Tuman (2003, 5) and Schmid and de Graaf (1982, 15).
19. See, for example, Tuman (2003); Alexander and Picard, eds. (1991); Nacos (1994); Combs (2003); and Alali and Eke, eds. (1991).
20. Schmid and de Graaf (1982, 9).
21. Schmid and de Graaf (1982, 14).
22. Schmid and de Graaf (1982, 15).
23. Schmid and de Graaf (1982, 15).
24. See, for example, McQuail (2000, 52–53), for a description of this model as the "transmission model"; and Schirato and Yell (1996, 1–21), for a discussion of this model as the "process model."
25. This model of communication has been a useful ally of the media effects tradition, which has historically sought to draw conclusions about audience responses to messages based on content analyses of media texts.

26. McQuail (1982, ii).
27. See, for example, Ang (1991) and Seiter (1999).
28. Schmid and de Graaf (1982, 15).
29. While Schmid and de Graaf conceptualize the audience as the "public" in the quotation above, I am referring to both terrorism's popular and its "official" audiences.
30. Gupta (2002, 14–15).
31. Gupta (2002, 15) (my emphasis).
32. Baudrillard (2002, 30). See also Debord (1994).
33. Baudrillard (2002, 6).
34. Cooper (1979, 150).
35. Derrida in Borradori (2003a, 107).
36. Borradori (2003b, 139).
37. Derrida in Borradori (2003a, 91).
38. All forms of "violence" and "criminality" can be understood as forms of communication. See, for example, Bardsley (1987). However, in the case of terrorism, the communicative dimension is explicitly foregrounded.
39. Baudrillard (2002, 5).
40. Baudrillard (2002, 5).
41. Borradori (2003b, 148).
42. Terdiman (1985, 57).
43. Foucault (1977a, 27). See also Hall (1997).
44. O'Sullivan et al. (1994, 93).
45. Hall (1997, 44).
46. Foucault (1977b, 200).
47. Said (1986, 153).
48. Throughout this book, when I refer to "dominant discourse," I draw upon Terdiman's definition.
49. Terdiman (1985, 93).
50. Terdiman (1985, 92–93).
51. Hall (1997, 50).
52. Terdiman (1985, 78).
53. Terdiman (1985, 87).
54. For example, Laqueur, perhaps the preeminent scholar on terrorism, whose 1977 text, *Terrorism*, has been a touchstone for many analyses of terrorism, has recently published *The New Terrorism* (Laqueur, 1999), *History of Terrorism* (Laqueur, 2001), *No End to War* (Laqueur, 2004a), and *Voices of Terror* (Laqueur, 2004b). See also Jenkins (2003) and Hoffman (2006).
55. Here I distinguish between the "traditional political economy" approach and the "critical political economy" approach. For an elaboration of the differences, see Golding and Murdock (1991).
56. Herman and O'Sullivan (1989, 55).
57. Herman and O'Sullivan (1989, 55).
58. Zwerman (1992, 136).

59. Zwerman (1992, 136).
60. Herman and O'Sullivan (1989, 8).
61. Zwerman (1992, 136).
62. Zwerman (1992, 134).
63. Jenkins (2003, 139).
64. Jenkins (2003, 150).
65. Jenkins (2003, 18).
66. MacDonald (1991, 2).
67. Townshend (2002, 2).
68. Hage (2003, 126).
69. That is, disproportionate given that terrorism has historically directly affected very small numbers of victims. As Charles Townshend notes, "something about terrorism makes its threat inflate, genie-like, way beyond its actual physical scale . . . [However] the physical threat posed by terrorism [is] dwarfed by other more quotidian dangers" (2002, 2). See also Laqueur (1978, 5).
70. Jenkins (2003, 27).
71. Laqueur (1977, 79).
72. Cruise O'Brien (1983, 91).
73. Jenkins (2003, 25) (my emphasis).
74. Hage (2003, 127).
75. Giddens (1985, 121).
76. Herman and O'Sullivan (1989, 44) (my emphasis).
77. Dror (1983, 68) (my emphasis).
78. Horowitz (1983, 49).
79. Herman and O'Sullivan (1989, 38).
80. Laqueur (1977, 7).
81. This idea echoes Rubenstein's claim that terrorism results from "a widening gap between a group's 'value expectations' and the political system's 'value capabilities.'" (1989, 308–09).
82. Laqueur (1977, 11) (my emphasis).
83. See also Herman and O'Sullivan (1989). When this literature refers to "democracy," it does not typically distinguish between the different forms of democracy that exist globally.
84. Herman and O'Sullivan (1989, 42).
85. Herman and O'Sullivan (1989, 39).
86. Even where scholars acknowledge that terrorism is not necessarily the sole preserve of nonstate actors, it is nonetheless conceptualized in relation to the political institution of the state. See, for example, Bassiouni (1983, 178).
87. Jenkins (2003, 28).
88. Jenkins (2003, 28).
89. Jenkins (2003, 28).
90. Crenshaw (1983a, 1–37).
91. However, it needs to be acknowledged that not all states are understood as beyond terrorism. Indeed, Western terrorism studies has often emphasized the terroristic

tendencies of communist and fascist nation-states. However, democratic states are usually positioned as the expression of popular political will, and hence outside the potential to be labeled "terrorist."
92. Terdiman (1985, 63) (my emphasis).
93. Terdiman (1985, 78).
94. Terdiman (1985, 58).
95. Terdiman (1985, 79).

2 Constructing the Terrorist: The Threat from Within

1. Counterterrorism Threat Assessment and Warning Unit (1999, 4–5).
2. See, for example, MacDonald (1991); Zwerman (1992); and Greenhalgh (1990).
3. Elshtain (1987, 169).
4. Wilkinson (1978, 241–42).
5. As Hall has noted, "discourse itself produces 'subjects'—figures who personify the particular forms of knowledge which the discourse produces" (1997, 56).
6. For this definition, see Jenkins (2003, 28).
7. Laqueur (1977).
8. Hage (2003, 126).
9. Wilkinson (1978, 241).
10. Johnson (1978, 274).
11. Freedman (1983, 3) (my emphasis).
12. Laqueur (1978, 256–57).
13. Laqueur (1978, 257).
14. Laqueur (1977, 125).
15. Zwerman (1992, 134).
16. Zwerman (1992, 134).
17. Jenkins (2003, 151) (my emphasis).
18. Hozic (1990, 73).
19. Hozic (1990, 73).
20. Hozic (1990, 73).
21. Hozic (1990, 78). The kidnapping of Aldo Moro by the Italian Brigate Rosse in 1978 is one example of the ways this plays out. See Wagner-Pacifici (1986).
22. Rubenstein (1989, 310).
23. Hocking (1988, 94).
24. Laqueur (1977, 5).
25. Rubenstein (1989, 310) (my emphasis).
26. Counterterrorism Threat Assessment and Warning Unit (1999, 25).
27. Payne (2005).
28. Counterterrorism Threat Assessment and Warning Unit (1999, 35). Note that these figures are approximate because, according to the same report, "the FBI did not begin to formally record annual terrorism figures until the mid-1970s" (ibid., 34).
29. Rubenstein (1989, 307–08).
30. Laqueur (1977, 207).

31. The moral panic around this "new breed of terrorism" articulated with similar concerns about the rise of the "counter-culture" and were primarily concerned with the failure of the US middle classes to adequately socialize the next generation into good bourgeois citizens. Despite 1970s panic claims, it appears in general that "disaffected members of the political establishment are the principal agents of rebellion in the modern world" (Gurr, 1989c, 118).

32. Alongside predominantly white middle class terrorist groups such as the Weather Underground and the Symbionese Liberation Army, at least two other terrorist groups representing so-called minority interests were active in the United States in the late 1960s and early 1970s: the Puerto Rican national liberation group, the FALN, and the black liberation group, the Black Panthers. While these latter groups did not stem from within the dominant class per se, the Weather Underground and the Symbionese Liberation Army both claimed solidarity with their anti-imperial platform. This apparent alignment of interests around the "liberation" of subaltern groups only further exacerbated the threat associated with white middle class terrorism.

33. Laqueur notes that there was a spate of bombings in the United States in the 1890s by anarchist "propaganda by deed groups" that had the support of segments of the population (1977, 11). Further, there had been other left-wing attacks in the early twentieth century, but "terrorism in the US was limited in scope and purpose; there was no intention of overthrowing the government, killing the political leadership or changing the political system" (1977, 15), and by the 1970s, these attacks had all but been erased from popular memory.

34. Zwerman (1992, 134).

35. Gurr (1989b, 205–06).

36. Historically, right-wing terrorism in the United States does not target society as a whole nor the institutional legal, economic, and political apparatus of state power, but seeks to intimidate subaltern groups into complicity with an order that both produces and relies upon their subordination. In this sense, right-wing terror, as Gurr suggests, defends the status quo. By contrast, 1970s left-wing terrorism claimed to advocate for those very same groups that right-wing terror traditionally targets in the United States.

37. These terrorist groups often had a problematic relationship to subalterneity in that their membership was drawn predominantly from the educated middle classes. See Hacker (1983, 26).

38. This was particularly true of the threat posed by terrorist groups with a racial agenda, such as the Black Panthers and the Symbionese Liberation Army.

39. Arguably, this politics of labeling terrorism undergoes a transformation in the post-1970s era. For example, the 1995 right-wing Oklahoma bombings were distinctly labeled as terrorist. And Gurr notes that there were a number of right-wing groups active in the United States in the 1980s; many of which were classified as terrorist by the FBI (Gurr, 1989b, 211). There is no space to elaborate the circumstances of this transformation here; however, this would be a productive avenue for further research.

40. This is further illustrated by the fact that individuals participating in "home-grown" left-wing political bombings, such as those carried out by the Weathermen in the United States in the late 1960s and early 1970s, are routinely described as terrorist incidents, whereas abortion and birth control clinic bombings by right-wing "pro-life" groups historically are not. See Gurr (1989b, 211). In US culture, abortion and birth control have been crucial sites of feminist contestation since the late 1960s and can be read, not as threatening, but reasserting, the dominance of the Judeo-Christian moral imperatives that structure dominant cultural under-standings of gender. They are not constructed as "terrorism" because they are complicit in the reproduction of hegemonic gender relations: they are "terror in defense of the status quo."

41. Freedman (1983, 7).

42. Grosz as cited in Naffine (1997, 8). Grosz writes: "Men have functioned as if they represented masculinity only incidentally or only in moments of passion and sexual encounter, while the rest of the time they are representatives of the human, the generic 'person.'"

43. Laqueur (1977, 121).

44. Jenkins (2003, 151).

45. Greenhalgh (1990, 161) (my emphasis).

46. Greenhalgh (1990, 161).

47. Zwerman (1992, 135).

48. Freedman (1983, 7). Indeed, terrorism studies proponents sometimes describe the terrorist organization as a "pseudo-family" founded on deviant notions of family and domesticity. This constructs the terrorist organization within domi-nant discourse as a unit that undermines and threatens the nuclear family struc-ture and, therefore, social order. I return to this point in Chapter Seven.

49. Greenhalgh (1990, 161).

50. Cooper (1979, 151).

51. While the discourse on female terrorism that I outline here has its origins in the late 1960s and early 1970s, it continues to be reproduced unmodified in many fora in current times. See, for example, the sections dealing with female terrorists of the "Hudson Report" on the sociology and psychology of terrorism commis-sioned by the US Library of Congress and published in 1999 (Hudson, 1999, 45–50).

52. On the gendering of crime in Western culture, see Young (1996).

53. We must acknowledge that all crime is gendered, whether committed by men or by women, and, as do Allen (1989) and Naffine (1997), that the gendering of men's crime remains largely invisible within both criminological analyses and popular cultural representations of crime.

54. Young (1996, 27).

55. Naffine (1997, 2).

56. Zwerman (1992, 136).

57. Cooper (1979, 151).

58. See, for example, Georges-Abeyie (1983, 72–73).

59. See, for example, Cooper (1979, 152).
60. Laqueur (1977, 121, and 207).
61. Cooper (1979, 151) (my emphasis). In the post–September 11, 2001 climate, there is a similar preoccupation with the female suicide bomber. While suicide bombing has long been a tactic of terrorist groups, the female suicide bomber is often constructed as a new phenomenon.
62. Greenhalgh (1990, 161–62).
63. Cooper (1979, 152–53).
64. Creed (1993, 106).
65. Zwerman (1992, 135).
66. Cooper (1979, 151).
67. As cited in MacDonald (1991, 4).
68. Galvin as cited in Zwerman (1992, 139).
69. MacDonald (1991, 4)
70. Zwerman (1992, 134–35) (my emphasis).
71. De Cataldo Neuberger and Valentini (1996, 1).
72. This idea has been fundamental to French feminisms/postmodern feminisms, in particular. See Tong (1989).
73. Irigaray (1985b, 69).
74. Irigaray (1985b, 70).
75. Irigaray (1985b, 72).
76. Young (1996, 27).
77. Young (1996, 29).
78. Pateman (1994, 108–19).
79. De Lauretis (1987, 3).
80. Hart (1994, 8).
81. Here, what I refer to as "excess" parallels what Derrida calls *différánce* or the "supplement." See Derrida (1982).
82. Hart (1994, 8).
83. Irigaray (1985b, 70).
84. Irigaray (1985a, 90).
85. Dollimore (1991, 141). The concept of abjection provides another way of thinking about the fear generated by the "proximate." See Kristeva (1982). I discuss abjection further in Chapter Six.
86. See MacDonald (1991).
87. Georges-Abeyie (1983, 82).
88. Georges-Abeyie (1983, 82). I discuss this claim further in Chapter Three.
89. Robin Morgan's feminist analysis also makes this argument, positing that the female terrorist is seduced by the "demon lover" into participating in male-dominated violence. See Morgan (2001).
90. Zwerman (1992, 138). The study referred to here is Weinberg and Eubank (1987).
91. MacDonald (1991, 9).

92. MacDonald (1991, 9).
93. See, for example, Georges-Abeyie (1983, 77), and my discussion in Chapter Three.
94. See, for example, MacDonald (1991, 8). These claims were brought to bear upon Patricia Hearst's decision to join the Symbionese Liberation Army, which I discuss in detail in Chapter Seven.
95. See, for example, Lloyd (1993), Pateman (1988), and Chesler (1989).
96. MacDonald (1991, 8).
97. Irigaray (1985b, 84).
98. Irigaray (1985b, 76).
99. Hart (1994, 9).
100. Irigaray (1985b, 175–76).
101. For a detailed explication of the nineteenth-century alignment of Man with Reason and Woman with sexuality and the body, see Dijkstra (1986).
102. In other words, Woman, for the nineteenth-century modern white male, destined but struggling for spiritual enlightenment, is the abject. See Kristeva (1982).
103. Hall (1994, 395). Hall discusses the ways that colonialism continues to structure the representational economy of (post)colonial cultures. However, we can extrapolate from Hall's argument a more general argument about the ways that historical formations affect the modes of representation within contemporary culture.
104. J. K. Zawodny as cited in Morgan (2001, 192).
105. Hart (1994, 43).
106. Young (1996, 27).
107. Young (1996, 28). What criminology knows about femininity is that it is deviant. As Young states, femininity "is known in that it is continually measured, recorded, examined and inspected for evidence of its necessary deviance, its waywardness" (Young, 1996, 27). However, the nature of femininity's deviance is ultimately obscured, it eludes the "truth"-seeking criminologist:
Women have been represented as analytic opacity: their nature is not open to be read by the criminologist, who is thus unable to know them. Women have also been represented as hysterical, thus rendering their real natures hidden to themselves as well as to the analysing criminologist who is forced to interpret behaviours as symptoms and symptoms as traits. Finally, women have been conceptualised as withholding their natures from analysis, exercising an innate ability to dissemble and dissimulate (making their nature one of deception). Woman is thus simultaneously impenetrable enigma, displacement and dissimulation (Young 1996, 27–28).
To illustrate her argument, Young turns to Lombroso's *The Female Offender* (Lombroso and Ferrero, 1895).
108. Lombroso and Ferrero (1895). Lombroso and Ferrero's work marks the inception of the criminological preoccupation with the female criminal. Deploying physiognomical and phrenological methods, Lombroso set out to establish the

identifying physical features of the female criminal. However, despite the excruciating detail of his investigation, he failed to determine a pattern that would enable the identification and prediction of female criminality, confessing, "these figures do not amount to much" (Lombroso and Ferrero 1895, 74). Indeed, in Lombroso's final analysis, female criminals could not be physically distinguished from law-abiding women. Thus, for Lombroso, who began his project with the intention of unveiling its secrets using the tools of science, female criminality, and by extension femininity, remained obscure.

109. In this sense, terrorism studies treatments of the female terrorist parallel Lombroso's nineteenth-century analysis of the female criminal. See footnote 108 of this chapter.

110. Zwerman (1992, 148).

111. Zwerman (1992, 148).

112. Zwerman (1992, 136).

113. MacDonald (1991, 3).

114. See, for example, Georges-Abeyie (1983, 82), on the former, and Pearlstein (1991), on the latter.

115. MacDonald (1991, 3).

116. MacDonald writes: "The vast majority of the [terrorist women I interviewed] seemed to be *extremely ordinary*. They were married, or had boyfriends, or were gay; they loved their children; they were shy or gregarious; and on the whole welcoming. *In all they bore a remarkable similarity to the rest of the female species*" (MacDonald 1991, 10–11) (my emphasis).

117. Also known as the Rote Armee Fraktion (Red Army Faction).

118. Finn (2002). Peter Finn, 'Germans Studied Brains of Radical Group's Leaders', *Washington Post* online, 19 Nov. 2002, p.15. For a critical analysis of this incident, see Third (2010).

119. Finn (2002, 15).

120. Indeed, in Meinhof's case, scientists "declined to release the full report on the brain" (Finn 2002, 15), contributing to the secretion of the female terrorist.

121. This anxiety has historically characterized treatments of the generic female criminal. As Ann Jones has argued, Lombroso was "haunted by the fear that an apparently good woman might, at any unexpected moment, turn out to be bad" (Jones 1980, 6). Similarly, Young has suggested that "Lombroso's manifestations of Woman are liminal figures that mark out borders between typologies. Much of the anxiety that drives *The Female Offender* derives from the uncertainty of predicting which individual woman might fall into which category" (Young 1996, 30).

122. Zwerman (1992, 141).

123. Zwerman (1992, 141). I discuss this idea further in Chapter Three.

124. Zwerman writes: "Significantly, the elasticity of this definition has the greatest impact on the women . . . Charged with 'sedition', 'conspiracy', and 'criminal racketeering' . . . regardless of their actual level of participation in the actions, previous criminal record, or demonstrated behavior within the courts and prisons, [they] are subject to an array of exceptional, erratic, and experimental procedures within the criminal justice system, where no measure of security is deemed too harsh or inappropriate" (1992, 141).

125. Turner as cited in McClintock (1995, 24).
126. MacDonald (1991, 10), referring to Russell and Miller (1977).
127. Taylor (1988, 132).
128. Zwerman (1992, 155).
129. I discuss the idea of the everyday as a site of transgression and resistance in close detail in Chapter Four.
130. As Hart writes, "The 'violent' woman is not an exceptional figure. Rather, she is a handy construct that serves white patriarchal heterosexuality. She is essential to this discourse and functions most usefully as a specialized and hence containable category" (1994, 17).
131. Žižek cited in Hart (1994, 9).

3 Feminist Terrorists and Terrorist Feminists: The Crosswiring of Feminism with Terrorism

1. Radical feminist Carol Hanisch as cited in Evans (1979, 207).
2. In this chapter, the "religious right" and the "New Right" refer to the Christian Religious Right in the United States, which Durham configures as an expression of mainstream conservatism, distinct from the "far right" (Durham, 2003, 97).
3. Harris (2001). John F. Harris, "God Gave US 'What We Deserve,' Falwell Says," *Washington Post*, September 12, 2001 (my emphasis). This news article was first drawn to my attention by Carole Ferrier.
4. I use the term "subaltern" here to indicate the ways that North American second-wave feminism has, since the late 1960s, typically claimed to operate on behalf of women who, within feminist discourse, are positioned outside the formal power structures of dominant culture. However, I acknowledge that the term "subaltern" is not unproblematic here, in that the movement's key protagonists were white, middle-class women, and thus technically, members of the dominant class, even as they claimed to speak on behalf of a broader, subaltern group.
5. "Feminism Meets Terrorism," Phyllis Schlafly, *Eagle Forum* online, accessed 28 July 2003, http://www.eagleforum.org/column/2002/jan02/02-01-s23.html. All further quotations in this paragraph are drawn from this newsletter (all emphases are mine). In this newsletter, Schlafly triumphantly declares that the death toll of firefighters—men 343, women 0—is a nail in the coffin for the feminist agenda of affirmative action.
6. Reverend Pat Robertson as cited in "Positive Atheism's Big Scary List of Pat Robertson Quotations," accessed 28 July 2003, http://www.positiveatheism.org/hist/quotes/revpat.html.
7. This concern about women's involvement in terrorism unfolded against the backdrop of a broader criminological concern with what was perceived as a significant rise in women's perpetration of, and prosecution for, "violent crimes." Whether or not prosecutions of women committing violent and/or terrorist crimes increased in the 1970s is debatable. See Simon and Sharma (1979, 392).
8. Throughout this section, I refer to the New Left. While the term might suggest a single and coherent political movement, it in fact comprised a wide range of groups

with diverse, and sometimes conflicting, political aims and objectives. Most of these groups were issue- and/or identity-based groups. I discuss the composition of the New Left, also known as the Movement, in closer detail in Chapter Six.

9. Zwerman (1992, 140).
10. In the Western world, this is often the case in the aftermath of a "wave" of terrorism. The introduction of special legislation to "combat" the problem of terrorism often impinges on the democratic rights of citizens to organize by creating a situation in which organizations that advocate civil protest and other such means of "peaceful" resistance potentially fall within the ambit of government definitions of "terrorism." See Hocking (2003).
11. Zwerman (1992, 140).
12. Methvyn as cited in Zwerman (1992, 140).
13. Laqueur (1977, 147) (my emphasis).
14. Laqueur (1977, 205). For Laqueur, "American terrorism"—by which he means the specific form of urban terrorism of groups such as the Black Panthers and the Weathermen in the United States in the late 1960s and early 1970s—was indebted to the New Left not just in terms of its ideological orientation, but also in terms of its organizational structure (Laqueur, 1977, 208). Laqueur notes that the decline of the New Left led to the simultaneous rise of urban terrorism in a number of nations, including Japan, Germany, Italy, and England (Laqueur, 1977, 206).
15. Rubenstein (1989, 308–09).
16. Hacker (1983, 25).
17. "The Symbionese Liberation Army: Terrorism and the Left" (1974, 24).
18. As I elaborate further in Chapter Five, the first spate of systematic terror attacks in the United States did not occur alongside the *rise* or the *consolidation* of the New Left but as the energies of the organized left began to fragment and the always already tenuous cohesion of the Movement gave way to factional disputes and general despair.
19. This linkage of the New Left and terrorism articulated with North American Cold War fears about Soviet-inspired Communism. See Nadel (1995).
20. Cooper (1979, 151) (my emphasis).
21. Feminists have sometimes articulated similar ideas about the connections between feminism and female terrorism. While feminist readings do not go as far to suggest that feminism might have been the direct cause of female terrorism, the idea that women's participation in terrorism is linked to the spirit of female emancipation is a subtext of a number of feminist analyses. See, for example, Mullaney (1983, 55). Feminist commentaries express an ambivalence toward the figure of the female terrorist. She has sometimes been celebrated by feminists. For example, Valerie Solanas was considered an inspiration by many radical feminists in the late 1960s (see Chapter Five). At other points in history, feminists have been reluctant to validate the female terrorist's violent methods and have been keen to assert female terrorists as victims (as opposed to perpetrators) of patriarchal forms of violence (see Morgan, 1979).

22. MacDonald (1991, 5) (my emphasis).

23. Georges-Abeyie (1983, 77).

24. Georges-Abeyie lists the following feminist motivations for female terrorism: Terrorist organizations provide an opportunity for upward mobility, in leadership and an active role in formulating the group's policies, opportunities that are absent or extremely limited in the white male-dominated world of legitimate activity; . . . Terrorist organizations offer change and a renunciation of the current male-dominated chauvinistic mores; . . . The traditional American stereotype of women as weak, supportive, submissive, silent, and of lower intelligence and drive is absent in the philosophies of many terrorist organizations; . . . Membership in a terrorist organization is the *natural* outgrowth of membership in extreme feminist organizations; . . . Women are rejecting stereotypic roles and thus adopting traditional male roles that include revolutionary and terrorist violence; . . . Hormonal disturbances, caused by excessive sexual freedom; . . . Economic, political, and familial liberation due to the trend toward greater justice and equality for women plays a role (Georges-Abeyie, 1983, 77) (my emphasis).

25. For example, Pearlstein (1991) analyzes the personal histories of Patricia Soltysik (SLA) and Susan Stern and Diana Oughton (both members of the Weathermen) to establish their psychological motivations.

26. An important figure in the study of female criminality, Adler authored what was considered to be a landmark text entitled *Sisters in Crime* (1975), and a number of articles dealing with a perceived rise in female crime in the United States.

27. Adler (1979a, 415–16). Adler goes on to imply that the first woman to be included in the FBI's "Ten Most Wanted Fugitives" list was a "politicized female." However, this does not appear to be the case. The first woman to be listed was Ruth Eiseman-Schier, who, along with her male lover, orchestrated the kidnapping and live burial of millionaire heiress Barbara Mackle in Gwinnett County, Georgia in 1968 ("FBI Most Wanted—the FBI's Ten Most Wanted Fugitives—Frequently Asked Questions," Federal Bureau of Investigation, accessed 19 March 2014, http://www.fbi.gov/wanted/topten/tenfaq.htm#9).

28. Adler (1979b, 409). See also Simon (1979); and Lopez-Rey (1979). NB: Simon disagreed with Adler's hypothesis that women's crime would continue to rise at an increased rate into the future.

29. Adler (1979a, 91). She later goes on to assert that "there is a darker side . . . to this movement for equality," namely that, "it took a general social movement sweeping the world with egalitarian forces to provide women with the opportunity for a more equal footing in the criminal hierarchy. And it appears that women have used this opportunity" (Adler 1979b, 407–08). See also Simon and Sharma (1979, 391).

30. As cited in MacDonald (1991, 6).

31. Zwerman (1992, 140).

32. Faludi (1991, xii).

33. She argues that "a backlash against women's rights is nothing new in American history. Indeed, it's a recurring phenomenon: it returns every time women begin

to make some headway toward equality, a seemingly inevitable early frost to the culture's brief flowerings of feminism" (Faludi, 1991, 46).

34. Faludi (1991, xviii).
35. Faludi (1991, xx).
36. Dr Jean Baker Miller as cited in Faludi (1991, xx).
37. Petchesky as cited in Faludi (1991, 232–33) (my emphasis).
38. Faludi (1991, xix).
39. Faludi (1991, 233).
40. Faludi (1991, 232) (my emphasis).
41. Faludi (1991, 232).
42. Hacker (1983, 24).
43. This is the structural version of agency, as opposed to the liberal individualist version of agency that I identified with Hacker earlier.
44. MacDonald (1991, 232).
45. Georges-Abeyie (1983, 82).
46. The idea that terrorist groups attract feminist women, and that feminism shapes the goals and objectives of such terrorist organizations, continues to circulate in contemporary analyses of terrorism. See, for example, Griset and Mahan (2003, 163).
47. Cooper (1979, 152–53) (my emphasis).
48. For example, see Alpert (1981).
49. See, for example, Morgan (2001) (in particular Chapter Six, "Token Terrorist"); and Hearst (1982).
50. See Chapter Six.
51. In referring to these groups as "white," I use the term to describe how they were positioned within dominant discourse, as opposed to an essentialist understanding of the group's membership. It can be argued that all terrorists are racialized. We have seen this most recently in the racialization of "Islamic terrorists" within the spaces of Western popular culture. Both the SLA and the Weather Underground were racialized as "white" within popular culture.
52. Cooper (1979, 153).
53. Adler (1979b, 415–16) (my emphasis).
54. Adler, we should recall, advocates that the increase in women's crime, including the rise of the "politicized female," was the consequence of the women's liberation movement.
55. Georges-Abeyie (1983, 74).
56. Gitlin (1987, 384).
57. Laqueur (1977, 4).
58. Cooper (1979, 153) (my emphasis).
59. This contention constitutes the central political claim of Michel Foucault's *Madness and Civilization: A History of Insanity in the Age of Reason* (1973). Jacques Derrida makes a parallel argument in *Writing and Difference* (1978). Henri Lefebvre has also argued that dominant order responds to threats by constructing them as perversions (Lefebvre, 2000, 147). See also antipsychiatry scholar, Thomas Szasz, who states:

Whether a person is considered "mentally ill" or "committable" [is] bound up with issues of power and value . . . Today people may be segregated in mental hospitals because they are "sick" but also because they . . . espous[e] values and goals too sharply at variance with those dominant in the culture at a given time (Szasz, 1971, 18).

Phyllis Chesler makes a similar argument about women's "madness" in *Women and Madness* (1972).

60. Here, when I refer to "containment" I am referring primarily to a representational strategy by which subversive elements are rendered "safe" for popular consumption. We can understand containment as a form of recuperation, which Dick Hebdige defines as the process by which threats are "*returned* . . . to the place where common sense would have them fit" (1998, 94) The idea of containment, particularly as it related to the threat of communism, had great currency in the United States during the Cold War and, as a function of discourse, translated into a range of material practices, giving rise to what Alan Nadel describes as "containment culture" (1995, 3).

61. Cooper (1979, 153–54).

62. MacDonald (1991, 239). It is precisely this threat of feminism taken to its extreme that Valerie Solanas invokes in *The SCUM Manifesto*, when she declares that "if a large majority of women were SCUM, they could acquire complete control of this country within a few weeks" (Solanas, 2004, 69–70). See Chapter Five.

63. Georges-Abeyie (1983, 82).

64. Georges-Abeyie (1983, 77).

65. Georges-Abeyie (1983, 74) (my emphasis).

66. Georges-Abeyie (1983, 73).

67. Georges-Abeyie (1983, 74) (my emphasis).

68. I discuss this threat in detail in Chapter Seven, where I analyze the SLA's kidnapping of Patricia Campbell Hearst as an event that articulates as a threat to the structure of the nuclear family.

69. Gitlin (1987, 218).

70. For example, Morgan argues that within North American terrorist groups "pressure for rejection of monogamy and for lesbian acts (but never for *male* homosexuality) as forms of "sexual liberation" emanated *from the male leadership of those groups as direct orders*" (Morgan, 2001, 194). Piercy expresses a similar view (Piercy, 1970, 483–84).

71. Gitlin (1987, 109).

72. For example, Lydon's essay on "The Politics of Orgasm," which draws upon the groundbreaking work of sexologists Masters and Johnson, attempts to debunk commonly held beliefs about women's sexual nature. See Lydon (1970).

73. Piercy (1970, 489–90). See also Radicalesbians (2000, 235–36).

74. Although it had support from some feminist quarters, Gerhard notes that the value of lesbianism, as a "form of resistance to male oppression" was contested within both radical and liberal feminist circles (2001, 112).

75. Radicalesbians (2000, 236–37).
76. Shelley (1970, 343).
77. See Irigaray (1985b). I discuss this essay in Chapter Seven.
78. For example, Shelley writes, "I do not mean to condemn all males. I have found some beautiful, loving men among the revolutionaries, among the hippies, and the male homosexuals" (1970, 346).
79. See Shelley (1970, 346).
80. Radicalesbians (2000, 234).
81. As Radicalesbians argued, "lesbian is the word, the label, the condition that holds women in line. When a woman hears this word tossed her way, she knows she is stepping out of line. She knows that she has crossed the terrible boundary of her sex role" (2000, 234).

4 Terrorist Time: Terrorism's Disruption of Modernity

1. Amon (1983, 13).
2. Hage (2003, 126).
3. Jenkins (2003, 18).
4. Borradori (2003b, 149).
5. Derrida in Borradori (2003a, 90).
6. Derrida in Borradori (2003a, 90).
7. Derrida in Borradori (2003a, 90).
8. Derrida in Borradori (2003a, 93).
9. See Baudrillard (1998, 34).
10. Derrida in Borradori (2003a, 96).
11. I discuss this idea in detail in Chapter Five.
12. Conrad (2000, 64).
13. Conrad (2000, 67).
14. Frost (1999).
15. See Lippincott, ed. (1999, 146).
16. Conrad (2000, 69).
17. See Mulry (2000, 43–44). For further details of the Greenwich Bomb Outrage, see also Frost (1999).
18. See, for example, Derrida in Borradori (2003a, 103).
19. Bauman (2001b, 30).
20. Lyotard (1984, xxiii).
21. Bauman (2001a, 169).
22. Beilharz (2001, 6).
23. Bauman (1989, 93).
24. Bauman (2001c, 283).
25. Bauman (2001c, 284).
26. Bauman (2001a, 164).
27. Lyotard (1992, 90).
28. Bauman (2000, 110).

29. For example, as Jon Stratton notes, for Hegel, the state is "the inevitable effect of the working out of reason in history . . . The Hegelian state is the manifestation of universal reason . . . In addition, he associated the state with a particular idea of historical time" ("The Reasonable State and the End of Time," Chapter Seven, *Modern Time*, unpublished manuscript). My sincere thanks to Jon for sharing this manuscript with me.
30. See, for example, Anderson (1991).
31. This idea can be read as the secularization of Christian time, and is the essence of the liberatory promise of modernity.
32. In post-revolutionary France, the birth of the French Republic replaced the birth of Christ as the reference for calendar calculations. Similarly, Mussolini declared the fascists' march on Rome of 1922 as the origin of Italian time.
33. See Bauman (2000, 112–13).
34. Bauman (2000, 115).
35. Bauman (2000, 111).
36. See Virilio (2002).
37. Virilio (2002, 15).
38. Derrida in Borradori (2003a, 86).
39. Derrida in Borradori (2003a, 96–97).
40. Derrida in Borradori (2003a, 96–97).
41. See, for example, Boyarin (1995, 42). On the secularization of the apocalypse, see Bull (1995a).
42. H. H. Rowley as cited in Rowland (1995, 45). Rowley juxtaposes the apocalyptic tradition with the prophetic tradition that foretells "the future that should arise out of the present" (Rowland, 1995, 45).
43. Amon (1983, 15).
44. Amon (1983, 15).
45. Amon (1983, 15–17) (my emphasis).
46. Hence, the anxious claims that we will defend our "freedom," our "way of life," our "democracy," which we saw asserted by Western leaders in the aftermath of September 11, 2001, and more recent terrorist attacks.
47. Bauman (2000, 115).
48. Bauman (2000, 115).
49. Baudrillard (2002, 5).
50. Derrida in Borradori (2003a, 96).
51. See "'Making Do': Uses and Tactics," in de Certeau (1988, 35–39).
52. De Certeau (1988, 35–36).
53. De Certeau (1988, 36).
54. Lefebvre (2000, 24).
55. See Ball (1987).
56. Lefebvre (2000, 145).
57. Lefebvre (2000, 32).
58. De Certeau (1988, 37).
59. De Certeau (1988, 29–30).
60. De Certeau (1988, 36–37) (translation modified).

61. To clarify, the terrorist act disappears. However, its impression remains and gets magnified, particularly in the rhetoric of the state. We continue to replay the terrorist act and to talk about it—obsessively. In this sense, terrorism operates in similar ways to sex as theorized by Foucault (1990).
62. Baudrillard (2002, 19).
63. Baudrillard (2002, 19–20).
64. Baudrillard (2002, 20).
65. Derrida in Borradori (2003a, 93).
66. See Borradori (2003a, 94–95).
67. Amon (1983, 17).
68. Hobbes, (1968, 186).
69. Hobbes (1968, 186).
70. Derrida in Borradori (2003a, 103).
71. Laqueur cites that "the meaning of terrorism was given in the 1798 supplement of the Dictionnaire of the Académie Française as *système, régime de la terreur* (1977, 6) (my emphasis).
72. Laqueur (1977, 6).
73. See Herman and O'Sullivan (1989, 38).
74. To give Laqueur his due credit, he never claims to be interested in analyzing so-called state terrorism. Indeed, he goes to some length in *Terrorism* (1977) to specify that he is concerned primarily with the phenomenon of "urban terrorism," a form of terrorism "from below."
75. See Herman and O'Sullivan (1989).
76. Lefebvre (2000, 147).
77. Lefebvre (2000, 148) (my emphasis).
78. Lefebvre (2000, 147).
79. Lefebvre (2000, 146).
80. Lefebvre writes: "[In Protestantism,] God and Reason were the portion of each individual, everyone was his own mentor, the control of his instincts . . . Protestantism provided the images and the language that capitalism, unobtrusively, adopted" (Lefebvre, 2000, 146).
81. Lefebvre (2000, 146).
82. Lefebvre (2000, 35). He further suggests that the monotony and misery of the everyday is "reflected in the lives of the working classes and especially of *women*, upon whom the conditions of everyday life bear heaviest" (2000, 35) (my emphasis).
83. De Certeau, Giard and Mayol (1998).
84. Lefebvre (2000, 147).
85. Lefebvre (2000, 44).
86. Lefebvre (2000, 44) (my emphasis).
87. Lefebvre (2000, 44).
88. Lefebvre (2000, 147).
89. In making this claim, Lefebvre is drawing upon the Gramscian tradition of Marxism, which argues that the continuity of society through time is based not on force but on a consensual complicity produced through the mechanism of negotiation.

90. It is useful to compare the parallels here with Foucault's concept of power through surveillance.
91. See Derrida in Borradori (2003a, 90).
92. Hage (2003, 127).
93. See Weber (1994, 310–11).
94. Conrad (2000, 64–65).
95. Derrida in Borradori (2003a, 186). We should note here that Derrida's statement can be read as a description of the ways terrorism invokes the terror of abjection.
96. Conrad (2000, 66).
97. Conrad (2000, 66–67).
98. Foucault (1977a).
99. Crick (first name unknown) as cited in Wilkinson (1978, 241).
100. Conrad (2000, 67–68).
101. Lefebvre (2000, 37).

5 Conjuring the Apocalypse: Radical Feminism, Apocalyptic Temporality, and the Society for Cutting Up Men

1. Solanas as cited in Harron and Minahan (1996, 115).
2. In North America, "radical feminists" comprised two groups: "politicos" and "feminists." "Politicos" argued that women's liberation was an important arm of the Movement proper, while "feminists" insisted that women needed to organize separately.
3. Willis (1989, vii). See also Echols (1989, 243).
4. Gurr (1989c, 108).
5. Reverend Pat Robertson as cited in *Quotes from the Religious Right*, accessed 8 April 2004, http://www.geocities.com/CapitolHill/7027/quotes.html.
6. Phyllis Schlafly as cited in "People for the American Way Celebrates Women's History Month," *People for the American Way*, accessed 8 April 2004, http://www. pfaw.org/pfaw/general/default.aspx?oid=9442 (my emphasis).
7. Feminist commentators since the mid-1990s have noted that feminist principles are now embedded in dominant US culture as fundamental rights of women. See the work of feminists who engaged in the "generation debate" in the mid-1990s, such as Brooks (1997).
8. Solanas (2004, 35).
9. Solanas (2004, 76–77).
10. Solanas (2004, 35).
11. Solanas (2004, 67).
12. Solanas as cited in Baer (1997, 55).
13. Susan Brownmiller's term as cited in Echols (1989, 158).
14. It must be noted that, while Solanas was a key inspiration for many radical feminists, she remained fiercely antimovement. See Fahs (2008).
15. Florynce Kennedy was a civil rights lawyer who was active in both the Black Liberation movement and the Women's Liberation movement. Kennedy was

cofounder of "The Feminists." In the early 1970s, Kennedy published several works of feminist analysis.

16. Kennedy as cited in Baer (1997, 54).
17. Atkinson as cited in Baer (1997, 54).
18. See Echols (1989, 168).
19. Echols (1989, 104).
20. Echols (1989, 105) (my emphasis).
21. As Gerhard suggests, "from the very beginnings of radical feminism, different groups with different trajectories . . . claimed the mantle of feminism" (2001, 103).
22. See Echols (1989).
23. Firestone (2000, 95).
24. DeKoven (2004, 256).
25. DeKoven (2004, 256).
26. Echols notes: "The Youth International Party (or Yippie) was formed in December, 1967 and functioned primarily as a vehicle for Abbie Hoffman and Jerry Rubin, two Movement activists who delighted in offending middle class sensibilities. Their guerrilla theatre actions were not designed to raise the consciousness of average Americans whose 'straightness' put them beyond the pale as much as they were calculated to capture time on network news programs" (1989, 76).
27. Raskin (1998, 220).
28. DeKoven (2004, 256).
29. Evans (1979, 213–14). This is the event that inspired the widespread myth of feminist bra burning, even though feminists did not set any undergarments on fire.
30. Echols (1989, 93).
31. Greer (1971, 308). Robin Morgan, Florika, Peggy Dobbins, Judy Duffett, Cynthia Funk, and Naomi Jaffe were among the 13 "heretical women" who founded WITCH. See Echols (1989, 96).
32. Echols (1989, 76). For a discussion of the Yippies, see, for example, Bodroghkozy (2001), Spigel and Curtin (1997), Raskin (1998), and Gitlin (1980, 146–79).
33. The Situationists practiced a politics of disruption. Their key theorist was Guy Debord who, in 1968, published *Society of the Spectacle* (1994) in French. Lefebvre's early work on the everyday was an attempt to theorize the politics of Situationism. See Ball (1987). For further discussion of Situationism, see Marcus (1989) and Plant (1992).
34. Evans notes that "media coverage in 1969 and 1970 provoked a massive influx of new members into all branches of the feminist movement" (1979, 214).
35. WITCH description, "Who We Are: Descriptions of Women's Liberation Groups," *The CWLU Herstory Website Archive*, accessed 22 March 2014, http://www.uic.edu/orgs/cwluherstory/CWLUArchive/natconference.html (my emphasis).
36. Felski (1995, 16) argues that feminism, despite its critique of the impact of modernity on women's experiences, is deeply imbricated with the project of modernity.

37. See Lyotard (1992).
38. For a discussion of the ways apocalypse and utopia are interconnected, see Lasky (1976)
39. Stavrakakis (1999, 100).
40. In this sense, it differs from its premodern religious precursors that set up the return to the Garden of Eden or the attainment of Paradise as something to be revealed by God.
41. The history of the concept of utopia is tracked by Kumar (1987).
42. Marin as cited in Stratton (2000a, 166).
43. Kumar (1991, 101).
44. Kumar (1991, 101).
45. The issue of representation is also a key issue of the feminist project. While feminism strives for the problem of representation to be resolved, it is simultaneously dependent upon the discursive distinction between men and women as its fundamental organizing category. If utopia represents the final resolution of the problem of representation, utopia is thus problematic for feminism.
46. Felski (1995, 148).
47. Felski (1995, 148).
48. Felski (1995, 170). I juxtapose "evolution" with "revolution" here, but the distinction between these two paradigms of social change is not always clear-cut. As Felski notes, revolution may be understood as a form of the dialectic operating in history. That is, the existing, flawed society gets cast as the "thesis," the feminist call for change as the "antithesis," and the society that incorporates the utopian/desired feminist transformation gets cast as the "synthesis," at which point the process begins all over again until, at some point in the (often distant) future, the feminist utopia is produced. In this configuration, "the metaphor of revolution can itself easily be assimilated back into a progressive teleology and a salvation history consisting of a sequence of revolutionary stages" (Felski, 1995, 170), which resonates strongly with the notion of progress and linear history that is characteristic of the evolutionary paradigm. In this way, revolution is incorporated into the evolutionary history of the state. However, within the representational economy of modernity, revolution nonetheless signifies as the negation of evolutionary teleology.
49. See Bull (1995, 1–17).
50. Amon (1983, 15).
51. See Boyarin (1995, 42).
52. Boyarin (1995, 42).
53. Kolakowski as cited in Kumar (1991, 94).
54. Enzensberger (1978, 74).
55. Echols (1989, 55).
56. Gitlin (1980, 373).
57. Gitlin (1987, 375).
58. Kaye (1986, 8).
59. Morgan (1970, xxxviii).

60. Gornick (1971) (my emphasis).
61. DeKoven (2004, 254). See also Firestone (2000, 90).
62. Enzensberger (1978, 79).
63. DeKoven (2004, 267).
64. "What is Liberation?" in Crow, ed. (2000, 81).
65. See, for example, Gurr (1989b).
66. Echols (1989, 185).
67. Echols (1989, 54).
68. Lefebvre (2000, 73).
69. Lefebvre (2000, 35).
70. Firestone as cited in DeKoven (2004, 264).
71. Firestone as cited in DeKoven (2004, 264).
72. DeKoven (2004, 256).
73. DeKoven (2004, 255) (my emphasis).
74. Echols (1989, 93).
75. Kristeva (1986, 193–94) (my emphasis).
76. Kristeva (1986, 200) (my emphasis).
77. Kristeva (1986, 203).
78. Pateman (1988, 58).
79. In seventeenth-century political theory, Reason forms the very basis of social organization. Although the state is often theorized in terms of the structural organization of violence, Reason provides the legitimating discourse for the modern state.
80. For further discussion of this point, see Stratton (1990, 210).
81. Pateman (1988). See also Lloyd (1993).
82. In this context, Woman operates in terms of the symptom—enabling the entity of the state to function as a relatively coherent symbolic construct, but also operating as a necessary site of the state's instability.
83. Pateman (1994, 108).
84. Pateman (1994, 108–09). The nature of the threat women pose to dominant order is grounded in the historical linkage of "women's nature" with their reproductive physiology. In the modern Western patriarchal imagination, the female body is constructed as a (potential) site of excess—elusive, fluid and requiring constant surveillance lest it escape the roles prescribed for it by patriarchal culture. See, for example, Young (1996) and Hart (1994).
85. Pateman (1994, 114).
86. The construction of women as a subversive force requires their separation from "civil" society and their relegation to the private sphere. However, simultaneously, modern gender divisions of labor entrust women with the responsibility of child rearing, placing the onus of reproducing morality from one generation to the next on the fundamentally untrustworthy figure of Woman.
87. Hegel as cited in Pateman (1994, 108).
88. MacDonald (1991, 239).
89. Kristeva (1986, 203).

90. "15 Minutes Later . . . (or: The Short Sad Life of Valerie Solanas)," in *In Focus*, accessed 3 January 2006, http://www.geocities.com/SoHo/2904/reviews.html.
91. Harron and Daniel (1996, xxv).
92. Harding, (2001, 142).
93. Baer (1997, 53).
94. Baer (1997, 53).
95. Harding (2001, 144).
96. Greer (1971, 308).
97. On this note, Solanas' attack, it seems, was in part motivated by what she saw as Warhol's personal betrayal of her. Under the impression that Warhol would direct a film based on a script she had written entitled "Up Your Ass," Solanas had reportedly given Warhol her only copy of the manuscript to read. Warhol subsequently misplaced the script. When he told Solanas, she accused him of appropriating it as his own (see Baer, 1997). The manuscript was located in 1998 ("Solanas Lost and Found," *Village Voice*, 12–18 January 2000, http://www.villagevoice.com/2000-01-11/news/solanas-lost-and-found/)
98. This image was further reinforced by Olympia Press' decision to publish the *SCUM Manifesto* following the shooting. Its cover featured a reproduction of the front-page story from the *New York Post*, with the headline, "ANDY WARHOL FIGHTS FOR LIFE." Publisher Maurice Girodias' preface stated, "this little book is my contribution to the study of violence," as if the text represented a psychological critique of the mind of a fanatical murderer (Harron and Minahan, 1996, xxvii).
99. For a normative theory of the role of madness in the modern nation-state, see Szasz (1971 and 1968). For a political-philosophical analysis of the discourse of madness in modernity, see Foucault (1973).
100. Young (1996, 29).
101. Solanas (2004, 75–76).
102. Parkinson Zamora (1989, 133).
103. Parkinson Zamora (1989, 17).
104. Solanas (2004, 47).
105. Solanas (1997, 4).
106. Gornick (1971).
107. Gornick (1971) (my emphasis). Although Gornick, a feminist, expresses sympathy with the manifesto's politics, she nonetheless constructs it as a text that is "beyond reason," buying into dominant cultural constructions of Solanas as mad.
108. Enzensberger (1978, 79).
109. Lloyd (1993).
110. For a history of eugenics, see Kevles (1985).
111. Solanas (2004, 35–36).
112. Aristotle, for example, claimed that "only embryos that had sufficient heat could develop into fully human form. The rest became female. In other words, woman was, in Aristotle's words, a 'misbegotten man' . . . and literally half-baked" (Weitz, 1998, 3).

113. Solanas (2004, 36).
114. This work argued, for example, that women are incapable of intellectual activity, and that this deficiency is inextricably tied with the "imperfection" of women's bodies. As late as 1905, "the president of the Oregon State Medical School, F. W. van Dyke . . . claimed that hard study killed sexual desire in women, took away their beauty, and brought on hysteria, neurasthenia, dyspepsia, astigmatism, dysmenorrhea" (Weitz, 1998, 6). See also Polster (1992, 73).
115. See Giddens (1985, 121).
116. Solanas (2004).
117. Solanas (2004, 75).
118. I mean here that the modern democratic nation state is patriarchal and excludes women not only from sites of power, but also, as Pateman (1988) argues, from the very political system on which the state is based.
119. Solanas (2004, 35).
120. Solanas (2004, 55).
121. Solanas (2004, 77) (my emphasis).
122. Solanas (2004, 76).
123. Solanas (2004, 76).
124. Solanas (2004, 69–70).
125. Kristeva (1986, 203).
126. Gornick (1971) (my emphasis).
127. Solanas (2004, 70).
128. Irigaray (1993, 12).
129. Greer (1971, 308) (my emphasis).
130. I draw here upon De Lauretis' Foucauldian reading of gender (1987).
131. DeKoven (2004, 260).
132. See, for example, Lyotard (1991).
133. Stratton (2000a, 119) (my emphasis).
134. Stratton (2000a, 120).
135. Bauman (1989).
136. Boyarin (1995, 43).
137. Lemkin as cited in Stratton (2000c, 237).
138. Stratton (2000c, 237).
139. Boyarin (1995, 43).
140. Solanas (1997, 79).
141. Gornick (1971).
142. Harron and Minahan (1996, x).
143. See, for example, Chesler (1989).
144. The San Diego State University established its Department of Women's Studies in 1970 and lays claim to the oldest women's studies program in the United States. Many other universities soon followed. In the early 1970s, "some 600 courses and 20 programs were identified by *Female Studies II*, a collection of curricula and syllabi" ("Program History Timeline," San Diego State University Women's Studies web site, accessed 14 January 2006, http://www-rohan.sdsu.edu/dept/wsweb/timeline.htm#1970s).

145. See, for example, Alpert (1974).
146. Morgan (1989).
147. See Echols (1989).

6 Abjecting Whiteness: "The Movement," Radical Feminism, Genocide

1. Gitlin (1987, 376).
2. Morgan (1970, xxxix–xl).
3. DeKoven (2004, 260).
4. Atkinson (2000, 86).
5. Here, the "Movement" (with a capital "M") refers to the broad constellation of left-leaning political organizations aspiring for social change that were affiliated with the civil rights movement, the antiwar movement, the free speech movement, the black power movement, and the North American counter-culture of the late 1960s/early 1970s. Where I refer to the feminist movement specifically, I have not used a capital, for example, "movement."
6. Morgan (2001, 217–18).
7. Judith Brown in Jones and Brown (2000, 55).
8. For a discussion of apocalyptic thinking within US culture, see Stratton (2000b, 21–51).
9. Raskin (1998, 219).
10. Evans (1979, 102).
11. Students for a Democratic Society was a nation-wide campus-based organization that "became the dominant institutional expression of the student new left" (Evans, 1979, 109). Its membership came from "middle-class and professional class families" (Kopkind as cited in Evans, 1979, 130). It is fair to assume that most of them were "'white.'"
12. This meeting was attended by "two thousand activists from 200 organizations" (Evans, 1979, 196).
13. Evans (1979, 102).
14. The "beloved community" was defined by SDS as "an interracial movement of the poor" (cited in Evans, 1979, 128).
15. Evans (1979, 135).
16. Judith Brown in Jones and Brown (2000, 55–56).
17. The Movement, in this sense, worked with an understanding of the individual as the agent of history's transformation, which is a feature of the modern apocalyptic (see Chapter Five).
18. Muncie (1984, 39).
19. Wolin (1997, 153).
20. Roszak (1970, 1).
21. Gitlin (1997, 291).
22. Nelson (1989, 114). Nelson is referring to the British counter-culture, but the same could be said of the North American social protest movement of the 1960s.

23. See Evans (1979, 196–97).
24. See, for example, Gurr (1989a, 17); and Raskin (1998, 255).
25. See, for example, Dyer (1997).
26. I use "race" to describe the discursive mechanism through which physical differences between embodied subjects assume (political) meaning.
27. For further discussion of this idea, see Stratton (2000a).
28. See Brodkin (1994).
29. See Gitlin (1988).
30. Evans (1979, 197). Black activists frequently called for black separatism; a call that would later be paralleled by some North American feminists' call for women's separatism.
31. See also Echols (1989, 36–37).
32. Evans (1979, 197).
33. Echols (1989, 47).
34. Echols (1989, 40).
35. Kopkind as cited in Echols (1989, 41).
36. Evans (1979, 157).
37. See Evans (1979, 133–34).
38. Gitlin (1988, 218). The 1970 Kent State University incident, when National Guardsmen fired on student protesters, killing four, "was chilling and seems to have moderated the frequency and the tactics of subsequent protest" (Gurr, 1989b, 214).
39. Echols (1989, 29).
40. Evans (1979, 196).
41. Evans (1979, 197).
42. Here again, we confront the problem of how to define the borders of an identity position. I use the term "Jewish" here in a cultural, as opposed to a racial, sense (see Stratton, 2000a). While many of the activists involved in the Movement may have identified as Jews, this did not necessarily translate into membership of Jewish political, religious, and/or community organizations or into a sense of membership of the Jewish community more generally (Novick, 1999, 173). However, in the context of the broad policy of Jewish assimilation into mainstream American society that was adopted by both individual Jews and Jewish organizations, Jews were encouraged to identify *as members of American Jewish culture* without necessarily practicing that identity in public (see Brodkin, 1994).
43. Indeed, it was precisely this kind of event that fueled Jewish organizations' concerns about black militant anti-Semitism. As Peter Novick notes, the formation of the Jewish Defense League was a direct response to this kind of verbal attack (Novick, 1999, 174).
44. Novick (1999, 174).
45. Gitlin (1988, 218).
46. Echols (1989, 45).
47. Gitlin (1988, 218).
48. Gitlin (1987, 376). See epigraph to this chapter.
49. Gitlin (1988, 218).

50. Echols (1989, 29).
51. Rabkin (1997, 54). Nixon was sworn in as president on 20 January 1969.
52. Evans (1979, 211).
53. Echols, (1989, 145).
54. Early women's liberation was not only a white movement, but also very much a middle class movement. Given that black women were more often than not also working class, the blind spots of race and class operated together to produce the feminist movement's "whiteness."
55. Echols (1989, 33).
56. See, for example, McClintock (1995).
57. See Gerhard (2001, 99). For radical feminist accounts of their decision to organize as a result of their experiences of the sexism of the left, see Morgan (1978); and Piercy (1970).
58. Evans attributes the rise of radical feminism in part to white women's experiences organizing in the civil rights movement. This history is tracked by Evans (1979, 82–101).
59. Evans (1979, 221).
60. Friedan (1973, 266–67).
61. Friedan (1973, 266).
62. Rabkin (1997, 66).
63. Firestone (2000, 90).
64. Solanas (2004, 67).
65. Solanas (2004, 39).
66. "What is Liberation?" in Crow, ed. (2000, 81) (my emphasis).
67. Atkinson (2000, 87) (my emphasis).
68. Rabkin (1997, 66). See also Echols (1989, 44 and 98–99).
69. Echols (1989, 45).
70. Morgan (2001, 224).
71. Grosz (1990, 89) (my emphasis).
72. Morgan's whiteness defines a boundary that is characteristic of the abject. As Kristeva suggests, "we may call it a border" (1982, 9).
73. Kristeva (1982, 6).
74. Kristeva (1982, 3).
75. Grosz (1990, 80–103) (my emphasis).
76. Kristeva (1982, 4).
77. Morgan (1970, xvii).
78. Grosz (1990, 86).
79. See, for example, Freud's story of the primal horde in *Moses and Monotheism* (1955a) and *Totem and Taboo* (1955b).
80. Kristeva (1982, 10).
81. Kristeva (1982, 7).
82. Grosz (1990, 93).
83. Kristeva (1982, 9).
84. Kristeva (1982, 4).
85. Kristeva (1982, 2).

86. Kristeva (1982, 8) (my emphasis).
87. Brown in Jones and Brown (2000, 56).
88. Atkinson (2000, 83) (my emphasis).
89. See, for example, Gerhard (2001, 98).
90. Firestone as cited in Gerhard (2001, 97). Firestone continues, "in our new society, humanity could finally revert to its natural polymorphous sexuality— all forms of sexuality would be allowed and indulged" (as cited in Gerhard, 2001, 97).
91. Gerhard (2001, 155).
92. Washington (1979, 239–40).
93. See also Gerhard (2001, 102).
94. Echols (1989, 218).
95. Washington (1979, 239).
96. Evans (1979, 196).
97. Greenhalgh (1990, 164).
98. LaHaye as cited in Faludi (1991, 239).
99. Rivers (1986, 89) (my emphasis).
100. Falwell as cited in Faludi (1991, 234) (my emphasis).
101. "State-sponsored terrorism" describes a government's backing of terrorism carried out on the soil of other nations, in the form of directly funding or providing political and diplomatic support for either state terrorism or revolutionary organizations seeking to overthrow foreign governments (see Herman and Chomsky, 1988).

7   Nuclear Terrorists: Patricia Hearst and the (Feminist) Terrorist Family

1. Boulton (1975, 9).
2. Patricia Campbell Hearst was known as Patty Hearst in the mass media. However, Hearst has repeatedly and publicly insisted that she finds the public's use of her shortened name overly familiar and presumptuous, and that she wishes to be known as Patricia. I have tried to abide by Hearst's preference here, except where it is necessary to distinguish between Hearst and a separate, fictional Patricia; Hearst and her parents, or Hearst's two "personalities"—"Patty" and "Tania."
3. See, for example, Alpert (1981). Alpert identifies her troubled childhood relationship with her parents and an abusive relationship with her lover, Sam Melville, as causes of her decision to participate in political violence as a member of the Jackson-Melville Unit, a small terrorist group loosely affiliated with the Weather Underground.
4. James (1974, 19).
5. Ellenberg (1974, 9).
6. James (1974, 49).
7. Ellenberg (1974, 5).
8. Ellenberg (1974, 8).
9. James (1974, 158).

10. Ellenberg (1974, 8).
11. James (1974, 86).
12. Ichord as cited in West and Belcher (1975, 25).
13. Brainwashing is the popular term for what is also known as coercive persuasion, thought reform, or psychological reprogramming.
14. Morgan (2001, 189).
15. Ellenberg (1974, 5). For further details of the similarities between the two texts, see Ellenberg (1974) and "The Strange Case of *Black Abductor*," Keck, accessed 28 January 2002, http://www.claykeck.com/Patty/articles/abductor.html.
16. The distributor was San Diego News Service.
17. For one such conspiracy theory, see "Mae Brussell's World Watchers International," Mae Brussell website, accessed February 28, 2002, http://www.maebrussell.com/Bibsheets/348349s1.html.
18. James (1974, 21).
19. James (1974, 130).
20. Ellenberg (1974, 14).
21. *Citizen Kane*, directed by Orson Welles (Los Angeles, USA: RKO Radio Pictures, 1941), 35-mm film.
22. See Boulton (1975, 82).
23. Boulton (1975, 94–95) (my emphasis).
24. West and Belcher (1975, 35).
25. Boulton (1975, 9). See epigraph to this chapter.
26. Boulton (1975, 82).
27. Alexander (1979).
28. Alexander (1979, 6).
29. See, for example, Comte (1974, 503).
30. So too, the al Qaeda attacks of 11 September 2001 in the United States, the Bali bombings of 12 October 2002 and 1 October 2005, and the London bombings of 7 July 2005 were often interpreted in terms of the impact of the attacks on individual families.
31. Freud draws the tale from Charles Darwin (*The Descent of Man*, 1871) and J. J. Atkinson (*The Primal Law*, 1903).
32. I allude here to MacCannell's argument that, in modernity, patriarchal order is replaced by a fraternal order (1991).
33. Freud (1955a, 81).
34. Freud's reading of the primal horde parallels Rousseau's "state of nature" as that which predates the social.
35. Freud (1955a, 81).
36. Freud (1955a, 81–82).
37. Marcuse (1970, 44).
38. Freud (1955a, 82).
39. Freud (1955b, 108).
40. Freud (1955a, 82).
41. See Chapters One and Two of MacCannell (1991).
42. Marcuse (1970, 67).

43. Freud (1955b, 30).
44. Freud (1955b, 29).
45. Marcuse (1970, 65).
46. Irigaray (1985b, 171).
47. Irigaray (1985b, 171).
48. Irigaray (1985b, 31).
49. Irigaray (1985b, 31).
50. Irigaray (1985b, 173).
51. Alexander (1979, 11) (my emphasis).
52. Remiro and Little had been arrested for the murder of Marcus Foster on 10 January 1974.
53. For the full text of the communiqué, see West and Belcher (1975, 338–41).
54. Szasz (1976, 10).
55. West and Belcher (1975, 214).
56. Marcus (1966, 285).
57. Freud (1955b, 35).
58. The Oakland siege was frequently referred to as a "holocaust," highlighting the state's violence toward the SLA. In this labeling of the state's response to the SLA, we can see how the Patty Hearst event, like Solanas' *SCUM Manifesto* and other radical feminist calls for genocide discussed in Chapter Six, blurred the distinction between legitimate and illegitimate violence.
59. Isenberg (2000, 640).
60. Hearst (1982, 97).
61. Barry (1984, 144).
62. Isenberg (2000, 656).
63. Isenberg (2000, 651–52).
64. The publication of these photographs privileged a narrative about the normalcy of the Hearsts' family life and cut across the class divide that threatened to separate the Hearsts from potentially sympathetic audiences.
65. Randolph Hearst as cited in Isenberg (2000, 655).
66. Isenberg (2000, 655).
67. Isenberg (2000, 655) (my emphasis).
68. Bob Dylan, "The Times They Are A-Changin'," *The Times They Are A-Changin'* (B0009MAP9A Sony, [1964] 2005), compact disc.
69. Clarke et al. (1976, 74).
70. Femia (1988, 3).
71. See, for example, the documentary, *Berkeley in the Sixties*, directed by Mark Kitchell (Berkeley, CA: Kitchell Films/P.O.V. Theatricals, 1990), video.
72. Clarke et al. (1976, 62).
73. Many women embraced the counter-culture as an opportunity to explore alternative modes of organizing everyday life that encompassed feminist ideals. However, the counter-culture did not necessarily translate into more congenial circumstances for women—indeed, often to the contrary.
74. See Mailer (1969).
75. Morgan (1970, xxxiv).

76. Lefebvre (2000, 147).
77. I have bracketed the term "radical" in order to signal draw attention to the dominant cultural tendency to conflate all forms of feminism with radical feminism.
78. Evans (1979, 221–22).
79. Faludi (1991, 233).
80. I take the term "mind share" from Naomi Klein (2001).
81. Gerhard (2001, 152).
82. For example, radical feminist activism had given rise to a significant underground press that helped to distribute the feminist message widely and in a way not possible via mainstream media outlets that, in general, remained hostile to feminist ideas and practices.
83. Evans (1979, 222).
84. Evans (1979, 215).
85. Evans (1979, 217).
86. Terrorism is also frequently configured in terms of contagion. See, for example, Picard (1991, 40–48); and Midlarsky, Crenshaw and Yoshida (1980, 262–98).
87. For example, Phyllis Schlafly proclaimed that "women's liberationists operate as Typhoid Marys carrying a germ" (Schlafly as cited in Faludi, 1991, 239). Jerry Falwell denounced feminism as "a sinister female web . . . spreading its tentacles across the Free World" (Falwell as cited in Faludi, 1991, 234).
88. Solanas (2004, 46–48).
89. Gerhard (2001, 97).
90. "About the Heritage Foundation," The Heritage Foundation, accessed 25 March 2014, http://www.heritage.org/about/.
91. Weyrich as cited in Faludi (1991, 232) (my emphasis).
92. The think tank's first legislative reform was the drafting of the Family Protection Act. This initiative came to epitomize the New Right's "pro-family" (for which we can read "antifeminist") agenda. As Faludi notes, the Act's proposals include to "eliminate federal laws supporting equal education; forbid intermingling of the sexes in any sport or other school-related activities; require marriage and motherhood to be taught as the proper careers for girls; deny federal funding to any school using textbooks portraying women in nontraditional roles; repeal all federal laws protecting battered wives from their husbands; and ban federally funded legal aid for any woman seeking abortion counseling or a divorce" (Faludi, 1991, 235).
93. Faludi (1991, 230).
94. A notable example of this in the cultural sphere was the release of the 1975 film, *Stepford Wives*, directed by Bryan Forbes (London: Cinema Club, 1997, VHS video). This film can be read as a backlash against the crisis in the gender relations underpinning the nuclear family that was brought on by the consolidation of feminism in the mid-1970s. See Stratton (1996, 224).
95. See Brenner (1996, 25).
96. The SLA comprised three men (including Cinque, the group's leader) and, when "Tania" joined them, five women.
97. Barry (1984, 155).
98. Cooper (1979, 153).

99. See Hearst (1982).
100. Isenberg (2000, 642).
101. "Symbionese Liberation Army Tape Transcripts," Icehouse online, accessed 1 June 1999, http://www.icehouse.net/zodiac/hearst/tape/21274.html.
102. On the impact of Hearst's pretrial psychological testing, antipsychiatrist, Szasz notes: "Between the time of her arrest, when she identified herself as an 'urban guerrilla,' and her appearance in court as a demure and dutiful daughter, Patty Hearst was no doubt influenced by her new captors and associates: no one calls this 'brainwashing'" (1976, 11).
103. Indeed, during her trial, recalling the mechanized women of *Stepford Wives*, one male juror commented, "we don't really know what she's like, whether we were looking at a live girl or a robot" (as cited in Isenberg, 2000, 664). "Tania," it seemed, was a feminist automaton and not, as she might seem, a "real girl."
104. "Symbionese Liberation Army Tape Transcripts," Icehouse online, accessed 1 June 1999, http://www.icehouse.net/zodiac/hearst/tape/21274.html.
105. Lane (1985, 79).
106. Arendt as cited in Gleason (1995, 95) (my emphasis).
107. Lefebvre (2000, 147).
108. The concept of "totalism" was developed by Erik Erikson, who defined it as "total immersion in a synthetic identity (extreme nationalism, racism or class consciousness)" (Gleason, 1995, 246).
109. Mao Tse Tung as cited in Gleason (1995, 96).
110. Orwell (1993). Although written before the term brainwashing was introduced to the English-speaking world, O'Brien's interrogation of Winston Smith mobilizes a concept of "washing the brain": "We make the brain perfect before we blow it up. No one whom we bring to this place ever stands out against us. Everyone is washed clean" (cited in Gleason 1995, 247).
111. Hunter claimed that the term was a direct translation of the words *hsi nao*, literally a "cleansing of the brain or mind."
112. Isenberg (2000, 642).
113. Lifton (1961, 5).
114. Gleason (1995, 100).
115. Isenberg (2000, 649). Commentators suggest that Bailey's legal strategy was confused. See Isenberg (2000, 649) and Lunde and Wilson (1977, 341–82).
116. Patricia's defense was also problematic because brainwashing was a "classed" phenomenon. The overwhelming majority of male POWs whose charges of collaboration with the enemy were dismissed were, as Congressman Wampler alludes in the quotation above, young men from average, if not below average, homes—certainly not from families of the Hearsts' economic and social status.
117. Isenberg (2000, 662).
118. Hall (1997, 44).
119. Szasz (1976, 11) (my emphasis).
120. See Terdiman (1985).
121. See Brown (1963). The term "counter-discursive" refers to Terdiman's definition in Terdiman (1985).

122. Roszak (1970); Marcuse (1964).
123. See Gleason (1995).
124. See my discussion of Lefebvre's concept of the "terrorist society" in Chapter Four.
125. Solanas (2004, 71).
126. "Songs from the Women's Liberation Movement," in Morgan, ed. (1970, 622–23).
127. Pear notes that in the confession "nearly always the father is to be denounced, both as a symbol of the exploiting classes and as an individual" (Pear, 1961, 129). Here Pear implicitly acknowledges that modern order is patriarchal—that "undoing" an individual's socialization in Western values and practices entails the (symbolic) rejection of the father.
128. For further discussion of the techniques of brainwashing, see Lifton (1961), Schein (1961), Brown (1963), and Gleason (1995).
129. Lifton as cited in Schein (1961, 214).
130. Solanas (2004, 48).
131. See footnote 92 of this chapter.
132. Embree (1970, 212).
133. Mainardi (1970, 502).
134. Morgan (1979, 61).
135. Hearst as cited in Morgan (1979, 60). This interview also forms the basis of Morgan's chapter on Hearst in *The Demon Lover* (2001, 180–216).
136. Isenberg (2000, 658) (my emphasis).

Postscript

1. On the Manson gang, see Bugliosi and Gentry (1975).
2. See Foss (1992).
3. See Echols (1989) and Willis (1989). The distinction between "radical" and "cultural" feminism is not clear-cut, and some commentators claim that the latter term signified the denigration by some radical feminists of other forms of radical feminism as "not really political" (Douglas, 1990).
4. Alpert (1974), *Documents from the Women's Liberation Movement: An On-line Archival Collection*, accessed 31 March 2014, http://scriptorium.lib.duke.edu/wlm/mother/
5. See Alpert (1981).
6. Alpert (1974), op. cit.
7. Alpert (1974), op. cit.
8. Alpert (1974), op. cit.
9. Morgan (2001).
10. Morgan (2001).
11. Alpert (1974), op. cit.
12. Alpert (1974), op. cit.
13. Morgan (1970, xl).

Bibliography

Adler, Freda. *Sisters in Crime*. New York: McGraw, 1975.

———. "Changing Patterns." In *The Criminology of Deviant Women*, edited by Freda Adler and Rita James Simon. Boston: Houghton Mifflin, 1979a.

———. "The Interaction between Women's Emancipation and Female Criminality: A Cross-Cultural Perspective." In *The Criminology of Deviant Women*, edited by Freda Adler and Rita James Simon. Boston: Houghton Mifflin, 1979b.

Alali, A. Odasuo and Kenoye Kevin Eke, eds. *Media Coverage of Terrorism: Methods of Diffusion*. Newbury Park: Sage, 1991.

Alexander, Shana. *Anyone's Daughter*. New York: Viking, 1979.

Alexander, Yonah and Robert G. Picard, eds. *In the Camera's Eye: News Coverage of Terrorist Events*. Washington: Brassey's, 1991.

Allen, Judith. "Men Crime and Criminology: Recasting the Questions." *International Journal of the Sociology of Law* 17 (1989): 19–39.

Alpert, Jane. *Mother Right: A New Feminist Theory*. Pittsburgh: Know, 1974, on *Documents from the Women's Liberation Movement: An On-line Archival Collection* website, accessed March 31, 2014, http://scriptorium.lib.duke.edu/wlm/mother/

———. *Growing up Underground: The Astonishing Autobiography of a Former Radical Fugitive and the Illumination of an American Era*. New York: Morrow, 1981.

Amon, Moshe. "The Phoenix Complex: Terrorism and the Death of Western Civilization." In *Perspectives on Terrorism*, edited by Lawrence Zelic Freedman and Yonah Alexander. Wilmington, DE: Scholarly Resources, 1983.

Anderson, Benedict. *Imagined Communities: Reflections on the Origin and Spread of Nationalism*. London: Verso, 1991.

Ang, Ien. *Desperately Seeking the Audience*. London: Routledge, 1991.

Atkinson, Ti-Grace. "Radical Feminism." In *Radical Feminism: A Documentary Reader*, edited by Barbara A. Crow. New York: New York University Press, 2000.

Baer, Freddie. "About Valerie Solanas." In *SCUM Manifesto*. Edinburgh, San Francisco: AK Press, 1997.

Ball, Edward. "The Great Sideshow of the Situationist International." *Yale French Studies* 73 (1987): 21–37.

Bardsley, Barney. *Flowers in Hell: An Investigation into Women and Crime*. London: Pandora, 1987.

Barnhurst, Kevin G. "The Literature of Terrorism: Implications for Visual Communication." In *Media Coverage of Terrorism: Methods of Diffusion*, edited by A. Odasuo Alali and Kenoye Kevin Eke. Newbury Park: Sage, 1991.

Barry, Kathleen. *Female Sexual Slavery*. New York: New York University Press, 1984.

Bassiouni, M. Cherif. "Problems in Media Coverage of Nonstate-Sponsored Terror-Violence Incidents." In *Perspectives on Terrorism*, edited by Lawrence Zelic Freedman and Yonah Alexander. Wilmington, DE: Scholarly Resources, 1983.

Baudrillard, Jean. *The Gulf War Did Not Take Place*. Translated by Paul Patton. Sydney: Power Publications, 1995.

———. *The Consumer Society: Myths and Structures*. Translated by Chris Turner. London: Sage, 1998.

———. *Fatal Strategies*. Translated by Editorial Board of Semiotext(e). London: Pluto, 1999.

———. *The Spirit of Terrorism and Requiem for the Twin Towers*. Translated by Chris Turner. London: Verso, 2002.

Bauman, Zygmunt. *Modernity and the Holocaust*. Cambridge: Polity, 1989.

———. *Liquid Modernity*. Cambridge: Polity, 2000.

———. "Modernity." In *The Bauman Reader*, edited by Peter Beilharz. Malden: Blackwell, 2001a.

———. "The Historical Location of Socialism." In *The Bauman Reader*, edited by Peter Beilharz. Malden: Blackwell, 2001b.

———. "The Quest for Order." In *The Bauman Reader*, edited by Peter Beilharz. Malden: Blackwell, 2001c.

Beilharz, Peter, ed. "Introduction: Reading Zygmunt Bauman." In *The Bauman Reader*, edited by Peter Beilharz. Malden: Blackwell, 2001.

Berendse, Gerrit-Jan and Ingo Cornils, "Introduction: The Long Shadow of Terrorism." In *Baader-Meinhof Returns: History and Cultural Memory of German Left-Wing Terrorism*, edited by Gerrit-Jan Berendse and Ingo Cornils. Amsterdam and New York: Rodopi, 2008.

Bodroghkozy, Aniko. *Groove Tube: Sixties Television and the Youth Rebellion*. Durham: Duke University Press, 2001.

Borradori, Giovanna. "Autoimmunity: Real and Symbolic Suicides: A Dialogue with Jacques Derrida." In *Philosophy in a Time of Terror: Dialogues with Jürgen Habermas and Jacques Derrida*, edited by Giovanna Borradori. Chicago: University of Chicago Press, 2003a.

———. "Deconstructing Terrorism: Derrida." In *Philosophy in a Time of Terror: Dialogues with Jürgen Habermas and Jacques Derrida*, edited by Giovanna Borradori. Chicago: University of Chicago Press, 2003b.

———. "Preface: Philosophy in a Time of Terror." In *Philosophy in a Time of Terror: Dialogues with Jürgen Habermas and Jacques Derrida*, edited by Giovanna Borradori. Chicago: University of Chicago Press, 2003c.

Boulton, David. *The Making of Tania Hearst*. London: New English Library, 1975.

Boyarin, Jonathan. "At Last, All the Goyim: Notes on a Greek Word Applied to Jews." In *Postmodern Apocalypse: Theory and Cultural Practice at the End*, edited by Richard Dellamora. Philadelphia: University of Pennsylvania Press, 1995.

Brenner, Johanna. "The Best of Times, the Worst of Times: Feminism in the United States." In *Mapping the Women's Movement: Feminist Politics and Social Transformation in the North*, edited by Monica Threlfall. London: Verso, 1996.

Brodkin, Karen. *How the Jews Became White Folks and What That Says About Race in America*. New Brunswick, NJ: Rutgers University Press, 1994.

Brooks, Ann. *Postfeminisms: Feminism, Cultural Theory, and Cultural Forms*. London: Routledge, 1997.

Brown, J. A. C. *Techniques of Persuasion: From Propaganda to Brainwashing*. Harmondsworth: Penguin, 1963.

Bugliosi, Vincent and Curt Gentry. *Helter Skelter: The True Story of the Manson Murders*. Toronto: Bantam, 1975.

Bull, Malcolm. "On Making Ends Meet." In *Apocalypse Theory and the Ends of the World*, edited by Malcolm Bull. Oxford and Cambridge: Blackwell, 1995.

Chesler, Phyllis. *Women and Madness*. San Diego: Harcourt Brace Jovanovich, 1989 (1972).

Clarke, John, Stuart Hall, Tony Jefferson, and Brian Roberts. "Subcultures, Cultures and Class." In *Resistance through Rituals: Youth Subcultures in Post-War Britain*, edited by Stuart Hall and Tony Jefferson. London: Hutchinson of London in association with the Centre for Contemporary Cultural Studies, University of Birmingham, 1976.

Combs, Cindy C. *Terrorism in the Twenty-First Century*. 3rd edn. Upper Saddle River, NJ: Prentice Hall, 2003.

Comte, Auguste. *The Positive Philosophy*. Translated by Harriet Martineau. New York: AMS, 1974.

Conrad, Joseph. *The Secret Agent: A Simple Tale*. London: Penguin, 2000.

Cooper, H. H. A. "Woman as Terrorist." In *The Criminology of Deviant Women*, edited by Freda Adler and Rita James Simon. Boston: Houghton Mifflin, 1979.

Cooper, H. H. A. and Lawrence John Redlinger. *Terrorism and Espionage in the Middle East: Deception, Displacement and Denial*. Lewiston, NY: Edwin Mellen, 2006.

Counterterrorism Threat Assessment and Warning Unit, Counterterrorism Division, US Department of Justice, Federal Bureau of Investigation. *Terrorism in the United States 1999: 30 Years of Terrorism, a Special Retrospective Edition*. Federal Bureau of Investigation, Reports and Publications, 1999.

Creed, Barbara. *The Monstrous-Feminine: Film, Feminism, Psychoanalysis*. London: Routledge, 1993.

Crenshaw, Martha. "Introduction: Reflections on the Effects of Terrorism." In *Terrorism, Legitimacy and Power: The Consequences of Political Violence*, edited by Martha Crenshaw. Middletown, CT: Wesleyan University Press, 1983a.

Crenshaw, Martha, ed. *Terrorism, Legitimacy and Power: The Consequences of Political Violence*. Middletown, CT: Wesleyan University Press, 1983b.

Cronin, Audrey Kurth and James M. Ludes, eds. *Attacking Terrorism: Elements of a Grand Strategy*. Washington, DC: Georgetown University Press, 2004.

Cruise O'Brien, Conor. "Terrorism under Democratic Conditions." In *Terrorism, Legitimacy and Power: The Consequences of Political Violence*, edited by Martha Crenshaw. Middletown, CT: Wesleyan University Press, 1983.

de Cataldo Neuberger, Luisella and Tiziana Valentini. *Women and Terrorism*. Translated by Leo Michael Hughes. Basingstoke: Macmillan, 1996.

de Certeau, Michel. *The Practice of Everyday Life*. Translated by Steven Rendall. Berkeley: University of California Press, 1988.

de Certeau, Michel, Luce Giard, and Pierre Mayol. *The Practice of Everyday Life. Volume 2: Living and Cooking*. Translated by Timothy J. Tomasik. Minneapolis: University of Minnesota Press, 1998.

de Lauretis, Teresa. *Technologies of Gender: Essays on Theory, Film and Fiction*. Bloomington: Indiana University Press, 1987.

Debord, Guy. *Society of the Spectacle*. Translated by by Donald Nicholson-Smith. New York: Zone Books, 1994.

DeKoven, Marianne. *Utopia Limited: The Sixties and the Emergence of the Postmodern*. Durham: Duke University Press, 2004.

Derrida, Jacques. *Writing and Difference*. Translsated by Alan Bass. Chicago: University of Chicago Press, 1978.

———. *Margins of Philosophy*. Translated by Alan Bass. Chicago: University of Chicago Press, 1982.

Dijkstra, Bram. *Idols of Perversity: Fantasies of Feminine Evil in Fin De Siècle Culture*. New York: Oxford University Press, 1986.

Dollimore, Jonathan. *Sexual Dissidence: Augustine to Wilde, Freud to Foucault*. Oxford: Clarendon, 1991.

Douglas, Carol Anne. "Review of *Daring to be Bad: Radical Feminism in America 1967–1975*, by Alice Echols." *off our backs* April 30, 1990.

Dror, Yehezkel. "Terrorism as a Challenge to the Democratic Capacity to Govern." In *Terrorism, Legitimacy and Power: The Consequences of Political Violence*, edited by Martha Crenshaw. Middletown, CT: Wesleyan University Press, 1983.

Durham, Martin. "The American Far Right and 9/11." *Terrorism and Political Science* 15, no. 2 (Summer 2003): 96–111.

Dyer, Richard. *White*. London: Routledge, 1997.

Echols, Alice. *Daring to Be Bad: Radical Feminism in America 1967–1975*. Minneapolis: University of Minnesota, 1989.

Ellenberg, Al. "Introduction." In *Abduction: Fiction before Fact*, edited by Al Ellenberg. New York: Grove, 1974.

Elshtain, Jean. *Women and War*. New York: Basic Books, 1987.

Embree, Alice. "Media Images I: Madison Avenue Brainwashing: The Facts." In *Sisterhood Is Powerful: An Anthology of Writings from the Women's Liberation Movement*, edited by Robin Morgan. New York: Vintage, 1970.

Enzensberger, Hans Magnus. "Two Notes on the End of the World." *New Left Review* 110 (July–August 1978): 74–80.

Evans, Sara. *Personal Politics: The Roots of Women's Liberation in the Civil Rights Movement and the New Left*. New York: Alfred A. Knopf, 1979.

Fahs, Breanne "The Radical Possibilities of Valerie Solanas." *Feminist Studies* 34, no. 3 (Fall 2008): 591–617.

Faludi, Susan. *Backlash: The Undeclared War against American Women*. New York: Anchor, 1991.

Felski, Rita. *The Gender of Modernity*. Cambridge, MA: Harvard University Press, 1995.

Femia, Joseph V. *Gramsci's Political Thought: Hegemony, Consciousness and the Revolutionary Process*. Oxford: Oxford University Press, 1988.

Firestone, Shulamith. "The Dialectic of Sex." In *Radical Feminism: A Documentary Reader*, edited by Barbara A. Crow. New York: New York University Press, 2000.

Foss, Karen, A. "Out from Underground: The Discourse of Emerging Fugitives." *Western Journal of Communication* 56, no. 2 (1992): 125–42.

Foucault, Michel. *Madness and Civilization: A History of Insanity in the Age of Reason*. Translated by Richard Howard. New York: Random, 1973.

———. *Discipline and Punish: The Birth of the Prison*. Translated by Alan Sheridan. New York: Pantheon, 1977a.

———. *Language, Counter-Memory, Practice: Selected Essays and Interviews*. Edited and translated by Donald F. Bouchard. Ithaca: Cornell University Press, 1977b.

———. *The History of Sexuality Volume One: The Will to Knowledge*. Translated by Robert Hurley. London: Penguin, 1990.

Freedman, Lawrence Zelic. "Problems of the Polistaraxic." In *Perspectives on Terrorism*, edited by Lawrence Zelic Freedman and Yonah Alexander. Wilmington, DE: Scholarly Resources, 1983.

Freedman, Lawrence Zelic and Yonah Alexander, eds. *Perspectives on Terrorism*. Wilmington, DE: Scholarly Resources, 1983.

Freud, Sigmund. "Moses and Monotheism." In *The Standard Edition of the Complete Psychological Works of Sigmund Freud Vol. 23*, edited by James Strachey. London: Hogarth, 1955a.

———. "Totem and Taboo: Some Points of Agreement between the Mental Lives of Savages and Neurotics." In *The Standard Edition of the Complete Psychological Works of Sigmund Freud Vol. 13*, edited by James Strachey. London: Hogarth and the Institute of Psycho-analysis, 1955b.

Friedan, Betty. *The Feminine Mystique: What the Married Woman Has—and What She Wants*. Harmondsworth: Penguin, 1973.

Frost, Mike. "The Accidental Death of an Anarchist." *MIRA* 51 (1999). http://www.covastro.org.uk/mira/mira-issue-51

Georges-Abeyie, Daniel A. "Women as Terrorists." In *Perspectives on Terrorism*, edited by Lawrence Zelic Freedman and Yonah Alexander. Wilmington, DE: Scholarly Resources, 1983.

Gerhard, Jane. *Desiring Revolution: Second-Wave Feminism and the Rewriting of American Sexual Thought, 1920 to 1982*. New York: Columbia University Press, 2001.

Giddens, Anthony. *The Nation-State and Violence: Volume Two of a Contemporary Critique of Capitalism*. Berkeley: University of California Press, 1985.

Gitlin, Todd. *The Whole World Is Watching: Mass Media in the Making and the Unmaking of the New Left*. Berkeley: University of California Press, 1980.

———. *The Sixties: Years of Hope, Days of Rage*. Toronto: Bantam, 1987.

———. "The Implosion." In *The Sixties*, edited by Peter Stines. Detroit: Wayne State University Press, 1988.

———. Afterword to *Reassessing the Sixties: Debating the Political and Cultural Legacy*, edited by Stephen Macedo. New York: WW Norton, 1997.

Gleason, Abbott. *Totalitarianism: The Inner History of the Cold War.* New York: Oxford University Press, 1995.

Golding, Peter and Graham Murdock. "Culture, Communications, and Political Economy." In *Mass Media and Society*, edited by James Curran and Michael Gurevitch. London: Edward Arnold, 1991.

Gornick, Vivian. "Introduction to the Olympia Press Edition of Valerie Solanas." In *SCUM Manifesto*, by Valerie Solanas. London: Olympia, 1971.

Greenhalgh, Susanne. "The Bomb in the Baby Carriage: Women and Terrorism in Contemporary Drama." In *Terrorism and the Modern Drama*, edited by John Orr and Dragan Klaic. Edinburgh: Edinburgh University Press, 1990.

Greer, Germaine. *The Female Eunuch.* London: Paladin, 1971.

Griset, Pamala L. and Sue Mahan. "Women as Terrorists." In *Terrorism in Perspective*, edited by Pamala L. Griset and Sue Mahan. Thousand Oaks: Sage, 2003.

Grosz, Elizabeth. "The Body of Signification." In *Abjection, Melancholia and Love: The Work of Julia Kristeva*, edited by John Fletcher and Andrew Benjamin. London: Routledge, 1990.

Gupta, Suman. *The Replication of Violence: Thoughts on International Violence after September 11th, 2001.* London: Pluto, 2002.

Gurr, Ted Robert. "The History of Protest, Rebellion, and Reform in America: An Overview." In *Violence in America*, edited by Ted Robert Gurr. Newbury Park: Sage, 1989a.

———. "Political Terrorism: Historical Antecedents and Contemporary Trends." In *Violence in America*, edited by Ted Robert Gurr. Newbury Park: Sage, 1989b.

———. "Protest and Rebellion in the 1960s: The United States in World Perspective." In *Violence in America*, edited by Ted Robert Gurr. Newbury Park: Sage, 1989c.

Hacker, Frederick J. "Dialectic Interrelationships of Personal and Political Factors in Terrorism." In *Perspectives on Terrorism*, edited by Lawrence Zelic Freedman and Yonah Alexander. Wilmington, DE: Scholarly Resources, 1983.

Hage, Ghassan. *Against Paranoid Nationalism: Searching for Hope in a Shrinking Society.* Annandale, NSW: Pluto/Merlin, 2003.

Hall, Stuart. "Cultural Identity and Diaspora." In *Colonial Discourse and Postcolonial Theory*, edited by Patrick Williams and Laura Chrisman. New York: Columbia University Press, 1994.

———. "The Work of Representation." In *Representation: Cultural Representation and Signifying Practices*, edited by Stuart Hall. London: Sage, 1997.

Harding, James M. "The Simplest Surrealist Act: Valerie Solanas and the (Re) Assertion of Avantgarde Priorities." *The Drama Review* 45, no. 4 (2001): 142–62.

Harris, Jonathan, ed. *The New Terrorism: Politics of Violence.* New York: Julian Messner, 1983.

Harron, Mary and Daniel Minahan. *I Shot Andy Warhol.* London: Bloomsbury, 1996.

Hart, Lynda. *Fatal Women: Lesbian Sexuality and the Mark of Aggression.* New Jersey: Princeton University Press, 1994.

Hawthorne, Susan and Bronwyn Winter, eds. *September 11: Feminist Perspectives.* Melbourne: Spinifex, 2002.

Hearst, Patricia Campbell and Alvin Moscow. *Every Secret Thing*. London: Methuen, 1982.

Hebdige, Dick. *Subculture: The Meaning of Style*. London: Routledge, 1998.

Herman, Edward S. and Gerry O'Sullivan. *The 'Terrorism' Industry: The Experts and Institutions That Shape Our View of Terror*. New York: Pantheon, 1989.

Herman, Edward S. and Noam Chomsky. *Manufacturing Consent: The Political Economy of the Mass Media*. New York: Pantheon, 1988.

Hobbes, Thomas. *Leviathan*. Edited by C. B. Macpherson. Harmondsworth: Penguin, 1968.

Hocking, Jenny. "Counterterrorism as Counterinsurgency: The British Experience." *Social Justice* 15, no. 1 (1988): 83–97.

———. *Terror Laws: ASIO, Counter-Terrorism and the Threat to Democracy*. Sydney: University of NSW Press, 2003.

Hoffman, Bruce. *Inside Terrorism*. New York: Columbia University Press, 2006.

Horowitz, Irving Louis. "The Routinisation of Terrorism and Its Consequences." In *Terrorism, Legitimacy and Power: The Consequences of Political Violence*, edited by Martha Crenshaw. Middletown, CT: Wesleyan University Press, 1983.

Hozic, Aida. "The Inverted World of Spectacle: Social and Political Responses to Terrorism." In *Terrorism and the Modern Drama*, edited by John Orr and Dragan Klaic. Edinburgh: Edinburgh University Press, 1990.

Hudson, Rex. "The Sociology and Psychology of Terrorism: Who Becomes a Terrorist and Why?" on Jill St Claire's HomelandSecurityUS.Net website. Washington: Library of Congress, 1999, 45–50, accessed March 11, 2014, http://www.totse.com/en/politics/terrorists_and_freedom_fighters/164765.html

Irigaray, Luce. *Speculum of the Other Woman*. Translated by Gillian C. Gill. Ithaca: Cornell University Press, 1985a.

———. *This Sex Which Is Not One*. Translated by Catherine Porter and Carolyn Burke. Ithaca: Cornell University Press, 1985b.

———. *Je, Tu, Nous: Toward a Culture of Difference*. Translated by Alison Martin. New York: Routledge, 1993.

Isenberg, Nancy. "Not 'Anyone's Daughter': Patty Hearst and the Postmodern Legal Subject." *American Quarterly* 52, no. 4 (2000): 639–81.

James, Harrison. "Black Abductor." In *Abduction: Fiction Before Fact*, edited by Al Ellenberg. 2nd edn. New York: Grove, 1974.

Jenkins, Philip. *Images of Terror: What We Can and Can't Know About Terrorism*. New York: Aldine du Gruyter, 2003.

Johnson, Chalmers. "Perspectives on Terrorism." In *The Terrorism Reader: A Historical Anthology*, edited by Walter Laqueur. Philadelphia: Temple University Press, 1978.

Jones, Ann. *Women Who Kill*. New York: Fawcett Columbine, 1980.

Jones, Beverly and Judith Brown. "Toward a Female Liberation Movement." In *Radical Feminism: A Documentary Reader*, edited by Barbara A. Crow. New York: New York University Press, 2000.

Kaye, Howard L. *The Social Meaning of Modern Biology: From Social Darwinism to Sociobiology*. New Haven: Yale University Press, 1986.

Kevles, Daniel J. *In the Name of Eugenics; Genetics and the Uses of Human Heredity.* New York: Alfred A. Knopf, 1985.

Klein, Naomi. *No Logo: No Space, No Choice, No Jobs.* London: Flamingo, 2001.

Kristeva, Julia. *Powers of Horror: An Essay on Abjection.* Translated by Leon S. Roudiez. New York: Columbia University Press, 1982.

———. "Women's Time." In *The Kristeva Reader*, edited by Toril Moi. New York: Columbia University Press, 1986.

Kumar, Krishan. *Utopia and Anti-Utopia in Modern Times.* Oxford: Basil Blackwell, 1987.

———. *Utopianism.* Buckingham: Open University Press, 1991.

Lane, David. *State and Politics in the USSR.* Oxford: Basil Blackwell, 1985.

Laqueur, Walter. *Terrorism.* London: Weidenfeld and Nicolson, 1977.

———. "Terrorism: A Balance Sheet." In *The Terrorism Reader: A Historical Anthology*, edited by Walter Laqueur. Philadelphia: Temple University Press, 1978.

———. *The Age of Terrorism.* Boston: Little Brown, 1987.

———. *The New Terrorism.* New York: Oxford University Press, 1999.

———. *History of Terrorism.* New Brunswick, NJ: Transaction, 2001.

———. *No End to War: Terrorism in the Twenty-First Century.* New York: Continuum, 2004a.

———. *Voices of Terror: Manifestos, Writings and Manuals of Al Qaeda, Hamas, and Other Terrorists from around the World and Throughout the Ages.* New York: Reed, 2004b.

Lasky, Melvin J. *Utopia and Revolution: On the Origins of a Metaphor or Some Illustrations of the Problem of Political Temperament and Intellectual Climate and How Ideas, Ideals, and Ideologies Have Been Historically Related.* Chicago: The University of Chicago Press, 1976.

Lefebvre, Henri. *Everyday Life in the Modern World.* Translated by Sacha Rabinovitch. London: Athlone, 2000.

Lifton, Robert Jay. *Thought Reform and the Psychology of Totalism: A Study of Brainwashing in China.* New York: WW Norton, 1961.

Lippincott, Kristen. "Mechanical Time: Standardising Time." In *The Story of Time*, edited by Kristen Lippincott. London: Merrell Holberton, 1999.

Lloyd, Genevieve. *Man of Reason: "Male" and "Female" in Western Philosophy.* Minneapolis: University of Minnesota Press, 1993.

Lombroso, Cesare and Guglielmo Ferrero. *The Female Offender.* New York: D. Appleton, 1895.

Lopez-Rey, Manuel. "The Expansion and Distribution of Crime." In *The Criminology of Deviant Women*, edited by Freda Adler and Rita James Simon. Boston: Houghton Mifflin, 1979.

Lunde, Donald T. and Thomas E. Wilson. "Brainwashing as a Defense to Criminal Liability: Patty Hearst Revisited." *Criminal Law Bulletin* 13 (1977): 341–82.

Lydon, Susan. "The Politics of Orgasm." In *Sisterhood Is Powerful: An Anthology of Writings from the Women's Liberation Movement*, edited by Robin Morgan. New York: Vintage, 1970.

Lyotard, Jean-François. *The Postmodern Condition: A Report on Knowledge*. Translated by Geoff Bennington and Brian Massumi. Manchester: Manchester University Press, 1984.

————. *The Differend: Phrases in Dispute*. Translated by Georges Van Den Abbeele. Minneapolis: University of Minnesota Press, 1991.

————. *The Postmodern Explained to Children: Correspondence 1982–1985*. Translated by Don Berry et al. Sydney: Power Publications, 1992.

MacCannell, Juliet Flower. *The Régime of the Brother: After the Patriarchy*. London: Routledge, 1991.

MacDonald, Eileen. *Shoot the Women First*. London: Fourth Estate, 1991.

Mailer, Norman. *Miami and the Siege of Chicago: An Informal History of the American Political Conventions of 1968*. Harmondsworth: Penguin, 1969.

Mainardi, Pat. "The Politics of Housework." In *Sisterhood Is Powerful: An Anthology of Writings from the Women's Liberation Movement*, edited by Robin Morgan. New York: Vintage, 1970.

Marcus, Greil. *Lipstick Traces: A Secret History of the Twentieth Century*. Cambridge, MA: Harvard University Press, 1989.

Marcus, Steven. *The Other Victorians: A Study of Sexuality and Pornography in Mid-Nineteenth-Century England*. London: Weidenfeld and Nicolson, 1966.

Marcuse, Herbert. *One Dimensional Man: Studies in the Ideology of Advanced Industrial Society*. Boston: Beacon, 1964.

————. *Eros and Civilisation: A Philosophical Inquiry into Freud*. London: Sphere Books, 1970.

McClintock, Anne. *Imperial Leather: Race, Gender and Sexuality in the Colonial Contest*. New York: Routledge, 1995.

McQuail, Denis. "Foreword." In *Violence as Communication: Insurgent Terrorism and the Western News Media*, edited by Alex P. Schmid and Janny de Graaf. London: Sage, 1982.

————. *McQuail's Mass Communication Theory*. 4th edn. London: Sage, 2000.

Midlarsky, Manus I., Martha Crenshaw, and Fumihiko Yoshida. "Why Violence Spreads: The Contagion of International Terrorism." *International Studies Quarterly* 24, no. 2 (1980): 262–98.

Morgan, Robin. "Introduction: The Women's Revolution." In *Sisterhood Is Powerful: An Anthology of Writings from the Women's Liberation Movement*, edited by Robin Morgan. New York: Vintage, 1970.

————. "Goodbye to All That." In *Going Too Far: The Personal Chronicle of a Feminist*. New York: Vintage, 1978.

————. "From Riches to Rags: A Conversation with Patricia Hearst." *Ms. Magazine* (March 1979): 60.

————. *The Demon Lover: On the Sexuality of Terror*. London: Mandarin, 1989. Reprinted as *The Demon Lover: The Roots of Terrorism*. London: Piatkus, 2001.

Mullaney, Marie Marmo. *Revolutionary Women: Gender and the Socialist Revolutionary Role*. New York: Praeger, 1983.

Mulry, David. "Popular Accounts of the Greenwich Bombing and Conrad's the Secret Agent." *Rocky Mountain Review* 54, no. 2 (Fall 2000): 43–64.

Muncie, J. *The Trouble with Kids Today*. London: Hutchison, 1984.

Nacos, Brigitte L. *Terrorism and the Media: From the Iran Hostage Crisis to the World Trade Center Bombing*. New York: Columbia University Press, 1994.

Nadel, Alan. *Containment Culture: American Narratives, Postmodernism, and the Atomic Age*. Durham: Duke University Press, 1995.

Naffine, Ngaire. *Feminism and Criminology*. St Leonards, NSW: Allen and Unwin, 1997.

Nelson, Elizabeth. *The British Counterculture 1966–1973: A Study of the Underground Press*. London: Macmillan, 1989.

Novick, Peter. *The Holocaust in American Life*. Boston: Houghton Mifflin, 1999.

Nye, Joseph S., Paul Wilkinson, and Yukio Satoh. *Addressing the New International Terrorism: Prevention, Intervention, and Multilateral Cooperation*. Washington, DC: Brookings Institution Press, 2003.

O'Sullivan, Tim, John Hartley, Danny Saunders, Martin Montgomery, and John Fiske. *Key Concepts in Communication and Cultural Studies*. 2nd edn. London: Routledge, 1994.

Orwell, George. *Nineteen Eighty-Four*. London: Compact Books, 1993.

Parkinson Zamora, Lois. *Writing the Apocalypse: Historical Vision in Contemporary US and Latin American Fiction*. Cambridge: Cambridge University Press, 1989.

Pateman, Carole. *The Sexual Contract*. Cambridge: Polity, 1988.

———. "The Disorder of Women." In *The Polity Reader in Gender Studies*, edited by Anthony Giddens et al. Cambridge: Polity, 1994.

Payne, James L. "Does Freedom Prevent Terrorism?" *The American Conservative*, April 11, 2005, accessed January 9, 2006, http://www.amconmag.com/2005_04_11/article.html

Pear, Thomas Hatherley. *The Moulding of Modern Man: A Psychologist's View of Information, Persuasion and Mental Coercion Today*. London: Allen and Unwin, 1961.

Pearlstein, Richard. *The Mind of the Political Terrorist*. Wilmington, DE: Scholarly Resources, 1991.Picard, Robert G. "News Coverage as the Contagion of Terrorism." In *Media Coverage of Terrorism*, edited by Alali A. Odasuo and Kenoye Kelvin Eke. Newbury Park, CA: Sage, 1991.

Piercy, Marge. "The Grand Coolie Damn." In *Sisterhood Is Powerful: An Anthology of Writings from the Women's Liberation Movement*, edited by Robin Morgan. New York: Vintage, 1970.

Plant, Sadie. *The Most Radical Gesture: The Situationist International in a Postmodern Age*. London and New York: Routledge, 1992.

Polster, Miriam F. *Eve's Daughters: The Forbidden Heroism of Men*. San Francisco: Jossey-Bass, 1992.

Puar, Jasbir. *Terrorist Assemblages: Homonationalism in Queer Times*. Durham: Duke University Press, 2007.

Quainton, Anthony C. E. "Terrorism: Policy, Action and Reaction." In *Perspectives on Terrorism*, edited by Lawrence Zelic Freedman and Yonah Alexander. Wilmington, DE: Scholarly Resources, 1983.

Rabkin, Jeremy. "Feminism: Where the Spirit of the Sixties Lives On." In *Reassessing the Sixties: Debating the Political and Cultural Legacy*, edited by Stephen Macedo. New York: WW Norton, 1997.

Radicalesbians. "The Woman-Identified-Woman." In *Radical Feminism: A Documentary Reader*, edited by Barbara A. Crow. New York: New York University Press, 2000.

Rapoport, David, ed. *Inside Terrorist Organizations*. London and Portland, OR: Frank Cass, 2001.

———. *Terrorism: Critical Concepts in Political Science*. London: Routledge, 2005.

Rapoport, David and Leonard Weinberg, eds. *The Democratic Experience and Political Violence*. London and Portland, OR: Frank Cass, 2001.

Raskin, Jonah. *For the Hell of It: The Life and Times of Abbie Hoffman*. Berkeley, Los Angeles, and London: University of California Press, 1998.

Rivers, Gayle. *The War Against the Terrorist*. New York: Simon and Day, 1986.

Roszak, Theodore. *The Making of a Counterculture: Reflections on the Technocratic Society and Its Youthful Opposition*. London: Faber and Faber, 1970.

Rowland, Christopher. "'Upon Whom the Ends of the Ages Have Come': Apocalyptic and the Interpretation of the New Testament." In *Apocalypse Theory and the Ends of the World*, edited by Malcolm Bull. Oxford and Cambridge: Blackwell, 1995.

Rubenstein, Richard E. "Rebellion in America: The Fire Next Time?" In *Violence in America*, edited by Ted Robert Gurr. Newbury Park: Sage, 1989.

Russell, Charles A. and Bowman H. Miller. "Profile of a Terrorist." *Terrorism: An International Journal* 1, no. 1 (1977): 17–34.

Said, Edward. "Foucault and the Imagination of Power." In *Foucault: A Critical Reader*, edited by David Conzens Hoy. Oxford: Basil Blackwell, 1986.

Schein, Edgar H. *Coercive Persuasion: A Socio-Psychological Analysis of the 'Brainwashing' of American Civilian Prisoners by the Chinese Communists*. New York: Norton, 1961.

Schirato, Tony and Susan Yell. "Communication and Culture." In *Communication and Cultural Literacy: An Introduction*, edited by Tony Schirato and Susan Yell. St. Leonards, NSW: Allen and Unwin, 1996.

Schmid, Alex P. and Janny de Graaf. *Violence as Communication: Insurgent Terrorism and the Western News Media*. London: Sage, 1982.

Seiter, Ellen. "Qualitative Audience Research." In *Television and New Media Audiences*. Oxford: Clarendon, 1999.

Shelley, Martha. "Notes of a Radical Lesbian." In *Sisterhood Is Powerful: An Anthology of Writings from the Women's Liberation Movement*, edited by Robin Morgan. New York: Vintage, 1970.

Simon, Rita James. "A Look to the Future." In *The Criminology of Deviant Women*, edited by Freda Adler and Rita James Simon. Boston: Houghton Mifflin, 1979.

Simon, Rita James and Navin Sharma. "Women and Crime: Does the American Experience Generalize?" In *The Criminology of Deviant Women*, edited by Freda Adler and Rita James Simon. Boston: Houghton Mifflin, 1979.

Solanas, Valerie. *The SCUM Manifesto*. Edinburgh, San Francisco: AK Press, 1997. Reprinted as *The Scum Manifesto*. New York: Verso, 2004.

"Songs from the Women's Liberation Movement." In *Sisterhood Is Powerful: An Anthology of Writings from the Women's Liberation Movement*, edited by Robin Morgan. New York: Vintage, 1970 (No author).

Spigel, Lynn and Michael Curtin, eds. *The Revolution Wasn't Televised: Sixties Television and Social Conflict*. New York: Routledge, 1997.

Stavrakakis, Yannis. "Beyond the Fantasy of Utopia: The Aporia of Politics and the Challenge of Democracy." In *Lacan and the Political*. London: Routledge, 1999.

Stratton, Jon. *Writing Sites: A Genealogy of the Postmodern World*. Ann Arbor: University of Michigan Press, 1990.

———. *The Desirable Body: Cultural Fetishism and the Erotics of Consumption*. Manchester: Manchester University Press, 1996.

———. *Coming out Jewish: Constructing Ambivalent Identities*. London: Routledge, 2000a.

———. "The Beast of the Apocalypse: The Postcolonial Experience of the United States." In *Postcolonial America*, edited by Richard King. Urbana: University of Illinois Press, 2000b.

———. "Thinking through the Holocaust: A Discussion Inspired by Hilene Flanzbaum (Ed.), the Americanisation of the Holocaust." *Continuum: Journal of Media and Cultural Studies* 14, no. 2 (2000c): 231–45.

———. "The Reasonable State and the End of Time." In *Modern Time* (unpublished manuscript). n.d.

Szasz, Thomas. *The Myth of Mental Illness: Foundations of a Theory of Personal Conduct*. New York: Harper and Row, 1968.

———. *The Manufacture of Madness*. London: Routledge and Kegan Paul, 1971.

———. "Patty Hearst's Conversion: Some Call It Brainwashing." *The New Republic* (March 6, 1976): 10–12.

Taylor, Maxwell. *The Terrorist*. New York: Brassey's Defence, 1988.

Terdiman, Richard. *Discourse/Counter-Discourse: The Theory and Practice of Symbolic Resistance in Nineteenth-Century France*. Ithaca: Cornell University Press, 1985.

"The Symbionese Liberation Army: Terrorism and the Left." *Ramparts* (May 1974): 21–7. (No author).

Third, Amanda. "Imprisonment and Excessive Femininity: Reading Ulrike Meinhof's Brain." *Parallax* 16, no. 4 (2010): 83–100.

Tong, Rosemary. *Feminist Thought: A Comprehensive Introduction*. London: Unwin Hyman, 1989.

Townshend, Charles. *Terrorism: A Very Short Introduction*. Oxford: Oxford University Press, 2002.

Tuman, Joseph S. *Communicating Terror: The Rhetorical Dimensions of Terrorism*. Thousand Oaks: Sage, 2003.

Virilio, Paul. *Ground Zero*. London: Verso, 2002.

Wagner-Pacifici, Robin E. *The Moro Morality Play: Terrorism as Social Drama*. Chicago: University of Chicago Press, 1986.

Washington, Cynthia. "We Started from Different Ends of the Spectrum." In *Personal Politics: The Roots of Women's Liberation in the Civil Rights Movement and the New Left*, edited by Sara Evans. New York: Alfred A. Knopf, 1979.

Weber, Max. *Weber: Political Writings*. Translated by Ronald Spiers and edited by Peter Lassman and Ronald Spiers. Cambridge: Cambridge University Press, 1994.

Weinberg, Leonard and William Lee Eubank. "Italian Women Terrorists." *Terrorism: An International Journal* 9, no. 3 (1987): 241–62.

Weitz, Rose. "A History of Women's Bodies." In *The Politics of Women's Bodies: Sexuality, Appearance and Behaviour*, edited by Rose Weitz. Oxford: Oxford University Press, 1998.

West, Don and Jerry Belcher. *Patty/Tania*. New York: Pyramid, 1975.

"What Is Liberation?" In *Radical Feminism: A Documentary Reader*, edited by Barbara A. Crow. New York: New York University Press, 2000. (No author).

Wilkinson, Paul. "Pathology and Theory." In *The Terrorism Reader: A Historical Anthology*, edited by Walter Laqueur. Philadelphia: Temple University Press, 1978.

———. *Terrorism versus Democracy: The Liberal State Response*. London: Frank Cass, 2006.

Willis, Ellen. Foreword to *Daring to Be Bad: Radical Feminism in America 1967–1975*, by Alice Echols. Minneapolis: University of Minnesota Press, 1989.

Wolin, Sheldon. "The Destructive Sixties and Postmodern Conservatism." In *Reassessing the Sixties: Debating the Political and Cultural Legacy*, edited by Stephen Macedo. New York: WW Norton, 1997.

Young, Alison. *Imagining Crime: Textual Outlaws and Criminal Conversations*. London and Thousand Oaks: Sage, 1996.

Zwerman, Gilda. "Conservative and Feminist Images of Women Associated with Armed, Clandestine Organisations in the United States." *International Social Movement Research* 4 (1992): 133–59.

Index

Printed in Australia
AUHW010613250619
313828AU00005B/12